THE FRAGMENTS OF MY FATHER

A memoir of madness, love and being a carer

SAM MILLS

4th ESTATE · London

4th Estate
An imprint of HarperCollins*Publishers*
1 London Bridge Street
London SE1 9GF

www.4thEstate.co.uk

HarperCollins*Publishers*
1st Floor, Watermarque Building, Ringsend Road
Dublin 4, Ireland

First published in Great Britain in 2020 by 4th Estate
This 4th Estate paperback edition published in 2021

1

Printed and bound in Great Britain by CPI Group (UK) Ltd, Croydon CR0 4YY

MIX
Paper from
responsible sources
FSC® C007454

This book is produced from independently certified FSC™ paper
to ensure responsible forest management.

For more information visit: www.harpercollins.co.uk/green

For L.K.

And in loving memory of my mother.

Author's Note

This is a true story, but I have altered some names and other details to protect the privacy, and conceal the identities, of certain individuals.

PART I

This world of human beings grows too complicated, my only wonder is that we don't fill more madhouses: the insane view of life has much to be said for it – perhaps its the sane one after all: and *we*, the sad sober respectable citizens really rave every moment of our lives and deserve to be shut up perpetually.

Virginia Woolf to Emma Vaughan, 23 April 1901

I

It's a Friday night in early 2016 and I am staring at the streaky paintwork of a toilet door. It is locked. It has been locked for the past two hours. The skin on my knuckles is pink from repeated banging.

I call out, 'Dad, are you okay?'

There is a long silence.

Then, eventually, comes a reply:

'I'm … okay … I'll come out … in … a …'

I go downstairs, but the moment I reach the hallway, I feel I should venture back up, though it will only lead to a dead-end: the blank face of the toilet door again. By now, I have become familiar with its streaky whiteness, the thick and fine delineations of brushwork preserved in the white gloss, my brother's DIY job. Through the hall window the sky is filled with the blue smoke of twilight. There is that sparkle in the air as people leave work and head for the pub or home. If they saw our house, what assumptions would they make? It's a semi-detached in a little cul-de-sac, with a neat garden: I would have assumed it was a house where conventional people lived out happy, boring lives.

I suffer the vertigo of uncertainty. Over the past six months,

I've spoken to several people on the phone for advice about my father. They've all asked the same question: 'Are you his carer?' And I've always replied: 'No, I'm his daughter.' The term 'carer' feels too clinical. I help my dad because he is my dad. But I'm also nervous of the term because it implies I am in possession of wisdom and medical knowledge and that *I know what I am doing*.

On the table in the living room is a card with 'Emergency Mental Health Support Line' printed on it in red letters. I dial the number. The man at the end of the line introduces himself as Joe. It isn't until I tell him that my dad has been locked in a toilet for two hours that I realise how panicked I am; I hear it lacerate my voice. Often, in the present tense of a shocking situation, we can only feel numbness; it is in the aftermath that emotions take shape.

Joe is clearly a little confused by what I am telling him. In his line of work, the story of a man who is ill and locked in a toilet nearly always follows the same plot arc: he is making a threat; he intends to take his life. But my father's condition is so odd and rare and complex – one that doctors have not come across in decades – that I'm not able to explain it on the phone. I just want someone to tell me what to do, even if they are ignorant of the context. I want instruction; I want a friend.

Joe tells me: stay on the phone, go back upstairs and speak to him. 'Tell your dad he *has* to come out.'

Even though I've already tried this, I obey.

'Dad, you *have* to come out,' I recite.

Silence.

'You have to put some *force* into the words,' Joe tells me, and I suppress an urge to laugh hysterically; I feel as though I am auditioning for a part. 'You need to say it with authority.'

I bellow the words. No reply. My dad has stopped speaking altogether: this is a bad sign. The echo of my voice makes it seem as though the tiny room has expanded into a vast space. I picture my dad sitting on the toilet in a state of zombie suspension. Or, perhaps he is standing on the seat, wobbling precariously – a rotund seventy-two-year-old, trying to escape through the toilet window.

'I don't think he can help it,' I say. 'I think it's probably got out of control now.'

'You're doing very well,' says Joe.

Joe tells me to ring for an ambulance. And then he tells me he is sitting in his office and he'll be there all night. I can phone him any time. I can update him and let him know my dad is safe. And, if I feel afraid, I can just call and talk to him. In that instant, I fall in love with Joe. It is something that has happened a few times over the past six months. Someone shines a light into the dark storm of crisis and we bond in the intimacy of that moment; it feels as though we have known each other all our lives, even though we are strangers.

Why did Edward choose the toilet? Does he have a weapon? Do you think he is suicidal? These were the questions the woman fired at me when I called 999.

I answered: don't know, no, and no.

They wanted his rejection of life to be defined as an absolute; but it was far more shadowy and ambiguous. The woman told me that the ambulance would take an hour to come. They were having a busy evening. I sensed a subtext in her tone: austerity and cuts were the cause.

I switched off the phone. The streaky white door stared back at me.

I called out to my dad once more. Once more, there was no reply.

For the third time that day I telephoned my younger brother Stefan. He worked long hours in the City, but I figured he'd be home by now; his flat was just a few streets away from Dad's. When he appeared on the doorstep ten minutes later, he was carrying a half-drunk bottle of beer. Stefan was in his mid-thirties. Our interactions usually followed the same pattern: we took the piss out of each other as though we were kids again. But this time we were both panicked.

The hour stretched out before us. We argued about solutions. In the end, we surfed the net and picked out a locksmith. Not available, we kept being told. It's a Friday night, we don't have anyone …

While I kept calling out to Dad, Stefan found a screwdriver in a toolbox under the stairs and slotted it between door and lock, trying to force it open. A presence by my legs made me jump: my cat Leo was purring and gazing up at me quizzically. Most of the time, she possessed the haughty, wilful air of a cat who regarded her owners as her butlers. In a crisis, however, she seemed to soften and do her best to offer purry support, to play her role as part of the family. I knelt down and stroked her, watching anxiously as my brother jiggled, flecks of white paint flying to the floor. The lock, which my father had screwed on himself, began to rattle as it bent away from the door. And then – *snap!* – the door swung open and I saw a look of shock on my brother's face.

Dad was wearing his pyjamas. He was standing upright, facing us, but he couldn't see us. His body was locked into a strange repetitive loop, like a machine programmed to do an assembly-line task: his left arm would raise, jerk above his head, and then his right foot would lift. His scarlet face was screwed into a fist of agony.

I flew to him. Negotiating past the jerks, I gave him a hug. I whispered in his ear that he would be alright. He was unable to reply. It was as though his mind and body had said goodbye to each other. His body was doing its own strange thing and he was trapped in it, helpless. I tried to take his arm and smooth out the spasms, but it ignored me and carried on. Stepping back, I thought I should let him be: to interfere any more might hurt him.

The doorbell shrilled. The ambulance – early? But when I hurtled down to open the door, I found a locksmith waiting, ready to assist. 'I'm sorry,' I said, giving him the bundle of notes my brother had passed me.

When the ambulance did arrive, the crew were wonderful. Like Joe, they exuded warmth; they genuinely cared. My father's state baffled them. They fired questions at us, and we did our best to explain his tendency to slip into catatonia. In the end they moved Dad into a wheelchair and wrapped him in a blanket. Then they eyed the stairs nervously. My father is five feet-five and weighs sixteen stone. One of my friends once remarked to me that he looked like Father Christmas, with white hair and a benign, round face that people found instantly endearing. How to carry him? They hummed and hawed. They brought up a transfer chair, a bit like a sack barrow, and strapped him in. The final turn of the stairs was tricky. Eventually, they got him to the bottom. They looked as though they wanted to cheer.

The house felt lonely and empty after they had gone; night rain was freckling the windows. I pictured my dad and Stefan at the hospital, stuck in some side room in A&E. My brother would be there until at least two or three in the morning, whilst nurses spirited in and out doing tests, asking questions.

In the living room, I gazed over at Dad's armchair, tucked away in the corner. The seat was hollowed from use and the arm on which he rested his head to nap, curled up like a big cat, was frayed to strings of cloth. Next to the chair was a wooden cabinet on which he'd placed a pair of chunky black reading glasses, his newspaper tokens, his Bible, a list of things to do and to remember, and his pocket diary. I picked it up and opened the front page. It contained that line that all diaries have and few people ever bother to fill out: who to contact in the event of an emergency. Perhaps those who do are the ones who are vulnerable, aware of the hairline cracks in their lives, the threat of fracture. I was touched to see my name and number written on this line, and then felt shadowed by fear: I thought of my father in the toilet and imagined what might have been if I hadn't been there.

I wandered into the spare bedroom. Once this room had belonged to my mother. Her presence was there still, in the pleats and shadows. A basket of make-up at the back of the desk gathering a thick layer of dust. Her dressing gown, a long leopard-print affair, hung on the back of the door. On her bookshelf sat a row of spine-cracked favourites: the *Lord of the Rings* trilogy, a textbook about Freud, Herman Hesse's *Siddartha*. Today, 19 February – the day Dad had spent locked in the toilet – was her birthday. She would have been seventy.

I grew up in this house, the neat semi in a cul-de-sac in a quiet town in Surrey, and stayed here until my university years. Mum was well then, and Dad – Dad was still stable. After graduating I headed north to a little place between Manchester and Liverpool called Appley Bridge, where I rented a room and wrote.

I had expected to reach my late thirties and suddenly metamorphose into Someone Sensible who wanted to put down roots and buy a property. It hadn't quite happened. I was still self-employed, a writer with a bank balance that hovered perilously close to the line; I had no family of my own; I was uncertain whether I wanted to be a mother. I was, however, in a long-term relationship. My boyfriend, Thom, was eight years younger than me, a book reviewer and a fellow book-lover. Our favourite thing was to wander around second-hand bookshops, rummaging the shelves for gems and stealing kisses in dusty corners. He lived in the north too, anchored there by a young daughter from a previous relationship.

At New Year, Thom had come down to stay with me. We'd had a party in the dining room, pushing the table to one side, taking it in turns to pick tracks on YouTube. His dancing style involved swaying on the spot, whereas I resembled a manic hare. He'd stayed in the spare room, and we'd made love quietly, self-conscious as teenagers, giggling and stopping halfway through if we heard my dad's heavy footfall on the stairs as he got up for a midnight snack. Thom had infused the house with energy, and when he'd left it had slumped back to flatness.

Since September 2015 I'd been living out of a suitcase, zigzagging between north and south, boyfriend and father, happiness and duty, pleasure and sacrifice. I'd grown out of the habit of hanging my clothes up. I washed them, folded them, put them back in the suitcase, which served as an improvised chest of drawers. For Valentine's Day, Thom and I had celebrated with a meal out in Manchester. I'd been looking forward to another trip to his place in Buxton, a town of grand green hills, ancient buildings, icy winds and clear spring water. Now it would have to be cancelled.

Thom would be sympathetic, I assured myself. But I felt the itch of worry: I was seeing less and less of him. I recalled how hard it had been last September, when Dad had fallen sick, and those strange catatonic symptoms had first made themselves known. He'd been taken to A&E at St Helier hospital, then transferred to a geriatric wing in Tolworth

Hospital. During those autumn months when he'd been hospitalised, life had been suspended, as though I had inhaled and I was still waiting to let out that gasp of breath. I'd found that nearly every email I sent began with the words *I'm sorry for the slow reply*, that I'd begged for work deadlines to be pushed into the week after next, and set aside my dreams for a future time when life might be normal again. That night, on my mother's birthday, as I sat and watched the sky turn from blue to black, I wondered for the first time if it ever would.

2

My first memory: I am four years old and sitting in our cosy living room with my parents and older brother, John. Our faces are reflected and superimposed onto the TV set as we watch *The Fall and Rise of Reginald Perrin*. One family sitting in suburbia looking at another version of suburbia. Suburbs were once a place for the poor, for those who overflowed from the cities. Then, as the rural poor migrated to industrial cities, the wealthy middle classes moved out to the fringes. Gradually, suburbia came to be associated with neat gardens, neighbours twitching at curtains, 2.4 children and nine-to-five jobs. In the late seventies, *Reginald Perrin* satirised the sheer boredom of it all; Reggie seeks to escape it by faking his suicide, leaving his clothes and belongings on a beach to be erased by the waves.

Suburbia was a place my parents had escaped to. My mother, Glesney, had grown up on a council estate in south London, at the Elephant and Castle; my father, Edward, came from a large working-class family in New Malden. My mum had been denied a good education by a chauvinistic father who said that university was a waste of time for a woman; my dad's education had been meagre, but he managed to get a good job at the local factory. When they'd bought our semi-detached house, the estate agent had looked bewildered and asked: 'Are you sure you want to buy this place?' It was a house on a fine street, but inside it was a mess of loose wires, crumbling brickwork and walls painted in those lurid colours that were inexplicably fashionable in the sixties, avocado green and bright orange. The last owner had been an old man whose eccentricity had intensified into madness. His fingerprints were still on the walls, black smudges of wrinkled digits that looked eerie in their muddling of the elderly and the juvenile. There seems something prophetic about them now. My parents were thrilled, however. They had nearly achieved social mobility. The scene we watched together on TV was aspirational, for Perrin's house showed how our place might look, his middle-class boredom the luxury my parents longed for.

Another memory: I am gazing out of the window and see a man walking up and down naked. His clothes have been discarded, like Perrin's on the beach, trailing down the hallway. (Or have the two merged together in my mind?) My mother takes me, my older brother and my new baby brother to visit Dad. The place he is staying in is a large, white building, with cranky radiators that gurgle. People are wandering about as though they are in the middle of some imaginary maze, seeking the centre. One woman has the cackling laugh of a fairy-tale witch. My dad has always been a playful parent, indulging me in my favourite game whereby he would grab me by the ankles, swing me like a pendulum and cry, 'Tick, tock, tick, tock!' as my long hair brushed his shoes. This new version of my father is sitting in a chair in his green dressing gown. When he finally raises his eyes to look at us, I see sadness fossilised in his pupils.

With my dad missing, the planned transformation of our home failed. The house sighed and slumped its shoulders, the paint peeled, and the fingerprints remained on the walls.

I never asked my mum what had happened to my father. I felt too afraid, and perhaps she felt afraid of how she might frame that story. She looked tired and had a habit of biting her nails to the pink. She had started to take on various cleaning jobs. On one occasion a letter landed on the mat that brought her to tears. The local tax inspector had demanded a meeting, unable to believe that we lived off so little. My brother and I were taken along with her to see him. The man was kind, but he looked shocked when he asked, 'Don't you ever go out to dinner?' and she replied in the negative.

Dad returned home some months later. But he did not go back to work and, a year on, he disappeared again. Once more, he became a mysterious figure in a dressing gown in that strange white institution that seemed to me a place somewhere between a hospital and a school for the anguished.

By now, I had started primary school, which made me conscious that I was different from the other kids. They were dropped off at school by parents who had swish cars; they lived in comfortable houses; their clothes were crisp and their shoes shiny. My shoes had holes in and when I changed out of uniform into my day clothes, they had a whiff of oddity about them. Someone once asked me why I wore clothes from jumble sales. Dressed in a ragged ra-ra skirt of mauve and lemon layers, which clashed with an off-white Mickey Mouse T-shirt, I wasn't entirely sure how to reply.

The solution arrived with books. My mother had learnt the art of living off very little. She returned from jumble sales with bags bursting with tatty, dog-eared novels which cost a penny each. I read at night in bed and in the garden in the summer days, lying on the overgrown daisy-studded lawn and under the shade of a lilac bush, before breakfast and during breaks at primary school. Everything was wrong in theory. But in practice I was happy. I had Enid Blyton, Anne Digby, E. S. Nesbitt and Roald Dahl. In *Matilda*, Dahl describes how his heroine escapes from the unhappiness of her childhood through a visit to the local library:

'The books transported her into new worlds and introduced her to amazing people who lived exciting lives. She went on olden-day sailing ships with Joseph Conrad. She went to Africa with Ernest Hemingway and to India with Rudyard Kipling. She travelled all over the world while sitting in her little room in an English village.'

I couldn't necessarily look to my parents for wisdom anymore. My father was hidden and my mother, though loving, was preoccupied with trying to keep us fed and not lose the house. My brothers were no help, either. My older brother was distant; my younger brother was still a toddler, though fun to tease.

Books became my glorious escape. Their invented narratives were coherent, where every detail of the plot contributed to a whole and all made sense in the inevitable happy ending. By contrast, the real world was puzzling in its chaos. I was acquiring a sense of how stories were shaped but my own family's narrative remained a confusion, a tale seemingly without logic.

'*What happened to your dad?*' was a question I was asked in the playground. Not knowing what to say, I made up a story. I was learning from my favourite authors the art of spinning a tale, of how to build anticipation and end with a cliffhanger. As Dickens advised, 'Make them laugh, make them cry, make them wait'. The story of my father was a serialisation that I embellished day by day. It was Worzel Gummidge with a macabre slant; he had been unexpectedly kidnapped by a band of savage tramps who had invaded the bottom of our garden. This had evolved into a hostage crisis. My father was trapped in a garden shed: would he ever return? At one point, I became so engrossed in my story that I forgot it wasn't real. I was taken to the sick room because I was crying. When I told the nurse my tale, I could see that she was trying not to laugh; she gave me a biscuit, patted me on the head and sent me on my way.

Even if I had known the term for my father's illness, it would have meant nothing to me. Children survive without science the way ancient societies did – making up stories which explained why sometimes the rain fell and sometimes there was a drought, where the stars came from and why humans were put on earth. When we are children we view our parents as our gods, and so they need grand narratives. To say that my dad was 'mad' felt simplistic and would have rendered him too fragile, too human. He needed to be a hero in a tragedy – and importantly, at the mercy of external forces rather than internal ones.

In the playground, I became an observer. The difference in class between me and my classmates had cleaved me from them. The turning-inwards of my energies was becoming habitual; I read books in break-times, or watched the others playing. Most of the games were about love and war – Kiss Chase or some variant on Cowboys and Indians. Or children played at professions, at Doctors and Nurses, or being a spy. Children do not play at being children, they play at being grown-ups; the playground is a dress rehearsal for the future. I watched them with envy. I read *James and the Giant Peach*, *Five Children and It*, *The Secret Seven* and wished the characters might be coaxed from the page into real life friends.

And then, suddenly, my dad was back home again.

It was a plot hole I could not fill. Every time he returned, I was simply glad that he was home, without worrying too much about the whys: why he had gone, why he took pills at night, or why his work suits hung in his wardrobe and gathered dust. I remember going on a family outing by car one day when I was about eight years old. I was sitting in the back with my brothers and I was reading Roald Dahl's *Danny*

The Champion of the World. My father was driving. I could see his face in the rear-view mirror and he was muttering to himself as though in conversation with a voice; I smiled, recognising that I mirrored his reflection, for I had the voice of Dahl running through my mind, and it was witty, rude, wry, and compassionate. Fiction can sometimes enrich us, leave us feeling full, but just as often a good book can leave us wistful, with a sense of absence. In *Danny*, the hero does not have a mother but he has an amazing father. His father teaches him how to fish and takes him on secret poaching trips in the middle of the night. At the end of the book, there is a concluding message: 'A stodgy parent is no fun at all! What a child wants – and DESERVES – is a parent who is SPARKY.' It was hard not to stare at the picture of Dahl on the back cover, sitting in his Buckinghamshire garden, a tall man with a twinkle in his eye, and imagine that he was the perfect incarnation of paternity.

Back home, I flipped through a tattered dictionary, wishing I could discover a word for my dad's idiosyncrasies. If I could only find it, I thought, it would be like turning a key in a lock. Despite discovering new words I liked the sound of (*peevish, aberration, crasis*), nothing enlightened me. The key would not turn.

3

*B*ang! Bang! Bang!

When I arrived at St Helier hospital, I made my way through the criss-cross of white corridors to the fifth floor. My dad had been brought here in the ambulance yesterday. As I approached the ward, I heard a noise that filled me with dread.

Bang! Bang! Bang!

There were eight beds. The other patients were all elderly men and, though sick, they appeared to be 'normal'. They were reading the paper, watching TV, or chatting with relatives, who sat in plastic chairs around their beds. My dad looked simultaneously elderly and infantile. He was drumming violently, fists flying up and crashing down on the bed, like an enormous white-haired baby in a cot. When I said hello, a faint smile quivered on his lips – his fists pausing for a few seconds – before he went back to his routine.

A nurse approached me and said that my dad would probably be discharged later that day.

'But look at him,' I said, my heart thumping with shock. 'Isn't he always like this?'

I tried to explain the man my father normally was: a man

who rose every morning and made his own breakfast, did his own daily shop, and cooked himself a poached egg for lunch, one of those simple recipes that involves a certain delicate skill, lest the egg collapse into a wobbly morass. The nurse looked sympathetic but wary, as though she couldn't quite equate these two versions of my father. If he'd been in with a broken limb, she might have been able to synthesise them. But madness tears a person's character into two, their sane self and their insane one, and it can be hard to make the join, perceive them as a whole. Here, in hospital, the staff were used to illness being tested, clarified, boxes ticked and clear prognoses made. Dad had had an operation for bowel cancer the previous year and the accompanying leaflet gave a window for recovery of five to seven days and then a prognosis for his health in three months' and six months' time. Now he was an enigma, someone suffering from something which might or might not be cured at any time in the future.

Last September, when my dad had been brought in with the same ailment – a mysterious catatonia – they had also been a little suspicious and bewildered at first. I think it was the result of government cuts. With so few beds, perhaps there were fears that we were just dumping him on the system, creating a bed-blocker.

'You can't discharge him, we'd have no idea how to look after him,' I said. 'And I'm worried about him eating and drinking.'

The nurse softened. She said he'd be assessed by a psychiatrist. She added that she'd try to feed him.

I sat down beside my dad. Unscrewing a bottle of orange juice, I pushed a straw into it and held it to his lips. They looked parched, chapped. He drank in gasping, slurpy bursts. Relief came over his face. But it didn't cease the relentless *Bang! Bang! Bang!*s. I unfolded a copy of *The Daily Telegraph*, his paper of choice, and attempted to read an article to him, lifting the paper high to hide my face as irritated patients and visitors glared over at us.

The hospital cafe was a Costa; I ordered a hot chocolate and sat down by the window. I was taking a break, for I hadn't been able to soothe my dad's relentless banging. From my bag, I pulled a copy of *Mrs Dalloway*.

Virginia Woolf's novel is set on a single day in June 1923 and captures the psyche of a nation in the aftermath of the First World War; it dives and swoops into the consciousness of various characters, shifting from one to another within a single paragraph. I suppose I was drawn to a reread because of its theme of madness. In the novel's early conception, the book's two main characters, Clarissa Dalloway and Septimus Smith, were one; then Woolf split this imaginative egg into two. Clarissa is a high-society woman planning a dinner party; Septimus is a soldier who fought on the Western front and lost a friend there just before the Armistice. Woolf notes in her diary that she wanted to sketch the 'world seen by the sane and the insane', showing how thin the membrane is between the two. Clarissa suffers from neurosis, Septimus from psychosis. She is more manic; he is more depressed. Clarissa represents the governing classes – 'civilised life' – who were left largely untouched by the war, whilst soldiers such as Septimus were left in a state of trauma and despair.

I found myself moved by the relationship between Septimus and his wife, Rezia, seeing echoes of my parents' marriage. They sit in Regent's Park together, gazing at the trees and sky. Rezia tries to cheer herself by recalling the reassurances of her husband's doctors, that he has 'nothing whatever seriously the matter with him but was a little out of sorts'. The narrative jumps to Septimus's viewpoint and we see just how disturbed he is, for he hears the birds singing in Greek, and imagines he sees his dead friend, Evans, behind the park railings. It is an evocation of the lonely ache of mental illness – lonely for both of them. Septimus's wife cannot fathom the depths of his despair, musing: 'To love makes one solitary'; he cannot share the state of his mind with her; they sit as man and wife, but they are strangers. Septimus ends up committing suicide, jumping from a window. His psychiatrist attends Clarissa's dinner party and there she learns of his patient's death.

The book pinpoints a time in history when attitudes towards mental health and gender were changing. In the Victorian era, women with mental health issues were often diagnosed with hysteria. Shellshock baffled a society in love with the romantic idea that men returning from the front were war heroes. When soldiers first began to exhibit symptoms of what would now be called PTSD – dizziness, depression, sexual impotence, nightmares, fits of shaking, paralysis – doctors initially reacted with denial. The military saw it as cowardice and veterans were threatened with court martial if they did not 'drop' or suppress their symptoms. By 1922, however, over a hundred special treatment centres had been established for veterans seeking help. The illness was first termed 'male hysteria', then 'neurasthenia' and, eventually, 'shellshock'. Doctors had to acknowledge that it might be a malady of the mind rather than the body. As a result, psychiatry gained in power and prominence.

A friend of mine once said that she would have loved to have had a husband like Leonard Woolf. He supported Virginia in her writing, rooted her during the wild winds of her illness. Leonard, I supposed, had effectively been her carer.

Carer: that word again. More and more, people were pinning the label on me, and it still felt odd. I associated the word with someone in a blue coat, stripping beds, wearing rubber gloves; a Florence Nightingale figure with endless reserves of patience, energy and love. When I'd googled the verb *to care*, I'd found it was of Germanic origin, relating to the High German *chara*, meaning grief, sorrow. To care involved suffering. Over time, its meaning softened as it also came to signify *to make provision or look out for someone.*

My mum had looked after my dad for years, but I don't remember her ever being called a carer. Clearly it was a term of the present day, one that was gaining currency. Recently I'd picked up on the white noise of a social care crisis in the press, though I knew little of the details. If I thought about it, however, I did know of friends who were going through something similar. One had a parent who was ill with Alzheimer's. At midnight she would suddenly be woken by a call from her mother's neighbour telling her that her mother was wandering about the road without a coat, and she'd have to jump into a car and drive across the night to rescue the situation. Another had a brother with Down's syndrome: his parents had given him a loving, stable environment, but as they'd grown old they'd become wrung out with tiredness and, after a lifetime of sacrifice, had been forced to give up and put their adult son in a home.

Carer: the term seemed an anomaly in our modern society – one that, since Thatcherism, has become so individualistic, amplified by Twitter and reality TV; one which prizes aspiration, self-reliance, getting ahead. Not one in which wages are down and inflation is high and life is moving so fast, for I was beginning to associate being a carer with losing chunks of time, getting behind, to-do lists forever unticked and multiplying. Perhaps that was why the label has evolved: as a way of defining duty, enclosing it, protecting it from life's pressures.

I told myself to get up and return to my dad's bedside, or head home. Reading Woolf felt like such an indulgence. When I wasn't with my father I fretted that I was neglecting him; when I was with him, I fretted that I was neglecting my other responsibilities. I was a conscientious type. Missing deadlines made me anxious; I hated to feel I was letting people down. I had so many things to do: emails, freelance editing, chap-

SAM MILLS

ters to write, chapters to edit, research, washing, housework. I imagined my Florence Nightingale alter ego, who would be back at my dad's bedside by now, saying soothing words, knowing how to calm his *banging*. I sat and read and felt guilty.

4

I remember the moment I discovered what was wrong with my dad – or, at least, found out what label his illness had.

I was fourteen years old. Now that my dad was working as a clerk – his first job in a long time – and my mum had part-time work as a medical secretary, our house was less of a dump and even had wallpaper in some places. My bedroom was the corner box room upstairs. In the evenings, I could hear the wind battering the side of the house and the thrum of a wasps' nest in the air vent. But I loved it in there; it was my hiding place, my cave. It felt more like a study than a bedroom. I had so many piles of books and lever arch files filled with my writing that I couldn't move more than three paces without bashing into them. I was already keen to be a published author, though most of the books I wrote were derivative, borrowing from the romances I read, with little idea of how fantastical they were. I hadn't the life experience to discern that men did not always bring happy endings.

Homework always came first, however. Mum had repeatedly impressed upon me that life had no future without a good education. Though I'd passed my eleven-plus I'd been destined for the local comprehensive school, until my mum intervened – fighting ferociously with the council to get me into the local girls' grammar school. I had been sulky about the idea at the time: Mum had explained that girls did not perform as well when they studied in classes with boys, for both sexes just ended up showing off to each other. I'd thought: *boys are just the thing I want in my class.*

As always, Mum was right. On my first day, I'd fallen in love with the school. It was set in the sprawling grounds of a park; in the playground you could hear the yowls of peacocks from a nearby mansion. Local geography highlighted the class divides. Those who came from wealthy families lived in the big, white birthday-cake houses near to the school; those of us who were in the poorer division headed for the bus to take us on the long journey home. But class did not seem to matter so much, not the way it had in primary school. On my first day, I sat between a shy girl called Lucy, and Henrietta, the daughter of a Surrey vicar; and I got the bus back home with a new Sri Lankan friend called Eshani. For the first time in a long while, I was lucky enough to have good friends, and I treasured them dearly.

It was almost 7 o'clock by the time I finished my homework that evening – an essay about Lady Macbeth. Hungry, I went downstairs for dinner. Just four plates had been set at the table, as my older brother had recently left home; the shouts and babble of dialogue from the TV next door suggested my younger brother was watching *Grange Hill.*

In the kitchen, I found my dad pulling a tray of chips from the oven. He set them down on the surface and stared at them gravely.

'You've burnt the chips, Dad,' I pointed out casually. I didn't really mind. I liked them that way, crispy and crunchy between my teeth.

My dad pulled off his oven gloves; I heard the pounding of his footsteps on the stairs. I watched the chips cool into a row of blackened fingers. As I ventured upstairs, I could hear weeping. I felt my heart thump, conscious that ignorance might be better than knowledge, that it might be safer to go back down.

The bedroom door was ajar. I crept closer. Dad was sitting on the bed, saying: 'I burnt the chips, I burnt the chips' over and over and Mum was there with him. Dad's face was red, as if the tears he was shedding had been wrenched from his gut, and Mum was making shushing noises as though he was her child.

I crept down the stairs. In the kitchen, I walked in circles and chewed nervously on an apple. When my mother eventually came down, she explained that my dad had 'schizophrenia' and that sometimes it was hard to get his medication right. The amazement on my face startled her. 'Didn't you notice all the pills he takes?' she asked. 'Don't you remember when he took off all his clothes and walked down the street and then none of the other children's parents let them come to play for a while...?' There was something oddly casual about her tone, as though we were exchanging gossip about someone else's family. Our discussion was brief; I was too shocked to summon any questions about my father's illness.

Later, after my parents had gone to bed, I sat in the bath and wept at this strange and sudden rewriting of our lives. Through the warped window glass, I could see the yellow lights of the house next door. I imagined the faint sounds of laughter as they sat and enjoyed dinner together: a conventional family, the one I'd fooled myself into thinking we were. At school I had been reading my nonsense poetry to my friends and they'd teased me for being 'mad'; did that mean his illness was weaving its way into my words?

That night I was finally able to find the correct word in the dictionary. It informed me that schizophrenia came from Greek roots, *skhizein* meaning split/tear and *phren*, the mind. The key had turned.

The next evening my dad made tea again. A trio of us at the table: Dad, me, my younger brother. We ate in silence. It was a Tuesday, which meant Mum had her evening class for A-level psychology. Without her, the house felt empty and eerie; she always created a sparkle, a warm energy, a love that gave our home an ambient glow.

After dinner, I stood in the hallway and watched my father from the slit between door and frame. The beard he was growing highlighted his gaunt cheekbones. He was sitting in his armchair reading the Bible; this was his new obsession, something he clung to as though it was keeping him afloat in the world. Looking back, I wonder if he combated his voices by reading about men who had heard the voice of God giving them divine instruction; while he was labelled mad, they had been celebrated as prophets.

Upstairs in my room I got to work: I took an envelope from my rucksack containing a passport photo of my friend Anil. Using a Pritt Stick, I carefully glued the photo to a square of card with a college logo watermarked on its background. The next bit was trickier; I carved lettering into a rubber and used ink from my fountain pen to paint over the letters, before stamping it over the photo. The final touch was a dash of *Blue Peter*: a wrapping of sticky back plastic. And there it was – another fake ID. Anil had already paid me 50p for this. It was a way of earning extra money, since my weekly allowance was considerably smaller than most of my friends. It meant we could get into nightclubs with 'proof' that we were over eighteen. Nightclubs meant alcohol, boys, smoking: all the things that we missed out on at a girls' grammar school where everyone was well behaved, wore coats that were the correct shade of navy, and where hems above the knee were forbidden.

I found myself thinking of Laura Palmer as I slotted the ID card back into the envelope. *Twin Peaks* was an obsession at our school. Laura lived a double life: her good girl, blonde, high-school sweetheart one, and her darker two-boyfriends-on-the-go promiscuous druggie one. (This splitting of people into two, normal self and doppelgänger, seemed to be a feature in the series as it went on.) That division was something I identified with. One half of me did my homework, achieved grade As, looked meek and innocent, was made form rep and obediently picked up the register each morning for my teacher; and the other smoked illicit cigarettes in the park on the way home, made fake IDs, lured boys on dancefloors, and shared fumbling trysts with them in dark corners in clubs. It seemed hard to allow the two to blur together and perhaps, I wondered, it was something the male sex found easier to do, to be whole, unified.

The ID card finished, I got stuck into my writing. It was becoming my addiction. When there was a knock at the door, I jumped. A stern silhouette appeared.

'You're not to have sex before marriage – it says so in the Bible,' my dad intoned in a robotic tone.

I rolled my eyes in exasperation. Dad looked upset, then he was gone.

The next day I recalled the incident and felt lost, as though the dislocated exchange with Dad had had nothing to do with me. When I told my mum about it, she just laughed and told me not to take any notice of him, which made me feel better. And this was how I survived growing up with my father. I saw the same process occur in my younger brother – a distancing, as though my father was an unfortunate and obscure relative staying in the house, someone we all had to tolerate.

Much of the time Dad was so quiet he was like a ghost – though sometimes, when he was doing the washing up, I'd hear him shout: '*Shut up! Shut up!*', trying to bat away the voices that swirled around him like a malignant wind. Once, on the bookcase by his chair, I found a list he'd made of rebukes to its torments –

> *I am not under house arrest*
> *I am not a Muslim*
> *I am a Christian*

– all written in small, jagged capital letters with his favourite Parker biro. After this, I would check the bookcase every so often, seeking more eerie rebukes, but there were only shopping lists and details of Bible services.

As an adult, whenever I came home to visit my parents, Dad would hover in the background in silence. A friend of mine who stayed with us later recalled: 'I remember your dad not saying a single word to me. It's as though he wasn't there.' I know now that this is a symptom of schizophrenia: an indifference, an ephemeral, unengaged absence. But at that time all I knew was that my mum was like a best friend to me, while my relationship with my father was virtually non-existent.

One year, we all went to the cinema on Boxing Day. We saw the film *Australia*, and as the credits rolled and we emerged from the dark, I was surprised by the animation on my dad's face. When I asked him if he'd enjoyed it, he said it was one of the best films he'd ever seen. Later, my mum explained: 'His voice suddenly stopped speaking to him – he had two hours of freedom.' Freedom: the word jolted me. Because he had stopped vocalising his battle, I often forgot that he was imprisoned in that cell, where a hostile figure talked at him all day. Whatever conversational tug of war was going on inside him had become a private anguish.

On the mantlepiece in our living room sits a photographic triptych of my mother, looking shy, smiling and pensive. After I'd returned from visiting my father at St Helier hospital, I found myself looking at her frozen expressions, wishing I could ask her for advice. Had she ever seen my father descend into catatonia? How would she have handled it?

We had lost my mother just over four years ago. Since she'd gone, I had not seen my father cry once.

My brothers and I had waited and watched him, always vigilant for signs of a breakdown. But he just carried on in his set routine. Over the years, the bandwidth of his attention and interests had narrowed down. He had no friends, only his family. He had no ambitions. Taking a trip to somewhere he didn't know would cause his hands to tremble with anxiety. Routine held him together. He slept the same sort of hours as a cat. At night, he would spend twelve hours in bed and often napped in the daytime. His day was bookended by the taking of medicines – Lansoprazole and Lactulose first thing in the morning, Amisulpride and Clozapine last thing at night. His physique was also shaped by them: he put on a huge amount of weight, a side effect of his pills. He went to the local supermarket several times a day, but rarely ventured beyond the town, except for hospital appointments; the parameters of his existence were more akin to those of someone who lived centuries ago. The only dramatic change after Mum died was that he stopped watching *EastEnders*, (he and Mum had always watched it together). My brothers and I were divided as to whether this was a sign of an improvement in his mental health.

When I was away in Appley Bridge I would call him every night. Our talks would last ten minutes or so. We always had the same conversation, cheerful and superficial: I would ask him how the weather was; he'd reply that it was sunny/rainy/grey. I'd ask him if he'd eaten/fed the cat/gone out. He'd reply yes/yes/yes. Then I'd say goodnight. He always seemed pleased that I had rung. When I was back living with him, I would cook him the occasional meal. There was a companionable warmth between us, in that we shared the house but didn't speak much. This continued for three and a half years, before suddenly, dramatically, things deteriorated.

September 2015 brought the first signs of trouble. My dad was taking weekly trips to the GP for remedies for corns, a tickle in his throat, a fit of dizziness, a small rash on his hand. Initially I felt anxious, because I knew from loved ones I'd lost that a tiny symptom can belie an illness that slashes and burns; and then I became immune to worry, because it seemed that minor illnesses were becoming my dad's hobby, something to collect, to fuss and turn over and label. Then his tendency to hypochondria became manic. Stefan took him to the GP over an indefinable illness; on their way out, Dad began to weep. He was taken to hospital, discharged a few days later. He seemed strange, blurry, slowed-down, tasks taking twice as long as usual. I thought if I cooked for him it might help. I thought that rest was the answer.

That day in September, when it first happened, I remember setting down plates on the dining-room table for lunch. My eyes skimmed a stain on the carpet. My mother had lived her last days in this room, and the stain had been created by – a spilt drink? – a splash of urine? – now faded to a watermark.

I went into the hallway and called upstairs: 'Dad, it's ready!'

Two plates on the table. The empty place where she once sat, at the head. My appetite was always sharp. Still standing, getting impatient, I speared a potato and chewed it quickly. I called to Dad again. When there was no reply, I hurried up the stairs. 'Come in,' his quavery voice replied to my knock. He was sitting on the bed, looking at the clothes neatly laid out next to him – trousers, braces, shirt – as though he had been given a set of bad letters at a turn in Scrabble and couldn't make a word out of them.

Kneeling down, I busied myself with peeling off his socks, pulling on taut crisp ones. But when I reached for his pyjama shirt, my hand paused. I hadn't seen my dad naked since I was a child.

'Why don't you have lunch in your pyjamas?' I suggested.

As he lumbered down the stairs, I thought: *hang on, has he even taken his morning medicines?* One of our kitchen cupboards now functioned as a medicine cabinet: I found a jumble of white boxes with scientific names and labels giving instructions for doses. In the dining room, Dad sat down before his plate of cooling chicken and vegetables. I passed him his pills. Silence; stasis. I poured him a glass of water and put the pills on a spoon. I raised them to his mouth. He opened it. I slipped them in and passed him the water.

I started to cut up his food. A piece of chicken on the end of my fork came up against his closed lips. He looked at me as though he couldn't hear the words I was saying: *Dad, it's good to eat, you need to keep your strength up.* For one surreal moment, I felt as though I was an apparition he did not believe in. When I called 999 they asked if he was breathing, if he was in pain, and I had trouble explaining his state: he seemed as though he was in a coma, yet he was awake. After I hung up, I took solace in the sound of him breathing in and out, but I could not make his eyes connect with mine. The fading light in them chilled me with a grief-flash: my mother lying in this room, on a makeshift hospital bed, the life seeping out of her. It was as though he was in a liminal state, body half-dead, mind in purgatory.

It took eight weeks for him to heal. Due to a lack of beds at the local psychiatric hospital in Tooting, he was transferred from St Helier to Tolworth hospital, where he shared a ward with elderly patients suffering from dementia. There he was medicated and nourished back to walking, talking, speaking health and discharged for Christmas. I had assumed then that the catatonia was a blip, a one-off. Perhaps he'd just got tired, run down, needed rest. Now that it was happening all over again, I could no longer dismiss it as an anomaly. This was the start of something new, a pattern I could neither name nor explain. I thought of all the years that my mother had looked after him. Why, after decades of stability, had he collapsed again – and why into such a strange state?

5

All couples have a Getting Together story. The one they fondly recount at parties, in answer to the question, *How did you …?* Over time, the details narrow and harden, acquire a lacquer of fiction. The story is something you repeat as the narrative of your love affair becomes complex and conflicted; it becomes a kind of origin myth.

In 2012, I had a book published called *The Quiddity of Will Self*. It was supposed to be the literary equivalent of the movie *Being John Malkovich*, only with Will Self as the centre of fascination. In interviews, I found myself telling people that I also saw it as a blueprint for a schizophrenic mind. No doubt this sounded a little pretentious, possibly wanky. But within the book, I felt that I was exorcising the ghost of my father's madness.

I used to joke to friends that I first noticed Thom when he wrote an online review of my book that was quasi-positive ('reading as a workable alternative to drugs'). I'd shoot him a sulky glance; he'd reply with a sheepish, conspiratorial grin. On our first date we'd gone to the Corner House, the arts cinema in Manchester, to see *Amour*, since we were both Haneke fans. It wasn't an ideal film to see when I was in the first year of grieving for my mother's death. The film depicts an elderly couple where the husband becomes carer to his wife after she suffers a stroke. Eventually, overwhelmed by exhaustion and despair, he murders his loved one with a pillow. Some furious critics argued that it was 'an advert for euthanasia'. This, too, evolved into anecdote: Thom would recount how I spent much of our first date sobbing in the toilets, 'the usual effect I have on women'.

At first, something inside me prickled resistance. I was not sure if I believed in monogamy. During the first few weeks of our relationship I would wake up from a nightmare, disorientated and wondering who I was lying next to (for I was so habituated to sleeping alone); the dream would involve Thom putting a lead or a noose around my neck and tugging tight. I tried to find reasons why he and I wouldn't work. The term of my relationships in the past had always been dwarfish. Normally the men/women I dated were more lukewarm about books, or became jealous of my writing, irked by my dreamy moods, my eccentricity, my absorption in research. I had grown used to treasuring my independence. But Thom's flat was crammed with bookshelves and he loved hearing about my book ideas. I was terrified that I was being tamed. I felt afraid of the loss of individuality; afraid of being one of those couples who start to blur into one, finish each other's sentences. I wanted to maintain the sharply defined edges of myself.

Three years on: on days when we are apart, we text every few hours. Silly pictures; quotes; politics; jokes; or sometimes just trivial details: what we ate for breakfast, what we ate for lunch. We have pet names for each other: he is Mr Rose and I am Miss Rossetti. One day when he leaves for work at the bank, leaving me to dream in his bed, I drift through his flat and become a composer. I tell him that it is a love song about him. I will never sing it in his presence, but when he gets home he will always be able to hear its echo in the walls. He hugs me very tightly when I tell him this.

After lovemaking we lie in the dark and discussions smoke between us, surreal and childlike. I ask him what colour his soul is and he says dark red. I tell him mine is the blue of the sea. Before sleep our noses bump as we say goodnight. I always borrow a T-shirt from his drawer, normally one decorated with an obscure band's offensive logo, and his tracksuit bottoms, which are too large and bag around my ankles. They are infused with his scent, a catnip to me. We joke that we have a pet Dodo, taking it in turns to look after him. I learn that Thom hates capers. That he loves the herb basil, is a night owl who can't bear the mornings; that he had once played guitar in a band called Billy Ruffian, and that he longed to have a pet wolf when he was a boy. Once, I have a dream that he is in a valley, and wolf howls are echoing through the hills, and he is laughing in joy at their sound.

On the way to see Dad in hospital, I texted Thom: 'taking *Mrs Dalloway* to read. Miss you xx'. It had been Thom who'd bought *Mrs D* for me, I suddenly remembered, as I sat on the bus and smoothed my hand over the cover. We often greeted each other with a surprise gift, usually a book or a sweet treat: chocolate for me, nerds for him.

Bang! Bang! Bang!

It was the second day since my dad had been whisked to St Helier in an ambulance, and the banging of his fists against the bed seemed to be more violent than ever. I observed a nurse – who I sensed was a kind woman but being driven a little mad by the noise – trying to lower his arms. They obstinately swung away from her and repeated their bangs with vehement determination. Sitting by his bed, I watched his face, his eyes closed, his expression a blank.

A memory from childhood: I am six or seven years old. Stefan grabs one of Dad's trouser legs and I hug the other. We anchor him to the living-room floor. 'Dad, don't go, don't go!' we cry, as though he is about to make an epic voyage instead of a trip to the supermarket around the corner. Perhaps we are afraid that he will take a detour and end up in a place with white beds where we can only see him during visiting hours. He smiles, benign.

Even though he was sick and shattered, we were able to connect with Dad through play and touch. It is when we became adolescents that the gap widened up, when we wanted sophistication instead of physical play, when we wanted answers to questions about people and the way the world worked, and he couldn't offer us those.

Bang! Bang! Bang!

Had he been fated to end this way? He had been born into a family of four children; he was the second youngest. They'd moved from Yorkshire to New Malden in his early childhood – two years before the end of the Second World War. His mother was an intelligent woman with a sharp mind and a love of Scrabble. His dad was a clerk by day, a talented musician by night. He played the piano in jazz bands, and had a go at the saxophone too, though 'he didn't quite have the puff for it'. When I was a kid I remember being handed a record called *Peter and the Wolf*, music my grandfather had composed for a play put on at our local theatre.

Bang! Bang! Bang!

My father had artistic talents too. In his peripatetic, patchwork career, he'd once worked as a sample-box maker, designing Easter egg boxes in various imaginative shapes. I remember us making special pillow boxes together: him laying down a piece of card on the dining-room table, his pencil scratching down the page in line with his ruler. These boxes were the shape of miniature pillows, with oval flaps at each end. I would paint designs on their sides – a sunset beach, a dragon, a love heart. They could hold odds and ends, paperclips, jewellery, or chocolate. Later, at school, I would often give decorated ones to my friends as presents.

Bang! Bang! Bang!

A funny thing about those boxes: some time before he'd been sectioned, Dad and I had been having lunch together, when I commented that he was artistic. He had blushed and immediately said: 'Oh no, I can't draw.' Dad was always determined to diminish himself. My brothers and I had all done well academically (oddly enough, this is common in families where a parent suffers from psychosis). But if I told Dad that he was clever, as I once did after he achieved an amazing score in a game of Scrabble, he would shake his head and assert: 'I'm not clever, I'm not talented.' Then, to prove his point, he'd tell me that he hadn't done well academically and failed to get into grammar school. But that was about luck as much as gifts. Maybe he'd just had a bad day when he took the exam; maybe fate had been scowling over him. Grammar school had lifted me up but had been a tragedy for him, putting him in a box that said *not as bright as my brothers*.

Was that why he put himself down, because he'd always compared himself to his older siblings? It was the same with social status. 'What class are you, Dad?' I once asked him. He said that he was working class (ish), but his children were middle class (definitely). There was a note of parental pride in his voice, but also, perhaps, a determination, in line with the character of his illness, not to be anything at all, not to define himself, as though he saw everyone around him as having technicolour lives of glory and intelligence and success, whilst his life was a silent, black and white movie with barely any plot.

My father's illness was a mystery. My father was a mystery.

Bang! Bang! Bang!

An idea came to me: the previous year, when my dad had his operation for bowel cancer, I would often read newspaper articles to him. When he discussed politics, it was one of the few occasions when he transcended his usual monosyllabic answers and responded with both energy and verve. Like most people, his views did not really fit into a box marked left or right wing but were a medley of contradictions: he was pro-Brexit, voted Lib Dem, believed education should be free and that immigrants should be welcomed.

Now I hoped that if I read to him it might work by a kind of osmosis, in the same way one reads to a loved one in a coma, hoping your voice might heal and stir. But he could barely hear the piece I was reading out, because of his helpless *Bang! Bang! Bang!*s.

I noticed that tears were oozing from my father's eyes.

'Are you okay, Dad?' I asked.

'I've just got a cold,' he said. It was one of the first fully formed sentences he'd spoken in a long time.

A cold? *Was he crying?* I wondered. *Is this some kind of breakdown?*

'Are you sad about anything?' I asked, but he had drifted below the dark surface of his catatonia again.

I stood up, leant over him and took hold of both of his arms. Slowly, I began to lower them to the bed. I felt the physical strength of my dad in resistance; we began to struggle. I leant in so close that my face was inches away from his. Our pupils reflected each other. I spoke to him through my eyes: *You're okay. I'm here. I'll always look after you.* I felt his fists pause. And then a change came over his face. The tension dissolved, and his expression summered into one of pure sweetness. Love shimmered between us. His eyes drifted shut. His hands twitched with the memory of compulsion, but lay still on the bed. As he drifted into sleep, I realised the pitch of his exhaustion, how hungry he had been for its release – his own desires thwarted by the peculiar perversions of his body.

6

This is a picture of a carer whom I admire very much: Leonard Woolf, the husband of a genius.

He was tall, thin and authoritative, yet he suffered a nervous tremor in his hands (inherited from his father) that could be so severe on some occasions, such as formal dinners, that the cutlery he held would rattle. He was clever and he was kind. He loved animals and had numerous pets. In Ceylon he adopted a leopard, in England he had dogs, and he once went on holiday with a pet marmoset called Mitzi which sat on his shoulders as he drove about in an open-topped car. He was a champion of the underdog. His socialism was in part inspired by the prejudice he suffered as a Jew (before they were married, this was one of Virginia's objections to him as she pondered his proposal). He noted that, unlike the aristocrats of the Bloomsbury circle in which he moved, unlike Lytton Strachey and the Stephens, he was 'an outsider to this class, because, although I and my father before me belonged to the professional middle class, we had only recently struggled up into it from the stratum of Jewish shopkeepers. We had no roots in it.' He had his flaws, too. He was obsessive about administration, which he regarded as 'the most precious flower and fruit' of civilisation; he loved doing his accounts. He could also be rather controlling and his dogs were always kept firmly to heel. He was an intellectual snob, but he wasn't a social one: he was happy, say, to chat about the League of Nations with his postman. At times, he has been caricatured as pompous and patrician, but this is unfair; he had a sparkling sense of humour and gave after-dinner speeches which left listeners (such as John Betjeman) rolling about with laughter. He became a feminist after his involvement with the Women's Co-Operative Guild and disagreed with 'one of the most inveterate and gross vulgar errors' that women were 'more emotional than men and more flighty'. It is hard not to like Leonard Woolf.

He married Virginia in 1912. Their marriage was one in which he tailored his life around hers. Over many decades, he nurtured her literary genius and she wrote masterpieces, such as *Mrs Dalloway*, *To the Lighthouse* and *Orlando*.

During my dark days of worry about my dad, Leonard became an inspiration. He had nursed Virginia through periods of breakdown and suicide attempts with great stoicism, love and loyalty. Being a carer can be a lonely duty; you can feel as though you are the only one in the world suffering its restrictions whilst everyone else around you are living lives of butterfly freedom. Leonard was a man I put on a pedestal. Knowing that he had to feed Virginia, that he sometimes floundered, that he questioned doctors, that his health suffered whilst he bettered hers, made him deeply human to me.

I read everything I could find about Leonard, eager to understand him better, but also to find answers to questions that haunted me: before marrying Virginia, did Leonard know that she suffered from mental health problems? Or was it something that he realised after they were married – did it come as a shock to him? A moment must have occurred in their relationship, as it did with my parents, when there was a subtle shift from husband/wife to carer/patient, the two blurring together. Was this hard for them both to accept these new roles?

I imagine Leonard as a young man in 1911. It is a summer evening and he is walking through Bloomsbury's Gordon Square to attend a dinner at the home of Vanessa Stephen, recently married to the art critic Clive Bell. The first time he met the Stephen sisters, back in 1900, was at Trinity College, Cambridge, when they came to visit their brother, Thoby. Both were dazzling in white dresses and big hats. In his autobiography, *Sowing*, he recalled how their beauty made everyone's breath stop, 'as it does when in a picture gallery you suddenly come face to face with a great Rembrandt or a Velasquez'. He recognised too their sharpness of mind, seeing in their eyes 'a look of great intelligence, hypercritical, sarcastic, satirical'.

Leonard has spent the last seven years in Ceylon, working for the civil service as a colonial administrator. When he left England, he was very much the 'innocent imperialist'; he has returned very much the anti-imperialist. In 1909 Lytton Strachey wrote to him declaring that Leonard ought to propose to Virginia – 'She's the only woman in the world with sufficient brains.' Lytton had planted a seed.

He dines with Vanessa and Clive. Afterwards, they are joined by Virginia and the artist Duncan Grant. Vanessa is now an artist; Virginia is still unmarried and working on a novel. Leonard is exhilarated by how much British society has changed in the time he has been away. The last time he visited 46 Gordon Square was back in 1904; then, he would never have dreamed of calling Vanessa or Virginia by their Christian names. Nor would they, as young women, have felt as confident to speak so freely, to spark and share and bat ideas. That fusty, oppressive Victorian atmosphere is gradually seeping away from society.

Aspasia. That is the name Leonard gives Virginia in his diary. Aspasia: the cultured, cerebral mistress of Pericles. Leonard is living with her now – albeit only as her lodger, having moved into Brunswick Square in December 1911. Duncan Grant and the economist Maynard Keynes are sharing the ground-floor; Virginia's brother Adrian is on the first floor, Virginia on the next floor, and he at the top. Virginia is one of his boarding housekeepers (polite society is shocked by her living in a house with single men).

Leonard has seen Virginia frequently over the last few months. They've spent a weekend in Firle, Sussex, together; courted each other in London squares. The Bloomsbury group is starting to take shape. Once, in Gordon Square, Leonard was thrilled to hear Virginia talking brazenly with Adrian about 'copulating' and 'fucking' (as Adrian gossiped later), as though to tease and shock. She can be crude; she can be cerebral; and sometimes in conversation there are wonderful moments where she can '"leave the ground" and give some fantastic, entrancing, amusing, dreamlike, almost lyrical description of an event, a place, or a person'. He's listened to her reading some of her novel-in-progress, *Melymbrosia*, and he thinks it is extraordinarily good. Just the sound of her voice has a physical impact on him. He tries to pinpoint it in words: it 'seems to bring things from the centre of rocks, deep streams that have lain long in primordial places within the earth'.

But he has proposed and she is uncertain. She needs time, indefinite time, to consider. He writes to her and declares all his faults – 'I see the risk in marrying anyone & certainly me. I am selfish, jealous, cruel, lustful, a liar & probably worse still. I had said over & over again to myself that I would never marry anyone because of this, mostly because, I think, I felt

I could never control these things with a woman who was inferior & would gradually enfuriate me by her inferiority & submission.'

They attend the theatre and the Russian ballet together. They share a love of the countryside, of the Sussex Downs. Reading is a joint passion; they both write; they share the same friends. He dares to hope that their intimacy is building towards an acceptance.

Virginia has turned down a number of proposals over the years; she does not want a marriage that feels like 'a profession'. As she becomes increasingly fraught, she suffers wild dreams, headaches, insomnia. A romantic suitor might have mistaken these for the agonies of romance. But Virginia is struggling with 'a touch of my usual disease, in the head', a mental agony which she describes as 'all the horrors of the dark cupboard of illness'. When Virginia is admitted to Burley Park, a nursing home in Twickenham, Vanessa writes to Leonard asking him to stay away.

Virginia sends him a disturbing letter from Burley Park: 'I shall tell you wonderful stories of the lunatics. By the bye, they've elected me King.'

Leonard is not deterred. When his request for leave is turned down, he resigns from his job, even though he is not certain of Virginia ever accepting him, nor of how he is going to survive financially. He misses her terribly and is grateful when Vanessa asks him to accompany her to see her physician, Dr Savage, to keep him involved.

In his memoir *Beginning Again*, Leonard muses that Virginia has a 'most sensitive and sophisticated mind', and that the Greeks recognised a connection between genius and madness. He recalls Seneca: *Nullum magnum ingenium sine mixtura dementiae fuit* (there has never been great genius without a mixture of madness in it), and Dryden's verse: 'Great wits are sure to madness near allied/And thin partitions do their bounds divide'. But at this stage in their relationship, whilst he can see that Virginia is sensitive, he is not fully aware of the extent of her mental health issues. Savage and Vanessa do not tell Leonard the whole story of her previous breakdowns. Vanessa is very keen for their marriage to go ahead. She has played the part of carer to her sister for many years, but now she herself is married, with a child and a lover and a career as a painter; she sees, perhaps, an opportunity for someone else to take on the responsibility of Virginia.

Virginia's stint in Burley Park was not the first time she'd stayed there: she also recuperated there in 1910. She had a history of mental health problems. *She suffered her first breakdown in 1895, after the death of her mother.* This is a sentence I came across often when I researched Virginia's life, and it is a cold, factual one. The more I read about the details of her childhood, the more empathy I felt for her; it isn't surprising, given the traumas that she suffered, that a breakdown occurred.

She was only thirteen when that first breakdown happened. Her mother, Julia Duckworth, had married Leslie Stephen, a widower thirteen years her senior. The family consisted of siblings Virginia, Adrian, Thoby and Vanessa and their half-siblings Laura, Stella, Gerald and George Duckworth. Losing a parent later in life is devastating enough; it can leave a wound that never fully heals. To lose a parent at such a tender age must have been particularly hard; furthermore, Virginia experienced the spiritual loss of a father alongside the physical loss of her mother. Leslie Stephen was infirm and nearly deaf and in need of a great deal of care. Stricken with grief and melancholy, he would sit at the dinner table and break down crying in front of the children, wishing he were dead. The children soon found themselves parenting him. The oldest daughter, Stella, in particular, virtually became a substitute wife.

Virginia referred to the death of her mother as 'the greatest disaster that could happen', and recorded how she lurched from mania to depression, from painful excitement to deep melancholia.

When her father died in 1904 – a third family death in less than a decade – Virginia's subsequent breakdown was even more severe. Three months after his passing, she fell into a manic state and heard voices ordering her to starve herself. Virginia was sent to Burnham Wood, Welwyn, to stay with Violet Dickinson, a family friend. Vanessa helped to look after her with the aid of three nurses. Whilst lying in bed, she imagined that she could hear King Edward VII lurking in the azaleas, swearing, and, like Septimus Smith in *Mrs Dalloway*, the birds singing in Greek. She made her first suicide attempt, jumping from a second-storey window, but was not seriously hurt. When she recovered from her breakdown, however, she returned to writing with characteristic fervour and dedication; by the end of that year she was beginning her prolific career in journalism by writing reviews and essays for the *Guardian*.

This time around, in 1912, Virginia also revives and returns to live in Brunswick Square. She and Leonard grow closer, bonding over their literary ambitions and finally, on 29 May, they are having lunch when Virginia tells Leonard she loves him and wants to marry him.

Afterwards, they travel to Maidenhead and take a boat ride up the river to Marlow, summer shimmering around them, gliding through the water so that, as Leonard recalled later, they seem 'to drift through a beautiful, vivid dream'.

When I told a friend that I was writing about Leonard Woolf as Virginia's carer, they immediately objected: 'But he was her husband,' as if the two roles were very separate things. It is true that the role of caring creates intimacy but also division within a relationship, with one person forced to step back and consider what is best for the other. When my parents were first married, they were equals, debating key decisions together. But, after my dad had a breakdown, the balance of power gradually shifted; as I grew up, I watched as my mother – quite reluctantly, at first – began to take charge, until she was making pretty much every decision for both of them. She paid the bills, controlled the money, decided where her children would go to school. The more she became a carer, the less she seemed to function as a romantic partner to my dad.

In 1913, Leonard *is* Virginia's husband: there is no doubt about that. They are happy newlyweds. They have honeymooned together in Somerset and travelled across Europe: France, Spain, Italy. Their sexual connection is shaky; but this does not diminish the depth and passion of their love. They have bestowed sweet pet names on each other: she is Mandril, he is Mongoose. Their writing lives tendril and flourish side by side; their daily routine is structured around their love of words and books. A typical day involves writing 750 words in the morning, followed by gardening in the afternoon and another 500 words between tea and dinner. In the evenings they enjoy reading, side by side, a routine that Virginia describes in her diary: 'L in his stall, I in mine'. Their lives dance between London and the countryside, parties and quieter living, Clifford's Inn, off Chancery Lane, and Asheham, a farmhouse in the Sussex countryside.

But, from time to time in the early days of their marriage, Leonard is also starting to flicker into the role of carer too. In January 1913, he pays a visit to Burley Park. He walks through its grounds towards the large Victorian house, the trees thin and stark with winter, the driveway crisp with frost. This is the private nursing home for ladies with 'nervous disorders' where Virginia battled the breakdown she suffered during their courtship. Is it a question of nature, or nurture? Leonard knows that mental illness is a zigzag in Virginia's genetic history. Her father is prone to periods of melancholy and 'fits of horrors' – headaches and insomnia. Her half-sister, Laura, is in an asylum. Leonard is seeking advice from

Virginia's doctors, from those who have cared for her and treated her in the past. He and Virginia have a decision to make.

Jean Thomas, the proprietor at Burley, welcomes him in and they sit down to discuss the issue: should he and Virginia have children? Would Virginia be able to cope? Or would it wreck her sanity and their marriage?

Yesterday Leonard sought the opinion of another physician, Dr Craig, who warned him that the risk would be very great. He knows that Jean is very fond of Virginia. A better verdict might be possible. But Jean is not positive: she also declares that it is a great risk. Nervous about making the right decision, Leonard is keen to hear a wide range of opinions. He doesn't just meet with Jean Thomas and Dr Craig; over the next week he hurries about from one doctor to another, receiving a kaleidoscope of opinions. Dr Savage says yes. Babies, he declares, would do Virginia all the good in the world. Dr Maurice Wright, a younger doctor, concurs and also gives his blessing. And Dr T. B. Hyslop suggests that they wait eighteen months before making a decision. That is two positives versus two negatives and a kind-of-maybe. Leonard consults family as well as doctors. He writes to Virginia's sister and Vanessa replies that she feels babies would be a mistake: 'One does plunge into a new and unknown state of affairs when one starts a baby and once it's started there's no going back.'

As Leonard darts between them, I imagine the words of Virginia's early letters echoing in his mind. 'I want everything –'

she wrote to him passionately, just before they were married, 'love, children, adventure, intimacy, work.' But after the doctors are consulted, he and Virginia are still uncertain. At first, Leonard is not fully persuaded by the doctors' fears, and Virginia remains hopeful, writing to Violet that they need to wait and spend six months in the countryside. As the months go by, however, Leonard observes Virginia becoming increasingly unwell, suffering agitation, headaches and all the symptoms of her old troubles. So it is he who seizes control and makes the final decision: they will not have children.

Virginia agrees to the decision with maturity and dignity, but the verdict is not without its heartbreak. Virginia has strong maternal instincts. She loves looking after Vanessa's children and, years later, she poignantly expresses her regret in a letter to a friend: 'a little more self control on my part, & we might have had a boy of 12, a girl of 10.'

The expression 'self-control' points to the fact that at times she unfairly blamed much of her illness on herself, even though it often rendered her quite helpless. Leonard describes how she thought 'that her mental condition was due to her own fault – laziness, inanition, gluttony'. In part, this was cultural, a hangover from the Victorian era, where asylums employed moral management, believing they could teach patients to develop rational control over their minds. No doubt, it was also symptomatic of a lack of general knowledge in society about mental illness.

But perhaps Virginia wanted to take on this blame because it implied that she had autonomy, for the more she fell sick, the more she was subjected to the decisions of doctors and her family. She was a formidably intelligent woman, and it infuriated her to have to submit to others. When writing *Mrs Dalloway* some years later, she noted in her diary that she was enjoying life more because she was feeling less 'coerced'. I've noted a similar streak in my father, a resistance to seeing himself as a victim. Once, just before he was about to collapse into a catatonic state – which I attempted to combat by suggesting he stay in his armchair – he tried to rise up in rebellion, declaring he didn't need to rest, wanting to affirm himself as active, in control, a victor over his illness. A second later, it swept him into darkness.

Did Leonard make the right decision? Perhaps he did the responsible thing. It is a choice that made things better but also made things worse. The sorrow of being denied parenthood may have been a factor in what Virginia suffered next, and the 'nightmare' that befell them.

7

Manchester is my favourite city in the world. I used to call it my muse because before my dad became ill, I would spend all day there, writing, wandering from library to cafe, converting caffeine into prose. It had the zing of our capital city, I felt, without the frazzle and the tiredness.

The day that I returned north, it was bitterly cold. Thom was waiting at Manchester Victoria Station with a roll-up tucked behind one ear. We hugged and kissed. We couldn't stop smiling. We knew that time was precious: my dad was still in St Helier, suspended in limbo, waiting for a verdict.

We walked to the Northern Quarter. The restaurants here were all the same, selling burgers with fancy names and upmarket fries and milkshakes, the hipster equivalents of McDonald's. Sometimes I thought the quarter was so trendy, it was like a parody; once we'd visited a cafe where you could choose a record to play on a gramophone, sip tea from jam jars, and your bill was chalked up on a large blackboard by a beehive-haired waitress.

I felt myself unwind. I was so used to seeing nurses and hospital beds that it was a novelty to be sitting in a place where the background noise was jazz and happy chatter. *Normal life*, I thought. An oasis. Thom rubbed my arm, then wound some strands of my long hair around his forefinger.

'How's the Dodo?' I asked him. 'Has he been behaving?'

'He's a nightmare. I hardly got any sleep last night, he pushed me out of bed and I ended up in his nest.'

The Dodo was a character I'd invented when *Quiddity* was published, the mascot of the Will Self cult: an irascible, opium-smoking, absinthe-swilling Soho beast. Like our imaginary kid, he would alternate between staying with me and Thom, and cause us no end of theatrical grief when he was arrested for drugs possession, or nearly set fire to an office by smoking his cigar.

After lunch, we walked arm in arm past buskers and street performers and passed a wig shop displaying row upon row of different styles and hues. I commented on how many people they must have beheaded to create the display. He laughed and I laughed and the blare of a trumpeting busker blasted our hearts and we were happy.

Back at Thom's small flat in Buxton, we colour-coded the books on his bookshelves. Later in the afternoon, his daughter came over. Aged nine, she was already an aspiring writer, stapling together sheets of paper to form mini chapbooks. When Thom encouraged her, I felt touched, reminded of the way my own mother had nurtured my creativity. I played with her whilst Thom cooked dinner, teaching her how to make pillow boxes, just as my father had once taught me.

The day was rushing by and as I came into the kitchen, Thom grabbed my hand: 'When will you come up again?'

How could I reply? With Dad in limbo, I felt as though I had no control over my future; it was being written for me.

'Can I check my email?' I asked, changing the subject.

I didn't have a smartphone; Thom, as a millennial, liked to tease me for being so Victorian. When I opened his laptop, he remarked, 'Emailing your *other* boyfriend, no doubt.' I rolled my eyes but felt a little sheepish. There was indeed an email from Z sitting in my inbox.

Thom and I were often jealous of our exes and past histories. My ex was a man I shall call Z, a prize-winning author. I emailed him on a daily basis. But he was a man my mum had thought of as a 'rogue', fling material, not boyfriend; and now he was no more than a close friend.

Later that night we lay in Thom's double bed. The wind outside – meek in the south – was a swearing banshee in Buxton. We listened to its squawls and then Thom said: 'Well, when your Dad's better, you can move in with me?' and I stroked his hand and the silence stretched out.

A home-cooked dinner, a DVD, morning croissants, a walk, a bookshop wander, and the weekend was gone. We kissed goodbye and then I was back on the train, watching my ghost double-stained on the passing landscape, on green slopes, cows and cars.

Thom's quiddity lingered with me. His scent on my coat and in my hair; I smiled as I recalled jokes and sweet moments; I carried on talking to him silently in my head, then translated the thought into a text.

I opened up a new book. Why had I never read up about schizophrenia before? My whole life I'd loved learning new facts, devoured non-fiction, enjoying the mind fizz of fresh ideas. As though in denial over my father's illness, I had avoided studying the subject, except where it was touched upon in novels. Recently, though, I'd tackled a few textbooks. I thought of the friend of mine whose partner had been diagnosed with Alzheimer's: within a few weeks she could speak about the illness with the authority of a professional. Now I wanted to become the expert too, to ward off these feelings of helplessness and confusion. I needed facts and figures to plug the gap; definitions to attempt to give outline to the smoky blur of my father's mysterious, absent personality. Most of the textbooks I'd read in recent weeks were often dry, and they said the same kind of thing over and over again:

Schizophrenia is an illness that affects one per cent of the population.

That said, around twenty per cent of us exist in a liminal area between psychosis and good mental health.

Schizophrenia is sometimes muddled with multiple personality disorder.

Think of the dramatic transformations of self in *The Strange Case of Dr Jekyll and Mr Hyde* – well, that is an entirely different illness.

It was first classified by the German psychiatrist Emil Kraepelin, a contemporary of Freud's, who named the illness *dementia praecox* in 1899, noting that many sufferers withdrew and sank to 'the life of a vagrant'.

This turned out to be wrong. Schizophrenia is quite different from Alzheimer's; the mind is afflicted, but it does not degenerate.

The Swiss doctor Eugen Bleuler disputed the idea of premature dementia, feeling that it in fact led to 'a heightened consciousness of memories and experiences'. He renamed the illness schizophrenia in 1911.

It is a biological illness, but its onset can be linked to stress. It develops most frequently in late adolescence/early adulthood. A tragedy, such as divorce or a job loss, can act as a match that strikes against genetic potential, lighting the full flame of illness.

The list of symptoms are:

Negative	Positive
Loss of concentration	Hallucinations
Socially withdrawn	Delusions e.g. thoughts are being controlled by someone else or planted in your mind
Emotionless and flat	
Loss of ambition	Unpredictable behaviour

I felt that it would be more apt to term them as the negative and the more negative.

Some books also include a separate category for 'disorganised symptoms' – including disordered speech and confused thinking. I could recognise some of these in my dad – the voices, the depression, the urge to withdraw. He struck me as a man who found the world a frightening place. By hiding away from it, he could continue to cohere, to keep himself together. Yet I would not call him a weak man. His blue eyes were always full of tenderness, as sweet as a boy's. Despite his odd behaviour when I was a teenager, he was never purposely cruel to me; and I never heard him say an ill word about anyone.

Here is R.D. Laing, writing in *The Divided Self*, on how the schizophrenic feels:

> . . . both more exposed, more vulnerable to others than we do, and more isolated. Thus a schizophrenic may say that he is made of glass, of such transparency and fragility that a look directed at him splinters him to bits and penetrates straight through him. We may suppose that precisely as such he experiences himself.
>
> We shall suggest that it was on the basis of this exquisite vulnerability that the unreal man became so adept at self-concealment.

Laing gave me richer insights than the textbooks, but I still had an itch to find the book that resonated, that gave a deeper understanding of where the voices came from, how the psyche was torn. That afternoon, as the train trundled on the tracks, passing through Crewe and Birmingham, I opened up *When the Sun Bursts* by psychoanalyst Christopher Bollas. The introduction made me tingle:

Most people I know who have talked with schizophrenics have noticed that these feel like conversations not with someone whose ailment is derived from the fog of symptomatic preoccupation, or the dulling repetition of character patterns, but with a person who seems to be existing on the edge of human perception. Take LSD and you see things you would ordinarily never perceive. Become schizophrenic and you see these things without the aid of drugs.

This is it, I thought, this is the book I've been searching for. Schizophrenia is an illness that is too idiosyncratic for the language of science; it needs poetry and imagination too.

Bollas was good at describing the slow onset of schizophrenia, the ways in which the self and body shifts and alters. 'Those on the verge of schizophrenia,' he writes, 'may experience profound changes in their way of seeing, hearing, and thinking. Early shocks may include an odd vividness of certain colors that can become eidetic or dreamlike in their intensity. This may be accompanied by an unusual sensitivity to sound.'

I thought of the American novelist Zelda Fitzgerald, who was diagnosed with schizophrenia in 1930, and detailed how she saw 'a new significance to everything ... colors were infinite, part of the air, and not restricted by the lines that encompassed them and lines were free of the masses they held'. Bollas describes the disorientation, the loneliness that comes with this strange metamorphosis: how sufferers feel afraid to tell their friends and family, at just the moment when they most need help. And he captures beautifully the sadness of this distancing: 'It is as if he is gradually leaving our world; although still present, he has transported himself across some unseen line, crossing over into another reality that totally absorbs his attention.'

For the schizophrenic, a breakdown can entail a painful collapse of the self, that central 'I' that underpins our daily narrative and creates the illusory story of our past, present and future. The self is lost, it fractures into voices; fragments of self might even be put outside of the sufferer, into objects (a tape recorder, a vacuum cleaner), the landscape (a tree). This creates a deep dislocation in the schizophrenic's sense of time and space – which is why they might create a mythology ('I am being given instructions by an alien') as a desperate substitute for the 'real' world they have lost. This is also why there is a loss of desire in pursuing goals – without an 'I' who is seeking achievement, and with the world around you not making sense anymore, perhaps they are no longer worth pursuing. The illness, then, is a vanishing act. For those left behind, families and friends and lovers, there is a grieving: 'Our type of mourning is unique as we are left holding the remnants of the person's former being.'

I thought of how it had been for my mother, marrying a man who was kind and sensitive and had a good job, who then became a wraith sporting a biblical beard, with no interest in her hopes, her fears or her desires. I thought of leaning over my dad's hospital bed, the moment when I looked into his eyes and saw love, as though the ferocity of my yearning had inspired him to fight back and show a flash of his lost self to me. But that had just been a fleeting moment: would Dad ever fully come back to me?

I set my book back on my lap as the train approached Euston, staring at the dour colours of London through the window. I recalled various people who had told me their stories of schizophrenics they'd known: a lover, a relative, flatmate. All of their tales were of schizophrenics at their worst, of withdrawal, chaos, hallucinations, destruction, suicide attempts. I knew people were highlighting these incidents in sympathy with me, as a way of saying, *we know what you're going through*, but I also felt sad. Nobody ever told me stories of schizophrenics who had healed and unified, who had got better.

8

It was dark when I arrived at Summerfields Hospital. The map by the entrance, lit by a fluorescent bulb, conveyed a vast, sprawling estate of blocks and buildings. The breeze was sharp, blowing my hair across my face as I wandered in the dark, following signs that weren't always clear, backtracking frequently, lost in the maze. Trees, wind-tossed, waved against night clouds. The buildings loomed over me; the lights within looked sinister and strange. I had received a call: my dad had been transferred here, sectioned for twenty-eight days by law. I checked another map. I was getting closer now.

Summerfields Asylum was opened in 1841; within five years it was full to bursting and needed an extension. Before the state-built asylums, those who were mentally ill ended up in madhouses. In the eighteenth century a new trade in 'lunacy' evolved. A growing middle class realised they could escape the stigma of mad relatives by having them locked up, and businessmen and medical men realised they could make a profit out of this. At the same time, the labouring classes were struggling with the burden of being carers. Many of them had moved to the cities, family ties were weaker, and there was a rise in wage labour – all of which meant they had less time and less energy for caring. A local parish authority could also decree that a 'lunatic' be moved to a madhouse if they had no family to take care of them.

These institutions were often run by practitioners with little or no medical training. They were not nurturing places. I shudder to think of what would have happened to my father if he had been alive then. Inside the madhouse he would have been chained to a cell, or put into a straitjacket. He would have been bitten by fleas and attacked by rats, and would have lived with the smell of faeces that had been rubbed onto walls. He would have witnessed female patients being raped by keepers; keepers who would have beaten him up. He might have suffered gangrene and, chances are, in the cold and the damp, he would have contracted tuberculosis. He might have been put into a coffin with holes drilled in the cover and then lowered into water and nearly been drowned, in order to engender fear in him. A highly influential doctor of the time, Thomas Willis, had decreed that the mad needed to suffer 'the emotion of fear' in order to be shocked back to reality. According to Willis, 'maniacs often recover much sooner if they are treated with tortures and torments in a hovel instead of with medicaments'.

As awareness of the mistreatment of 'lunatics' in the private madhouses grew, the Victorians were determined to build state-owned asylums which would be run by doctors and properly regulated. There was a developing realisation that illness was not caused by evil spirits but diseases of the body, prompting a more sympathetic attitude towards the mentally unwell. From 1845 – the year that it became compulsory for counties to build asylums – to the end of the nineteenth century marked an era of prolific asylum-building. 1851 saw the official opening of Colney Hatch: a huge institution, the size of a large village, built in the parish of Friern Barnet, the largest asylum in Europe and the most costly to date.

To the Victorians, the asylum came to be seen as a symbol of scientific advancement and human progress; Sir James Paget, Surgeon Extraordinary to Queen Victoria, called the modern lunatic asylum 'the most blessed manifestation of true civilisation that the world can present'. The writer Elaine Showalter has pointed out that whilst the construction of Colney Hatch disturbed some observers, others were puffed up with national pride that 'England, pre-eminent in art, in letters, in technology, and in trade, also led the world in madness. Both natives and foreigners agreed that as the richest and most advanced society, England necessarily had the highest incidence of insanity.' It was becoming accepted wisdom that mental health problems would be the inevitable side effect of a capitalist society as it shifted gears and the clock ticked ever faster.

At Summerfields there were dozens of wards, most of which seemed to be named after trees and flowers. When I finally found the right block, a vivacious staff member greeted me and looked up my father on her database: 'Oh, he's our new mystery guest!' she cried. 'We didn't know he had family. We didn't have any information about him.' She said he had been moved from their care unit to Crocus Ward.

Another map, and off I set again, into the cold, sharp night, to find my dad's new location. I had to press a buzzer to be allowed into the hallway, and before I could enter the main door, my bags were checked. I thought this was because patients weren't allowed plastic bags, or pens, or because I might be carrying something they could use as a weapon. I found out some weeks later that it was in case *I* might be carrying a firearm. Apparently a visitor had walked in and killed his relative with a few shots to the head (although when I googled this story, I couldn't find any details).

I entered a vast, long room, which comprised a dining area of tables and chairs, and an adjoining sitting room with a TV. About half a dozen nurses were in the room. Some months on I remember watching the third season of a favourite TV series, *The Fall*, and its inclusion of a scene that immediately jolted me out of my suspension of disbelief: *that doesn't look right*. The murderer is taken to a psychiatric unit, and some of the nurses in the ward are sitting on chairs, vaguely watchful. In my experience, nurses never have a chance to do this. They are always standing. There is simply too much going on for them to have the luxury of being observers; they have to constantly intervene.

Crocus Ward was a place of sound and fury. Some of the patients were sitting, talking to themselves. Others were walking about in agitation, hammering locked doors, rattling them. Some were crying. Some seemed on the verge of starting a fight. Overhead, garish fluorescent lights beamed down on this room that looked like some awful simulacrum of a suburban front room, as a cheery presenter on the TV babbled away, reflected in the eyes of staring, bewildered patients. I was afraid to make eye contact with anyone. My pupils skittered left, right, left, seeking, searching – there. On the sofa. There was my father.

Dad was lying down and his fists were still pounding away, beating at the orange leather. His eyes were closed, and they did not open when I knelt by him and said hello. Nor could he speak. The nurse I spoke to, a woman with pink hair, looked stressed. Edward had had a fall, she said. They'd sat him up in a chair, but then he'd slipped off, banging onto the floor. A doctor had assessed him and he was alright, aside from a few bruises. 'And he got moved into this ward without any notice,' she added. 'We don't really know anything about him.' She spoke as though he'd been rejected for membership for an elite club for schizophrenics.

Later, I laughed at the memory, but at the time I felt close to tears, being told that Dad didn't belong, just as our family had never fitted in when I was a kid. I felt like flicking her the V-sign and telling her we didn't want to be there anyway. But I could hardly grab my dad's hand and take him with me.

Instead, I asked in a measured voice if he had been fed.

She said he had arrived too late in the ward for dinner, which was served at 5.30.

I worried about him being dehydrated. I opened a bottle of fancy juice I'd bought on the way, put a straw into it and watched as my dad stopped his beating and drank eagerly. Behind me, I could hear one of the female patients saying: 'I know you're looking at me …' Was she talking to me? I risked a glance and figured she could be referring to anyone. Nobody was looking at her; the other patients were staring at the TV.

I turned back to Dad and chatted quietly, about a time when things would be better: he would be released and we'd go to a restaurant together, where he could have his favourite fish and chips followed by cherry pie. Then there would be my older brother's wedding, where he could buy a new suit and stand proud – and soon, I promised him, everything would be alright.

Skype's beepy siren rang out. I was in my bedroom back home. Two boxes flickered up on the screen: I saw Thom and I saw myself as he would see me, sitting on the floor, cat on my lap. Thom's fingers blibbled before his face in mock tentacles. I laughed, cheered up by his sea monster mime.

'How's your dad?'

'Well, it's a bit of a weird situation – the doctor there told me that they don't have proper records for him. It's been decades since he last had a major breakdown, so their history is patchy.' It seemed as though everything about my father was elusive, mysterious.

'So they don't know what will make him better?'

'They're giving him these drugs which should slowly bring him round … We hope. There's two theories – one is that he shouldn't have reduced his medicines, and the other is that it's caused by constipation.'

'That sounds odd.'

'I know.' The idea still sounded absurd to me, though I had googled it and found that it wasn't uncommon amongst elderly people. Severe constipation can cause delirium and become life-threatening.

'Stefan is totally set on the constipation theory,' I went on. 'But I think it's the meds.'

I broke off, worried that I was offloading too much. I knew that Thom was sympathetic but it was starting to feel as though all I thought and talked about these days was my dad. So I held up a book by our new favourite author, *Mrs Caliban* by Rachel Ingalls, about a bored housewife who falls for a six-foot-seven-inch tall sea monster who turns up at her house.

We chatted about books and work and, as it neared time for bed, I undressed on the edges of the screen, titillating Thom in a way I hadn't done for months. Our relationship had lost its sharper sexual edge over recent months; it had become more comfortable, verging on brotherly-sisterly. Thom teased me that he was taking screenshots. We said our good-nights and blew kisses and gestured hugs: now that we could no longer meet in person, mime had to suffice.

When I returned to Summerfields the following morning, it looked completely different in daylight. As I entered the tree-lined driveway, the elegant, grand buildings made me feel as though I were entering a National Trust property. The blocks were separated by expanses of lawn, framed with daffodils in shades of yellow and pale cream. It all looked so civilised.

This time I had brought a Scrabble set. It was a game my

dad loved. In his last incarceration at Tolworth Hospital, when he'd also been mute with catatonia, I had laid out the board in front of him and been startled by the swiftness with which he'd started playing. His words had been simple, mostly composed of three letters – *hat, cat, dog* – but his animation had delighted me.

But I was being too optimistic. I found my dad sitting upright in an orange leather chair, in the living-room area with the TV. His eyes were closed and he was drumming, drumming away at its wooden arms. His clothes looked odd – he was wearing grey sweatpants and a shirt with pinstripes. The pink-haired nurse grinned at me. She was a lot friendlier today and I warmed to her.

'Why's he wearing that?' I asked.

The answer was terrible.

She explained that in his catatonia he couldn't even use the toilet, so he was regularly soiling his clothes, and they kept cleaning him up. The clothes he was wearing right now were from their spare supply. She also said that he was resistant to taking fluids and had only been fed a little. I pulled a drink from my bag, another fancy concoction with cranberries and other exotic berries. I offered him the straw and he sucked in a little juice and then he let out a sound that curdled inside me. It was the weariest sigh I'd ever heard.

Seeing my shock, the nurse said: 'It's difficult – he doesn't really want to be alive right now.'

Her words were like a punch. My father's depression had always been veiled from me, his drugs softening it into a vague air of sedated melancholy. I had never seen him in such a state of naked despair and it broke my heart. I wanted him to be alive; I wanted him to want to live; I wanted him to want to be present for me and my brothers. Tentatively, I held his hand, as though some sort of spark and flow of optimism might travel from me to him. I suppose I was keen to replicate that moment in hospital, where he had been banging and I had looked into his eyes and soothed him. But like all spontaneous acts, an attempt to repeat it was futile. My dad's eyes remained closed. His fists kept on banging, oblivious, obstinate.

I got up to leave, feeling low. The nurse asked if I would wash his laundry, or if they should take care of it. I thought of my towering workload and – feeling oddly sheepish, as though it was a trick question, a test of my dedication as a carer – I asked if they would.

Back home, there was a call from St Helier. My dad was scheduled to have an operation on an aortic aneurysm. Now it would have to be cancelled. The woman on the phone sounded worried and agreed that he was in no fit state for it, but said: 'You must ring us as soon as he's well – it's urgent.' I went upstairs to my dad's bedroom feeling even more gloomy. An aneurysm – a dangerous balloon-like bulge in a blood vessel – could potentially rupture at any moment.

There was always an austere feeling to his room, even though we kept it tidy – there was nothing in it that displayed the usual stamp of character; no books, no paintings that he had chosen for himself, no treasures or knick-knacks, no noticeboard.

As I opened up his wardrobe it struck me that even his clothes suggested an absence. He habitually wore suits, a shirt and tie, no matter what the weather or occasion, even on a hot beach in the middle of summer. People often said that being next to my dad made them feel shabby, he was always so smart, but I had a feeling that he was simply determined to look respectable, to shield himself from being judged by doctors and strangers. They were clothes that hid him rather than made a statement.

As I folded them up and put them into carriers, as I stuffed his black socks into cracks, and coiled up his ties, I thought with sadness of the yearly trip we made to the beach together, a regular treat for his birthday. Would he be out of Summerfields by the summer? Would he ever get back to normal – or, at least, the normal that everyone had defined he needed to be?

9

Spring 1913. Leonard Woolf writes in his diary: 'V.n.v.w. b.n. [Virginia not very well bad night].' This was Leonard's habit when he was worried about Virginia: writing notes in code in his pocket diary. He is starting to notice warning signs: 'a peculiar "headache" low down at the back of her head, insomnia, and a tendency for the thoughts to race.'

At meal times he has to coax her to eat, noticing that she suffers 'some strange feeling of guilt' about food. He wonders whether its cause might be Virginia's turmoil over finishing her debut novel. Originally called *Melymbrosia* and now *The Voyage Out*, it is a book that Virginia has been working on for the last seven years. Between December 1912 and March 1913, she redrafted it once more in its entirety with a tortured intensity and feverish pace, retyping 600 pages. Leonard notes that she writes with an 'artistic integrity and ruthlessness which made her drive herself remorselessly towards perfection'. And the act of the finishing and letting go of a book – 'the shock of severing as it were the mental umbilical cord' – is always hard for her.

Recognising his wife's literary brilliance, Leonard praises the novel and passes it over to Gerald Duckworth, who has set up his own publishing house, Duckworth Press. But this only increases Virginia's worries: will anyone publish it? In order to empathise, we have to forget her colossal reputation and rewind time, remember that at this stage she has only proven herself as a journalist. She is hungry to succeed and terrified of publishing something that might be jeered at. Leonard's first novel, *A Village in the Jungle*, has been accepted for publication. She may have wondered whether she would end up being merely the wife of a novelist rather than a published author in her own right.

Even the acceptance of her novel by Duckworth doesn't bring her relief, for then comes the torture of going through her proofs over a period of several months, which she finds excruciating. Duckworth responds to Leonard's concerns (as well as other friends and family) by moving her publication date back by two years, to March 1915.

Victoria Glendinning, Leonard's biographer, captures the tragedy of the situation – 'life was opening out for him. At the same time, Virginia's illness was closing in on them both.'

I found this very poignant, finding an echo in my parents' marriage. When they moved from their maisonette to the house in Surrey, the place that epitomised their suburban dream, with a young son and a baby (me), they were so full of optimism, their future ahead of them. A friend told me how my mother took delight in all the details of their new home, from the curtains to my cot; she wanted to have more children, a brood of four, a big, happy family. But in the space of a few months all this had changed dramatically.

Leonard too, had returned from his honeymoon deeply in love. His debut novel had been published to good reviews, his journalism was flourishing (he had started writing for the *New Statesman*) and his political interests had found direction in socialism. It was a time for the Woolfs when optimism must have felt like the natural emotion, with their love new and tender, and their literary ambitions beginning to be fulfilled – and therefore such a shock for Leonard to suddenly find the woman he adored was now on the verge of suicide. I imagine his disorientation too: with no prior experience of mental illness, he now found himself on a steep learning curve. In *Beginning Again*, he describes it as the beginning of a nightmare that lasted for several months: 'One of those appalling nightmares which, because they belong to the world of reality and yet seem to be overlaid with unreality, have the double horror of the collapse of one's everyday life and, at the same time, of the most fantastic and devastating dream.'

Leonard Woolf has sometimes been unfairly maligned by critics, who have portrayed him as a controlling husband who censored Virginia's every move (one revisionist biographer, Irene Coates, even suggested that he dictated her suicide note). Many of the criticisms illustrate the main problems and dilemmas of being a carer which I came to face: how much liberty do you give your loved one, and how much control do you exert? This is a challenge that Leonard begins to grapple with in the early years of his marriage.

On the morning of 25 July 1913, Leonard writes in his diary:

'Went Savage w V morn said she ought to go Jean.' Dr Savage has recommended that Virginia should return to Burley Park, back to Jean Thomas. Virginia isn't happy. She accuses Leonard of beastliness. Whilst she 'liked her [Jean] up to a point', religion has weakened their friendship. In a letter to her sister Vanessa, Virginia describes how Jean sent her a copy of Tolstoy's *What I Believe*, enclosing 'a long serious letter with it, exhorting me to Christianity, which will save mé from insanity. How we are persecuted! The self conceit of Christians is really unendurable.' Jean's desire to save her soul has uneasy echoes of the medieval priests who argued that the mentally ill were possessed by demons, and hence needed priests to facilitate their repentance and healing. It reflects a desire to patronise and to control, to assume a position of superiority that was also practised by alienists in Victorian asylums.

Finally, Virginia agrees to go for a fortnight.

Leonard has to wait it out and hope the cure works. He is staying at their London lodgings, Clifford's Inn; he works in the mornings, and visits Virginia in the afternoons and evenings.

Given that there were no anti-psychotic drugs available in those days, Virginia's cure was tailored around healing through rest and diet. This regime was developed in the United States by the American neurologist Silas Weir Mitchell and often prescribed to patients suffering from neurasthenia (the condition Virginia had been diagnosed with) – an illness which covered, as Leonard put it, 'a multitude of sins, symptoms and miseries', from chronic fatigue to insomnia to irritability to headaches. Neurasthenia was regarded by many as a response to the pressures and pace of modern life, characterised by the telephone, the telegraph, the car, the plane.

Men and women were treated differently. It was thought that men would achieve balance by spending more time outdoors pursuing oh-so-'masculine' activities. In the States, doctors would often send men West to ride horses and rope cattle; Teddy Roosevelt took this cure before he became president. Women, on the other hand, were thought to suffer neurasthenia as a result of spending too much time *outside* of the home. Therefore, their cure required them to be cooped up indoors. It was recommended that female patients avoid reading and any intellectual activity, that a copious diet of milk-drinking should be followed (4–5 pints a day) and that the patient should be deprived of all communication with their family.

Leonard writes Virginia tender letters on a daily basis whilst she is in Burley. His love and devotion pour out onto the page; he declares himself 'in service' to her: 'I believe, Great One, you do want to take on your mongoose … for another year – & if you'll only let him grovel before you & kiss your toes, he'll be happy.' It's touching that Leonard's adoration isn't at all diminished by her illness; he is determined to see things through. He keeps looking ahead to the future, assuring her: 'Only rest quietly & dont worry about anything in the world, & it wont be any time before we're again having the best life that any two people can have.'

This was an approach I often found myself employing with my father when I visited him, when I would talk to him over and over about the future, trips to the coast, family events. I'm sure that Leonard repeated these reassurances in order to lift Virginia's spirits, but also to console himself, to make the present bearable by believing that it would soon be past, an experience they would both look back on.

He receives replies from Virginia. They are written in pencil, shaky, and on one side of the paper: 'I want to see you, but this is best' – and 'if only I weren't so appallingly stupid a mandril' – and 'Its all my fault' – and 'I have been disgraceful – to you'.

This meekness of tone reminds me of my father and his nervousness in psychiatric wards, of how he is always careful to show gratitude to staff, to his doctors – no doubt driven by the fear of a loss of control and his anxiety about when, and whether he will be released.

Leonard's replies are always kind, and he refuses to let Virginia blame herself. Whenever she worries about causing him misery and being a burden, he writes back: 'Never talk again, dearest, of causing me anything but the most perfect happiness, because literally & honestly that is what I get merely from sitting quietly reading by you.'

Virginia and Leonard stand on the platform at Paddington Station. It is 23 August 1913. Virginia has been released from Burley Park but she is still no better than she was when she entered the place. Vanessa waves them off cheerfully, but later she tells her husband: 'I don't think Woolf can go on for long alone, the strain of looking after her is so great.'

I picture them sitting on that train like Rezia and Septimus in *Mrs Dalloway*, like my parents: both bound and separated by the illness they are fighting. I imagine how Leonard must have been tempted by the thought of hauling their bags back onto the platform, slamming the carriage door, cancelling the trip.

The Woolfs are on their way to Holford in Somerset. Virginia is still resisting food, still unable to sleep and 'full of delusions'. But Dr Savage has recommended they go; Virginia has been promised a holiday as a reward for going to Twickenham, and Savage fears a broken promise might send her over the edge.

Does Savage know what he was talking about? Leonard is starting to lose faith in him as a doctor: he is Victorian, fusty, chauvinistic, old-fashioned. Feeling that he is 'in a hopeless quandary', Leonard has consulted with yet another physician, Dr Henry Head, who also thinks the trip is a bad idea but, like Savage, fears that Virginia might kill herself if denied it. Leonard is starting to suspect that beneath their white coats and air of authority, none of the doctors really have a clue how to define and predict his wife's illness. Nevertheless, the plan is agreed: Leonard will try to get Virginia to eat and rest at Holford, but if she gets worse, he will bring her back to see Dr Head and keep him updated on her state by letter. One of Leonard's few consolations is that he does not have to bear the burden of caring for his wife all by himself. Their family friend, Ka Cox, is on standby to join them if needed.

In Holford, they head for the Plough Inn, a cosy,

sixteenth-century inn with Tudor beams and an inglenook fireplace, situated at the foot of the Quantock Hills. Leonard must have found himself comparing past with present, for this is the place they had spent their honeymoon, enjoying little treats and delicious food: cream and butter and eggs and bacon making for voluptuous breakfasts. He surely didn't imagine then, in that blissful week, that they would end up returning in a state like this.

A few days on: it is 3.30 in the morning and Leonard is watching Virginia's breathing soften as she slips into sleep. It has been a long night and he's just given her a sleeping draught, 10 grams of Tripinal, to combat her insomnia. He has bromide and Veronal in his case of medicines too and he takes care to lock the case up, imagining terrible possibilities, should Virginia get her hands on the drugs … He feels the strain of being her carer, a role he must carry out covertly; he has to uphold the pretence of simply being her husband. 'I had to be on the alert continually, day and night,' he writes in *Beginning Again*, 'and yet, if possible, not give her the feeling of being watched.' Virginia is suffering from severe paranoia and delusions that people are laughing at her. The last thing she needs to feel is a sense of division between her and Leonard, to feel that he is playing doctor, analysing and assessing her.

Ka Cox has joined them on their holiday. Leonard ended up wiring her after a week. They attempt to have a quiet, simple time, reading and walking, but Virginia is resistant to rest or sleep, convinced that 'her condition was due to her own faults, and that eating and resting made her worse'. Leonard studies his wife and wonders how he might undertake the next challenge: persuading her to head back to London.

When he tackles the subject with Virginia, he is cautious and careful to respect her opinion. He gently advises her that they must return to home, but she can choose the doctor they see and 'she should put her case to him' and Leonard will put his. If the doctor says she is well, Leonard will accept the verdict and not worry her anymore about eating or resting. But if the doctor thinks Virginia is unwell, she must 'undergo what treatment he might prescribe'.

Virginia argues no, no, no. But after some time, she gives in and Leonard asks her to choose a doctor. She says Dr Head; Leonard is delighted and relieved, for Head is his choice too.

They sit on the train, the three of them: Leonard, Virginia and Ka Cox. Leonard can see that his wife is going through sheer hell, her despair so great that she is hanging on to life by a thread, and he must watch her at every moment, in case she decides to jump from the train. For Leonard, the journey has 'that terrible quality of the most real of real life and at the same time of a horrible dream'.

The relief of it, as Leonard closes the door to 38 Brunswick Square: they have got Virginia back safely.

They are staying at the lodgings of her brother, Adrian. The following morning, Leonard takes her to see Dr Maurice Wright, followed by an afternoon appointment with Head. Both tell Virginia that she is ill; Dr Head tries to reduce the stigma of mental illness by asserting that she is sick in the same way someone might suffer a cold or typhoid. She needs a rest cure; a trip to a nursing home. Once again, Virginia remains unconvinced, feeling she is entirely to blame – a continuing strategy, perhaps, to help her feel in control of a situation.

Later that day, Leonard and Vanessa leave Virginia behind and set off for a joint consultation with Dr Savage and Dr Head at Devonshire Place (a rather awkward situation given that Savage was unaware that Leonard had also been seeking the advice of the newer, younger doctor). Then the phone call comes. Ka Cox, whom they have left to keep an eye on Virginia, is on the line.

She tells Leonard that Virginia has fallen into a deep sleep –

Leonard jumps straight in a taxi.

Imagine the icy shock of it: Leonard flees back to Brunswick Square to find Virginia unconscious and is hit by the terrible realisation that, in the rush and turmoil of leaving the house for the doctors' meetings, he has left the case where he stores the medicines unlocked. Virginia has taken the Veronal tablets. A hundred grains of them.

On the top floor of Brunswick Square is another lodger, Geoffrey Keynes, Maynard's younger brother. He is also a surgeon. Leonard hammers up the stairs to call for help. Leaving Ka to watch over Virginia, they both leap into his car; with unpathetic fallacy, it is a beautiful sunny afternoon, all blue skies and soft clouds. They must get to St Bartholomew's Hospital, find a stomach pump. Leonard sits in the passenger seat, still in a state of shock, whilst Keynes drives, shouting: 'Urgent! Urgent!' through the window to disperse the traffic.

Dr Head and Keynes, together with a nurse, work into the early hours to save her life.

Leonard does not feel guilty. He knows that it is not his fault; a mistake was bound to happen sooner or later, given the stress and trauma of the situation. 'For the previous two months I had had to be on watch day and night to prevent a disaster of this kind,' he writes in his memoir. 'No person by himself could really do this, and even after Ka came and we were two, it was not enough.'

But the thought of Virginia never waking is unbearable. Utterly exhausted, he goes to bed, falls into a deep sleep … not stirring until he is woken by Vanessa at six the next morning.

Despite Leonard's deepest fears, Virginia pulls through. The next day, she is out of danger, and on Thursday morning, she regains consciousness.

Some months later, in the aftermath of shock, Leonard wrote to Virginia, 'You cant realise how utterly you would end my life for me if you had taken that sleeping mixture successfully or if you ever dismissed me.'

He concluded that her main motive for the suicide attempt was her dread of the doctors. It was a conclusion that would lead to Leonard making some key mistakes later in life as her carer.

That autumn of 1913, as Virginia revived over a period of days and regained her physical strength, her psychological problems worsened once again. Now Leonard was faced with a new quandary: could he continue to care for his wife or was it time to put Virginia permanently into an asylum?

10

I was tidying up one of the many book piles that teetered around the house when a postcard fluttered to the floor. On the front was a picture of Waterhouse's *Sirens*, their faces soft and nymphish with allure. On the back: 'Dear Miss Rossetti, may I thank you for such a superlative time together. We have feasted on Italian pizza, gone to see the *Medea* with the glorious Helen McCrory, watched the Dodo paddle in the Thames before insulting a swan ...' I felt a pang. Whenever Thom came to visit me in London, in that poignant hour before we parted, we'd sit in Victoria Station in a cafe and pen postcards: vignettes of the days we'd spent together. They would sing of picnics and theatre trips, bookshop adventures and moonlit walks. We'd pass each other our cards before goodbye kisses, and only read them after we'd parted.

It had been weeks since I had last seen Thom. Our contact was purely technological now: we texted and emailed and skyped.

I checked my laptop for an email from him, then reminded myself that he was at a concert this evening with a female friend. There was, however, an email from Z. He had sent me a limerick to cheer me up – rhyming Sam, clam and damn

– and then reassured me that, 'there would be better times ahead, there will be puddings'. I smiled and felt cheered, nostalgic for times when Z had wined and dined me, indulging my sweet tooth, candlelight echoing in our dilating pupils. Feeling disloyal, I flicked the email into a separate folder in my inbox.

Evening came. As I started the journey to Summerfields to visit Dad, I suffered a sense of resentment. I was carrying heavy bags of washed clothes and they were cutting red weals into my hands. (It hadn't worked out with Summerfields doing his washing, for some of his things had gone missing in the muddle of patients' laundry.)

A childish petulance came over me as I headed to the bus stop. I'd been working hard that afternoon, freelancing. I debated turning back, heading home, ordering an extravagant takeaway, pretending Summerfields didn't exist. Every trip to see my dad was three hours of the day: an hour to travel, an hour there, an hour back. I missed that winding-down time before bed, where I'd watch a box-set episode or read in the bath. My selfish side fought with my sense of duty. Duty won, but I was still pissed off.

It was that time between winter and spring when it gets dark early, the air stings cold and promising shoots emerge one day only to be spiked by frost the next. At the bus stop, I dug my hands in my pockets and felt the serrated edges of my house keys from my lodgings up north. A memory came, of being with Thom, him making a trip down to see me. We'd gone for an adventure in Hampton Court. I remembered us sitting on a bench under a tree, the sunlight dappling over us, reading together, doing the things we loved side by side.

On the bus, I read some of *Medea*, a book Thom had gifted me. I watched a mother trying to calm her errant kid, who insisted on pinging the bell for every stop, four or five times. My mum had once said that the great blessing of children was not having to think of yourself all the time. In an act of sacrifice, the ego has to dissolve. There were people who were having to care for their parents *and* balance kids, so I had it easy by comparison, I lectured myself sharply. And then there were kids who were carers, who came home from school and helped to cook and care for a family member, who lost the freedoms of childhood and adolescence: a role that one in five children now play.

I trudged down the road to Summerfields, shivered my way through its dark paths, fretting that it was the perfect place for a mugger to strike, before entering Crocus Ward and passing over the bags of clothes to the nurses and then—

Then I saw my dad, and he said, 'Hello.'

He was speaking again.

I wanted to cheer. I suffered a flicker of guilt that I'd nearly not come, nearly missed this wonder. It struck me again how our roles had truly been reversed; like a parent who is thrilled that their baby has started speaking, the moment seared into my memory.

Dad was sitting in one of the orange armchairs near the TV. A few feet away was a row of tables that they used at mealtimes; a quieter, more private area. I guided him to a table and we sat down together. We spoke in simple terms. Direct questions were pointless because Dad would always say he was happy and well, whatever his mood. I needed to play amateur psychiatrist, decode his words, follow my intuition through a maze of his replies and locate a centre. So I asked him about his routine, his food, his sleep. He described with enthusiasm how he'd been served a delicious shepherd's pie for dinner. He said he was sleeping well. It was odd, chatting like this, as though he was describing a nice hotel, when all around us were patients wandering about, and crying, and anxious carers trying to help them. I wondered how he could stand it, but his expression remained serene.

I could tell that the nurses were surprised too.

'Your dad's doing well,' said the pink-haired nurse. They were looking at him as though he'd emerged from a chrysalis; suddenly they had a sense of who he might be, if it were not for the obscuring mist of his illness. I think they were surprised to realise how much they liked him. When well, my father had a charisma, a kind, gentlemanly appeal.

I passed over a copy of the *Daily Telegraph*. He must be so isolated from the outside world in here, I thought. Sometimes the news confused him, because of his lack of social contact. Even in good health, he'd once phoned me up and said he was worried that the papers were printing lies. He had read an article, he said, about people in the Middle East being persecuted for their religious beliefs, which surely couldn't be true. For some reason this idea had rubbed against him, disorientated him. I explained that yes, religious persecution hadn't died away with the Crusades and the Inquisition. Without friends, without people to discuss politics with, without being able to use the internet, I suppose it was natural that he might some-times mistrust the papers – his only connection and regular source of information as to what was going on in the world. As his carer, I had to verify for him what was real and what was not.

I brought out the Scrabble set and his face lit up. We started a game, but I found it hard to concentrate. Two of the patients were arguing. I noticed that schizophrenia seemed to magnify introverts and extroverts; the patients either seemed to be quiet and melancholic, or angry and buzzing with a desire to confront.

A woman with wispy blonde hair, who looked somewhere in her forties, was particularly agitated. She wandered about the ward with a restless, manic energy, annoying the other patients by tapping them on the shoulder, stealing their things, or asking to go into the bedroom dorms, which were separated by a locked door, and then violently banging on the door to be let back in to the sitting-room area. My dad and I were just three or four word-zigzags into our Scrabble game when she picked up his *Telegraph* and hurried off with it.

Dad looked anguished – his paper, his treat, his connection to normalcy – stolen!

I rushed after her and took hold of one end of the news-paper. 'Can I take this back?' I asked nervously.

'It's my jumper,' she insisted, looking, but not looking into my eyes.

I appealed to a nurse, who stepped in and persuaded her to give the paper back to me.

Dad and I put down a few more words, before the woman swooped again; this time she picked up the Scrabble box, which led to another game of chase and retrieve. How can they stand it, I wondered, looking at the nurses with astonished admiration. They were so calm and patient, even though they had to intervene again, and again, and again. It looked to me like the most exhausting job in the world.

I said goodbye to my dad and hoped he'd be able to keep hold of his paper long enough to enjoy it.

Home. My cat, Leo, greeted me with ankle rubs and purrs. Before bed, I triple-checked that all the doors and windows were locked, feeling more vulnerable on my own.

I kept expecting to hear him, to hear the ting of plates as Dad washed up, a hummed snatch of a hymn. Feeling lonely, I made the mistake of looking at Twitter. A string of tweets can be fascinating and consoling, but it can also be alienating to watch everyone's vignettes scroll before you. Everyone seemed to be getting enviable publishing deals, reading the most fascinating books, and eating divinely delicious meals out. I started crafting a tweet about my dad. It was soon aborted. I was feeling low and seeking sympathy, which would probably attract trolls rather than consolation. 140 characters were hardly sufficient to sum up the complexity of the situation. Besides, whilst my close friends knew of his illness, there were plenty of people following me, vaguer acquaintances, who had no idea. It felt like an odd way to let them find out.

Instead, I flicked through *Medea*. I recalled seeing Helen McCrory on stage, dazzling in her white robes, the Chorus behind her, their voices an eerie babble. Twitter is the modern-day equivalent of that chorus. People narrate the minutiae of their lives and the public will judge, comment and retweet them, and if their thoughts/actions have been particularly 'sinful', they will attract the enraged, righteous masses, who descend like the Furies.

Upstairs, watching my reflection clean her teeth in the mirror, I thought of my father's nightly curfew on the ward. My freedom of choice felt luxurious by comparison. So often, those who are mentally ill lose control of their lives; much of what happens to them is governed by fate, that nebulous word that is a blur of society, medical opinion, public attitudes, family kindness, money. I thought of the Woolfs, and how, when the First World War began and there was a possibility of Leonard being conscripted, one of Virginia's friends worried that she would be left 'to her fate', fearing her death – her suicide – was inevitable without Leonard beside her. The average life expectancy of someone with schizophrenia is ten to fifteen years below the national average. To care for someone who is mentally ill is to battle fate; it is an intervention – or an attempt to intervene.

Once upon a time, whether or not you were a carer was not a free choice. In Greek and Roman times, it was expected that families would care for and take responsibility for their loved ones; in the *Laws*, Plato wrote: 'If a man is mad, he shall not be at large in the city, but his family shall keep him in any way they can.' When it came to the elderly, Athenian law required that children care for their parents. If they failed to do so, their punishment was a loss of citizenship. In our modern era, we appear to have the freedom to make a conscious choice as to whether or not we care for our mothers and fathers, although gender, class and money are also factors, played against personal conscience and the history of our relationship with our parent: whether they loved us as a child, whether we love them sufficiently now to make the sacrifice, and so on.

But, had I ever made a conscious choice? Caring felt like something that was happening *to* me, as though my father's illness had been an eruption that had flowed like lava over my life. I thought back to that moment when I first realised I would have to be a carer – the shock of it. Recently, I had been called it more and more: *You're Edward's carer? You're his primary carer?* I can't think of any other job where someone defines your role by conferring its title on you, as though they are holding out a mould that you must fill. Once upon a time it was a title mainly used for professionals; now it is increasingly becoming a personal one. By defining someone as a carer, it is a crafty way of the state shifting responsibility, and costs, onto families, of saying: *this is who you are now, this is what you do.* Eventually you are given leaflets – ones which you are invariably too tired to read – which confer and establish a sense of officialdom to your role, offering ways that local bodies might help you, further reinforcing your new status.

If I got up now and walked away, I doubt they would have chased me or berated me. Summerfields would just have started calling my brothers instead, and whoever answered the phone first would have picked up the baton of 'primary carer'. The more I acted as a carer, the more it felt as though I was being anchored, and the harder it would be to set sail and turn back. There was still a sense of faint disbelief, as though I was watching myself act a part that I was ill-suited to, that someone would soon fire me and say: *Who thought Sam could play this role, didn't you even audition her?* I was being driven by a mixture of guilt, conscience, pressure and love. Parts of me were willing; parts were rebelling. I was changing but, as so often when you undergo a rapid metamorphosis, the present was a confusing blur. It is only in retrospect that you can look back at the self you used to be.

II

O nce my father was speaking and eating again, I became anxious as to where the best place for him might be. Would it be better if he was released early and allowed to come home – even though there was always the danger that he might relapse and have to go through the system again? Or was the ward the safest place for him to heal?

It was the same question that had tormented Leonard Woolf in 1913. After Virginia recovered from her suicide attempt, he had to seriously consider the question of whether or not she ought to go to an asylum. His close friend Roger Fry, an art critic, painter and member of the Bloomsbury circle (who had an affair with Virginia's sister) put his wife, the artist Helen Coombe, into an asylum in 1910. She would stay there for the rest of her life. (Some decades later, T. S. Eliot also had his wife, Vivienne, committed, after they separated and she stalked him – though whether she was really certifiable remains doubtful, and it seems a convenient way of ridding himself of a woman who had become an embarrassment.) Leonard questioned whether he could cope with continuing to play the part of carer, whether putting Virginia away was a matter of choice or necessity.

Home or asylum: it's the eternal question that societies and families have debated when considering what is best for the mentally unwell. Before madhouses were built, if you had a mentally unwell relative in your family, you wouldn't be expected to care for them. Often 'lunatics' were kept in liminal spaces within the home: the cellar, the attic, or outside in the stables, or the pig pen. The classic example of this in literature occurs in *Jane Eyre*. Rochester keeps his wife, Bertha Mason (note that her maiden name is always used) locked up in his attic at Thornfield Hall. She never has a voice in the novel and for Jane, she is initially a mysterious apparition who makes terrifying appearances like a ghost in a Gothic melodrama.

If the lunatic in the family was harmless, they might also be sent out to wander and beg. Wandering lunatics were tolerated more in the countryside than the city. The mad, then, were viewed and treated much like animals, the difficult 'pet' of the family – if the lunatic was gentle, their family might allow them to scamper away, but if they were 'a savage beast', then they would have to be kept chained up.

As developments in science and medicine have given us greater insights into mental health, our sense of compassion and responsibility towards care has improved. Consider the difference in our attitude towards Alzheimer's today compared to Victorian times, when the disease had not yet been fully understood. In our current era, bed-blocking is a major problem with Alzheimer's patients, for 50,000 of them end up in the NHS each year – with our social care system in a threadbare state, they often fail to eat and drink properly and end up with dehydration or UTIs. I read of one woman who was so afraid of putting her Alzheimer's-afflicted mother into a care home in case she was treated poorly, that she shouldered a burdensome £1,000 a week to pay for a private nurse to keep her mother in her own home. But back in early Victorian times, if you had a parent with what we now know to be Alzheimer's, and you were from a lower class, they could easily have ended up in Bedlam.

Founded as Bethlem Hospital in the thirteenth century, by the seventeenth century the asylum, near London's Bishopsgate, had become a popular attraction mentioned in tourist guides; a day trip there was on a par with watching a public execution. Tourists would wander through this theatre of madness and mock the inmates, though families of the incarcerated also visited, bringing food and kindness to their loved ones.

When the Victorians ordered the mandatory building of asylums by local authorities, it signalled a sea change in attitudes, declaring that the state was better suited to caring than the individual. Early in the nineteenth century, the French physician Philippe Pinel, now known as the father of modern psychiatry, observed that 'deranged patients can hardly ever be cured in the bosom of their family'. Society had reached a point where madness could no longer be kept private, locked away, and hidden; the state was now in charge of what was best for the mentally unwell, and dictated as such.

* * *

'Hey!'

I was sitting in Summerfields with my dad, playing Scrabble, when the blonde woman stole the box again. I chased after her.

Her blue eyes bore into mine as she confided: 'I really want to plunge a knife into someone right now.'

I swallowed hard and returned to playing Scrabble with my dad, but I had trouble assembling words; in my shock, my letters just stayed letters. Although I knew, in theory, there were no weapons in Summerfields, I still didn't feel safe. I fretted that the blonde woman might somehow get hold of something – even if just a fork – and go for me. Here, within this world, I was an Other, a unfamiliar outsider, which was perhaps why she always made a beeline for me the moment I entered. Or, what if she went for my dad? Was he really safe in this place?

Increasingly, Dad seemed out of place on Crocus Ward. He'd gone from being the weakest, most seemingly tormented patient to one of the most civilised and calm. I would visit him and he'd sit there, serene, saying that he was fine and happy there, whilst all around him would be a varying chaos: paranoid patients bickering violently, someone openly masturbating, and now the threat of a woman with knife fantasies.

A day later I saw the blonde woman sitting at a table surrounded by visitors: her family. One of the friendliest nurses, a guy called Moses, stopped by my dad's table and told us that the woman had once been a brilliant snooker player, excelling in championships. All of a sudden, I had a glimpse of the person she was beneath the veil of illness. As time went by, this happened again and again. I'd hear a story about a patient who seemed in a ruinous state, and learn that they had been happy, creative, successful, run companies, before tragedy had struck and their lives had broken up, broken down.

Observing the patients, I thought: they have all the neuroses that we experience every day, but the volume is turned up. The woman who was so paranoid she snapped at everyone for looking at her – don't we all have that fear, scuttling around, that so and so doesn't like us, is judging us? It's one reason why there is such a stigma around mental illness; we may feel a sense of shame when we see someone losing their wits because we see ourselves in them. The difference between the so-called mad and the sane is in many respects a matter of censorship. The sane speak in sub-text; the mad don't filter their speech. They speak out all those little thoughts that the process of growing up has taught us to repress, and lock up inside. We grow up learning to lie, to flatter, to smile and say hi to the boss we hate, to play games with a lover. In their honesty, the mad break all our social codes.

It has been argued – most famously by Foucault – that the 'mad' are the scapegoats of society. After successes in combatting leprosy, we needed to create a new 'other' and started locking up those we described as insane. At one time, however, reason and insanity were not opposites; we celebrated 'wise' fools, but with the birth of madhouses and asylums, we created a distinction. That evening it struck me that this is also true of people inside psychiatric wards. Everyone was othering everyone else. If you know the history of someone with mental illness, it's a blip on their character; without this, it *is* their character. The family of the blonde woman probably looked at me and my father and thought we were the crazies. They had never seen my father outside of the ward. In their eyes, he was just the quiet, strange man who liked playing Scrabble. My father, too, often spoke to me as though he was one of the doctors instead of a patient. He'd tell me a story about two patients becoming violent and how he'd told a nurse and they'd been separated. There would be a quality of detachment in his tone, that of the wry observer.

Virginia Woolf showed a similar tendency when she was locked away at Twickenham. In 1910, she wrote a letter to Vanessa where she described how Jean Thomas takes in 'innumerable young women in love difficulties … I make Miss T. blush by asking if they're mad', playing the role of someone witnessing events around her. Woolf also wrote about seeing 'a long line of imbeciles' when she and Leonard were taking a walk along a Thames towpath. Unable to understand that she might be on the same spectrum with them, she declared that 'They should certainly be killed'. It is a horrific attitude, though not unusual for the time. As asylums were deemed a failure, eugenics was gaining popularity; even Winston Churchill argued for sterilisation of 'the feeble-minded'. Or, perhaps those 'imbeciles' horrified Woolf because she *did* see an echo of herself and her illness in them and resisted it fiercely. Her own half-sister, Laura Stephen, had been incarcerated in institutions since early adulthood, but Woolf always referred to her as an 'idiot', as 'Thackeray's grand-daughter' rather than a relation.

Home or psychiatric ward?

In the end, it was clear that the ward was the best place for my dad. Seeing him revive a little each day, I was grateful to the carers at Summerfields for doing a job that would have wrecked me. A friend of mine commented that it must be a relief to have my dad there, because 'the duty of care' was passed over to them. But it never felt like that to me. Dad was the backdrop to my every day, in my dreams at night, a constant tug of worry. I didn't feel I had let go at all – anymore than Leonard did when he hired nurses to help him with Virginia.

Rest was clearly a vital part of Dad's cure. Before my dad slipped into his catatonic state, I'd sensed that he was very tired, that he was suffering from a sort of deep exhaustion that made small tasks seem epic and gets into the blood of the soul. I could see that being free from all responsibilities, safe in the clockwork of a routine, given meals three times a day, set a curfew for his bedtime, was re-energising him. Being allowed to let go of the details of his life and to let the people around him organise it was giving him the space to heal.

A birthday celebration in honour of one of the patients left him radiant. When I visited him, he told me in an elated tone of how the nurse had brought in a cake and everyone had sung happy birthday. I asked if he felt happier in Summerfields;

I wondered if he needed more company. But he replied: no, he wanted to have his freedom back and return home, and when I saw his empty armchair in the living room, it looked lonely, as though waiting for the return of his warm body.

12

It lingered, Z's email.

He had sent it late the night before. He addressed me as 'Beautiful' and flirted, 'I wish I was a cat in your house'.

Z was an author whose name does not begin with z. I use his initial because he is a bright constellation in the literary world, a wonderful man with a zest for life, a brilliant mind and a sharp wit. I first met him over a decade ago. I sent a book to Faber and they pulled it off their slush pile and made an offer of publication. I turned up to a literary summer party fizzing with a kind of vivacious nervousness; Z took me under his wing. He made jokes under his breath about big name authors with airs and graces. He told me he liked my red dress. He asked to kiss my cheek several times. When I contacted him the next day, I recrafted my short email half a dozen times before sending it. Our love affair lasted three intense months before it burnt out.

But we kept on exchanging emails. This became a daily habit. By 2016 we'd been emailing every day for eleven years, over 3,000 of them. We alternated between cycles of flirtation and passion, friendship and chat. It was the ideal romance, as far as I was concerned – non-exclusive, intimate, free, warm, sexy, playful. During my early twenties, I had dated a guy who was disturbed by the anarchic energy of *Quiddity*, my work-in-progress, and instead wanted me to pen sweet stories for children. So I became wary of relationships, yet found solitude lonely. My relationship with Z seemed a perfect middle ground. If I had dated him, he certainly wouldn't have censored my work, but I suspected that I would have ended up playing the supporting role to a grand male writer, becoming muse rather than creator.

And then I met Thom – a man who loved my writing, who put a poster of my novel on his wall, who encouraged me to text him updates of whatever chapter I was struggling with. Once he told me, 'I'm in love with your mind' (which prompted me to complain teasingly, 'So you think I'm ugly then?'). Secretly, I loved the compliment. Here was a man who didn't want to control me or contain me or make me conform. It meant that the cycles Z and I were habituated to had to stall and freeze in the stasis of friendship.

There was a period of awkward transition. Z and I could never have announced to each other *I am dating someone else*. It would have been too painful; we always opted for a show, don't tell approach. Our emails simply shifted from flirtations to more neutral discussions about books, word counts, whether alcohol enhanced or impeded prose. Z knew I was devoted to my boyfriend, but he also liked to test me from time to time. In our last emails, we had exchanged photographs of ourselves from childhood, a curiously intimate sharing, touched by the sight of innocent faces, soft eyes.

The temptation was there: to send Z a flirtatious reply. Thom had recently been raving about a new female friend; the first thing he'd told me was that she was a 'submissive'. Cracks of jealousy and suspicion were spidering our relationship. Since my father had fallen ill in February, Thom and I had met just three times in two months. The better a carer I became for my dad, the worse a girlfriend to Thom; it was like a seesaw that would not balance.

When will my dad be discharged? was the silent question behind all our exchanges. How long would we have to wait before we could be a couple again, and by then, would it be too late?

I decided to escape to my local library. I would forget all my cares and just write, I resolved. I'd always worked at least forty hours a week on novels and scripts and articles to keep the bills paid but I'd recently taken off so much time visiting Dad that I was becoming anxious about money.

In the library cafe, I ordered a tea, pulling out my money in haste, convinced there was an impatient queue behind me. When I looked, I saw no one; my jittery anxiety had manifested in the form of phantom pressure.

Tea, notebook, wobbly table, creaky seat. My pen quivered; I felt rusty; circling on the surface. And then I began to write. I felt as though I was wriggling off the tight white coat of my carer persona, becoming myself again. They all dropped away, my worries over Dad and money and Thom and Z, and my pen scratched away as though with a will of its own, and my imagination began to fly and—

A call on my mobile. I checked the number. Summerfields. Putting down my pen in defeat, I answered.

The man at the end of the line was my father's psychiatrist. He was benign and very well spoken. He shared his thoughts about my father, but was diplomatic enough to say: 'I'd like to know what you think – you know your dad better than anyone else.'

It struck me that he was such a contrast to the doctors the Woolfs would have known. He wasn't interested in asserting his medical authority; he was willing to listen to my thoughts and work towards an understanding together.

In the thirty years of his career, he said, he'd only seen one other case of catatonic collapse. My dad's condition was rare and puzzling. Nobody could be certain as to what was causing it. It might be the Clozapine, a drug which had kept him more stable than anything he'd taken, but which could cause bowel problems in the elderly. Or it might be that he needed more of the drug, since his doses had been decreased in the past year. Or, or, or ...

Back home, I put Dad's clothes into the washing machine, followed by more writing, editing, emails. I yawned and I yawned. Normally my energy levels were quite steady; I did Transcendental Meditation twice a day which kept my mind zinging and fresh. I wasn't used to feeling this exhausted, raw in my eyes, hot in my stomach; it made me feel as though I was studying for an exam, only I wasn't sure when the exam would ever be.

* * *

Judging by Leonard Woolf's recollections of 1913, he seems to have been suffering something similar. He too must have been asking when the nightmare would ever end.

George Duckworth has loaned the Woolfs Dalingridge Place, his country house in West Sussex, along with a cook, parlourmaid, housemaids and gardeners, because their own lodgings are too small for live-in nurses. But even though there is more space and more help with Virginia here, the 'appalling nightmare' and 'collapse of one's everyday life' show little sign of letting up.

Lunchtime: Leonard and Virginia sit side by side in the dining room. Before them, on the table, is a plate of food. As Leonard's memoir records: 'In the first weeks at Dalingridge the most difficult and distressing problem was to get Virginia to eat.' Virginia is prone to sitting for hours, lost in melancholy, making no response when anything is said to her. Leonard takes her hand and puts a fork in it. He coaxes her gently: *please eat.* Virginia is unresponsive. So Leonard chides her a little more, very quietly, touching her arm as he does so. Finally, Virginia's fork spears a vegetable. She brings it to her mouth. Chews and swallows. Leonard's relief is short-lived as his eyes stray to the clock. It has taken her five minutes to eat one mouthful. He could call for help, ask the nurses to assist. But Virginia is prone to flying into rages against them. She is still paranoid, convinced the doctors and nurses have concocted a conspiracy against her. He eyes her slender frame: she is losing weight.

Just one more mouthful, he cajoles her. Why not try the meat this time?

Another five minutes, another mouthful.

The whole meal takes an hour.

Later that evening, having given Virginia her sleeping draught, Leonard enters his bedroom and gets into bed alone. He misses sleeping beside his wife. Dr Craig has recommended that Virginia should have someone in her room at night, but a nurse, not her husband. Sleeping in separate bedrooms becomes a habit they will maintain for the rest of their marriage.

This is the decision that Leonard has made – he will care for Virginia himself. He did visit some asylums, but felt they were 'dreadful, large gloomy buildings enclosed by high walls, dismal trees, and despair'. Her doctors have agreed that Leonard can look after her, provided that he is assisted by trained nurses. As a result, Virginia's illness remains defined by the firm label of neurasthenia, although Leonard suspects manic depression. But the word 'manic' is a dangerous one. Suicide is a crime and if Virginia is deemed 'manic' following her attempt, she might then be certifiable. Better that she is a neurasthenic. By taking on the duty of care himself, however, Leonard has set himself an exhausting challenge: he has to battle with her demons, and hope, on a daily basis, that he will win the fight …

A few weeks later, Leonard takes Virginia out onto the grand, sprawling lawn at Dalingridge. It is a beautiful autumn's eve. The view is exquisite and they play croquet 'in the warm, peaceful, soft and sunny evening'. A peace descends on them as they 'look towards the long hazy line of downs and the gap where Lewes lay'. Virginia is making fragile progress, beginning to eat, sleeping again. After two months here, she is starting to come back to him.

But the immense strain of it all has taken its toll on Leonard's health. He is in a state of nervous exhaustion, suffering headaches that are deep and dark. In my late teens, I remember my mother once confiding in me about a constant 'head pressure' that had come on. It wasn't a brain tumour, thank goodness – that was verified by some blood tests. It was more insidious than a headache, which comes and goes; more of a permanent ache in the backdrop of her mind, softened by the meditation retreats we went on, worsened by lack of sleep. Our GP said it was due to 'stress', which I translated as 'being a lifelong carer'. The 'head pressure' never disappeared; it lasted for decades.

In March 1914, desperate for a break, Leonard visits Lytton Strachey in Wiltshire for ten days. Even then he writes regularly to Virginia, telling her how much he misses her. In his absence, Vanessa, Janet Case and Ka Cox step in as carers. Sleep and rest and friendship slowly heal him. The separation only intensifies his devotion to his wife; though Lytton is one of his dearest friends, Leonard finds that: 'I've never been alone with anyone else for a few days without irritating & being irritated.' With Virginia, it is different: 'you can day after day & all day give me perfect happiness'.

January 1915: Virginia and Leonard are in the bedroom of their lodgings in Richmond. Leonard is playfully berating Virginia for attempting to cook breakfast in bed, for cookery classes are her new hobby. Virginia notes in her diary: 'I believe, however, that the good sense of the proceeding will make it prevail; that is, if I can dispose of the eggshells.'

Since the autumn of 1914, Virginia has been relatively stable. On 25 January 1915, they celebrate her thirty-third birthday and round the day off with tea at Buszard's Tea Rooms on Oxford Street. They decide that they will do three things. They will buy a bulldog and call him John; they will move into Hogarth House, a place they've had their eye on for new lodgings; and they will buy a printing press together. This is an idea they've been playing with for a while, and now excitement sparkles between them at the thought of becoming publishers together.

And then it happens: life breaks again.

February 1915: Leonard finds Virginia sitting on her bed, speaking gibberish, a jumble of dissociated words. It seems that she is trying to address her dead mother.

Leonard puts Virginia into Burley Park for a brief period, then hastily packs up their things so that they can move into Hogarth House at the earliest opportunity. They are renting rooms in Richmond and even though their landlady is a pleasant woman, Leonard realises that it is obvious 'we could not turn her house into a mental hospital'. Leonard and Virginia have bound their lives together through working from home, enjoying a writerly routine, but now home has become a place of uncertainty and turbulence, forcing them to become rootless, to keep moving and finding new places, and all against a backdrop of increasing money troubles.

The live-in nurses are expensive. They are forced to sell some of Virginia's jewellery. Leonard sits down and writes to Jack Hills, asking for an advance of £100. (Hills was briefly married to Virginia's half-sister, Stella, who died from peritonitis in 1897; after her death her wedding settlement was made over to Vanessa and Virginia.)

April comes. Leonard hopes that Hogarth House will have a calming effect on Virginia. It is a beautiful Georgian mansion split into two houses, a place of 'immense solidity with grace, lightness, and beauty'. He hires a maid, Lily, a cook and four nurses. He is worn out but still devoted, still prepared to bring Virginia back to good health.

But mental illness is never predictable. The horror of it: Virginia is in a new phase of her illness, quite different from the melancholic despair that she suffered at Dalingridge. Now she is like a fury, screaming, attacking one of the nurses. When she has visitors, she is malicious and cutting to them; her sister notes that she has taken against all men. What's more, she has turned against Leonard. He is now her enemy.

Leonard is in a state of shock. He can not even act as her carer anymore. Virginia can no longer bear to see him. Two months go by and they are estranged.

Why does Virginia take against Leonard? Is she struggling with a heterosexual relationship? This may have its roots in childhood trauma. It is difficult to be sure whether Leonard knows at this point what happened to Virginia in her past. When she was around six years old, her half-brother, Gerald, stood her on a ledge and explored her body – 'I remember how I hoped that he would stop', she recalled later in life, 'how I stiffened and wriggled as his hand approached my private parts. But it did not stop.' He wasn't the only brother who abused her: the death of her mother became an excuse for 'consoling embraces' from George Duckworth, fourteen years her senior, that crossed the fraternal boundary. When Stella died at the age of twenty-eight two years later, her father was grief-wracked and ill. So George took over as the unofficial guardian of Virginia and Vanessa, as they came out into society. Often these social occasions ended with George insisting on helping Virginia to undress, or lying on her bed and fondling her whilst she was undressed, 'to comfort' her for the fatal illness of her father.

Leonard and Virginia's relationship is tender and it is passionate, but it is not a sexual one. On their honeymoon, their first attempts at sex were aborted hastily after Virginia suffered 'a violent state of excitement', knowing these states 'were a prelude to her attacks of madness'. Later in life, Virginia would have an affair with Vita Sackville-West and Leonard was hurt but turned a blind eye to it. Years later Vita mused that Virginia 'dislikes the possessiveness and love of domination in men. In fact, she dislikes the quality of masculinity.' When Leonard made a decision that they should not have children, he also compromised his own sexual needs. A choice to conceive would have required them to explore and develop a more passionate relationship, if Virginia had been willing. Gerald Brenan, a friend, later reminisced that

'Leonard, though I should say a strongly sexed man, had to give up all idea of ever having any sort of sexual satisfaction. He told me that he was ready to do this "because she was a genius"'.

In Ceylon, Leonard had fought his despair by burying himself in his work. Now he does so again, taking solace in his reviews and politics (he is reviewing regularly for the *New Statesman*). I recognise the same impulse in myself. After my father became sick, I found myself increasing my working hours even though I had less energy – it was a way of distracting myself from tragedy, of having something of my own when the rest of my existence was diluted by caring; of having something I could control, and a project I could grow when the person I loved seemed to be withering.

In spring 1915, there is talk once more of Virginia being put in a home. Leonard is afraid of the neighbours being disturbed by the noise of her violent rages. But Leonard still resists. Dr Craig has assured him that Virginia will come around: that she will stop rejecting him.

And she does. Slowly, gradually, she begins to accept him again, until in August he is able to take her on a boat trip. Having been forced to glug considerable quantities of milk on the Weir Mitchell diet, she has put on weight – three stone. She is fragile but back in love with her husband; once more they are the Woolfs.

The stress of it all has its impact.

Leonard, lost in the 'labyrinth' of Virginia's illness, is

conscious of the public backdrop of the First World War – indeed, he is studying the causes and prevention of war – but the 'private nightmare' of being her carer predominates. He describes 1914 and 1915 as 'years which we simply lost out of our lives'.

In May 1916, Leonard sets off for a tribunal, armed with a letter from Dr Craig. He needs to avoid conscription. It isn't just a question of being a conscientious objector, it is a question of being a carer. He knows that Virginia will not be able to cope without him. His letter states that he is suffering from 'nerve exhaustion symptoms'. The (inherited) tremor in his hands is mentioned, as well as a list of other symptoms – his problems with sleep, the severe headaches that pound his mind. He has also lost weight and is now alarmingly skinny. The strain of being a carer has taken its toll. Leonard is – as Victoria Glendinning concludes – 'shell-shocked already'.

13

My dad was walking beside me, very slowly. He was wearing his suit and best tie, woven from blue silk. I felt there should have been trumpets blasting away as we entered the Tesco Express at the bottom of our road. There should have been violins and cellos swelling to vehement crescendo as he consulted his shopping list and dropped some bread into the basket I was holding for him. My father had been released! He was free, he was free. Summerfields was past, and I hoped I would never again have to drag myself up to that damned building and attempt to play Scrabble whilst the blonde woman stole the box and people moan-groaned around us.

Back home after our shopping pilgrimage, I was helping Dad put the food in the fridge when the phone rang.

Dad went to pick it up.

I hovered next to him, on edge. My dad loved to chat to the cold-calling salespeople who phoned him. He was so good-hearted and naive; he mistook their chatty tones for genuine friendliness. It was clear he'd been put on some sort of 'list' entitled 'the elderly, the vulnerable: suckers we can prey on'. From the con merchants who rang up to say there was something wrong with our computer so they could upload virus software, to fraudsters pretending to be from TalkTalk, to telemarketers, they were all sharking my father. Sometimes I had to intervene, write letters, make a noise, and declare that the £200 fine they were going to charge my dad for changing his gas/electricity/telephone/ after they'd persuaded him into a spectacularly bad deal, was a travesty and I would go to *Watchdog*, the papers etc. Last autumn, when my father was in Tolworth Hospital, a guy turned up on our doorstep, saying that 'he was in the area' and the roof needed fixing. His business card displayed an address right next to the hospital, a long detour to make to our house. He seemed to have got hold of a list of patients there, either from hacking in or maybe even bribing a member of staff, and driven over on the off chance that I was some little old lady who would naively agree to a new set of tiles. Even charities refused to take my dad's name off the database, despite my older brother and I phoning to explain that our father could not make sensible decisions and was giving them generous donations he could not afford. Everyone saw my dad as easy prey, and it made me furious. I was forever guarding him, barking the unscrupulous away.

My dad had been chatting for a few minutes now, responding to some kind of 'survey' from a guy who supposedly wanted to sell him the perfect washing machine.

'Yes, my date of birth is—' my dad was about to say; I yanked the phone line out of the socket before he could reveal it.

But, later that night, as I lay in bed, Dad's snores rumbling from the next room, I smiled into the dark. It was so good to have him home.

For all his psychological absence, my father has a strong physical presence. Close to midnight, I'd often wake to hear him getting up for snacks, then again at three, then five, when he'd drink milk or look for some cake to nibble on. He was like a high-calorie-consuming sleepwalker, wandering in a dazed state, failing to notice that he was dropping crumbs, or standing too close to the cat's dirt tray, so that in the morning I'd come down to find a trail of cake and cat litter across the hall, by his armchair, up the stairs. The new carpet we'd bought for his hallway looked as though it was a decade old within a matter of weeks.

By day, however, he looked like the retired CEO of a bank – smart and preppy in suit and tie, darting back and forth up the high street. My dad was definitely sane again, for he was shopping. Over the next few days, he visited Debenhams numerous times. He bought an apron, a new suit, an oven tray. He had needed the rigidity of Summerfields to get back on an even keel, and now he was exalting in his newfound independence. I think he was just so happy to be free to make his own decisions; his consumerism was a symbol of autonomy.

I made a new resolution to cook for my dad every day. He only had a limited repertoire of about two recipes and with his love for routine, tended to end up cooking the same dish day in, day out. I wanted him to have more variety in his diet, in the hope that the nourishment would anchor his mental health.

At lunchtimes, he was often quiet. I would have to interview him to elicit answers; he would rarely kickstart a conversation. His hands would tremble slightly as he held his knife and fork. It was one of the side effects of his medication: they gave symptoms akin to Parkinson's disease. Then there was his drooling at night, so I had to change his pillow regularly, and his weight gain, which I knew upset him (no doubt the midnight cake didn't help either), not to mention skin rashes and involuntary movements of his head, which would sometimes jerk abruptly. I could see why he'd wanted to cut the medication down; it was so sad that he could only leave the ward with the dose increased back up. His life was one of extreme states. Before medication, his illness had caused outrage; on it, he was beige, slowed down, wading through life. I recalled how Will Self, on being diagnosed as borderline schizophrenic in his early twenties, described how his anti-psychotic medication made him feel as if he 'were walking around buried up to [his] waist in mud with [his] brain full of sand'.

Medication made my parents' marriage easier, but it must have maintained the separation between them – my dad was strange when he was ill, but he was a stranger on his meds. If anti-psychotics had been available in Virginia Woolf's time, her marriage to Leonard might have remained more of a patient/carer relationship, with her in a sedated state, but her delightful eccentricity dampened down. Despite the harrowing experiences they went through, Leonard and Virginia had never wanted her to be entirely cured. Leonard was resistant to her being psychoanalysed by their friends, who had trained with Freud: 'Virginia's imagination, apart from her artistic creativity, was so interwoven with fantasises – and indeed with her madness – that if you stopped the madness you might have stopped the creativeness, too.'

Sometimes when Dad and I had lunch together, he would surprise me by blurting out a memory, often from his child-hood. It happened a few days after his return home. We were sitting at the table, eating the chicken pie I'd cooked, when Dad suddenly confessed: 'When I was at school, I won an elocution prize.'

'*What?*'

My dad was nervous of saying more than 'hello' to our neighbours. It seemed extraordinary that he would compete in such a contest.

He beamed and swallowed some chicken. 'I was twelve and I had to read a passage from Shakespeare.'

I had seen a photo of my dad as a child. He looked angelic, his face glowing with a delightful vitality and radiance. I pictured him at the lectern, reading slowly and passionately.

'So you were good at school,' I said, but he shook his head and went back to his usual refrain: 'I didn't do very well, only got a few O levels.'

'It sounds as though you were talented,' I insisted, but he shook his head sadly and shrank back inside himself, staring down at his chicken.

A few minutes passed and then I ventured a question that I had been asking over and over since his return: 'So are you feeling okay, Dad?' Then, knowing he'd automatically reply with a *yes*, I added: 'What kind of mood are you in?'

'I don't have moods,' he replied, laughing awkwardly.

I frowned, then carried on eating, lost for a response. His words shocked me, reverberated through me for weeks to come. I wondered if this was an honest representation of life on Clozapine, where the natural highs and lows of life are smoothed into a monotonous line, or if he just felt nervous of relating his emotions, for fear he'd be labelled 'mad'. The threat of being sectioned was a perpetual shadow over his life.

I, Mandril Sarcophagus Felicissima var. Rarissima, rerum naturae simplex (al. Virginia Woolf) swear that I will on June 16, 17 & 18 1. Rest on my back with my head on the cushions for a full half hour after lunch. 2. Eat exactly as much as if I were not alone. 3. Be in bed by 10.25 every night & settle off to sleep at once. 4. Have my breakfast in bed. 5. Drink a *whole* glass of milk in the morning. 6. In certain contingencies rest on the sofa, not walk about house or outside, until the return of animal illud miserrisimus, mongoosius communis. 7. Be wise. 8. Be happy. Signed: Mandril Sarcophagus Felicissima Var.rarissima, r.n.s. V.W. June 16th 1914. And I swear that I have so done in each & every respect. Signed: Mandril Sarcophagus F.V.R.R.N.S.V.W., June 19th 1914.

Leonard is anxious: he is about to go away. Virginia's recovery still seems fragile. So he gives her a contract and asks – sternly but sweetly – that she sign it.

He has grown in confidence as a carer. In the early days of her illness he felt lost, running from doctor to doctor, but he gradually came to realise that: 'what they knew amounted to practically nothing. They had not the slightest idea of the nature or the cause of Virginia's mental state, which resulted in her suddenly or gradually losing touch with the real world … Not knowing how or why this had happened to her, naturally they had no real or scientific knowledge of how to cure her.' Their advice on routine was some help; Dr Belfrage, for example, suggested that she ought to 'be in bed no less than 10 hours out of the 24'. Leonard has developed sensitive antennae for what keeps her stable – if Virginia lives 'a quiet, vegetative life, eating well, going to bed early, and not tiring herself mentally or physically', then she remains well. It might be a little boring – but it works.

I take issue with the bad press that Leonard has had for controlling Virginia from time to time. It is true that sometimes he did curtail her social life. In a letter he wrote to Lady Robert Cecil in the spring of 1916, cancelling a meeting she had arranged with Virginia on the basis that his wife had a headache, he asserted: 'She is absolutely forbidden by the doctors to do anything at all when these headaches return – & (though she would have flaunted their orders today in order to see you) I have stept in & insisted on her keeping in & doing nothing.' This was infuriating for some of their friends. Lady Ottoline

Morrell saw Leonard as Virginia's 'guardian' and was clearly irritated by the way he laid down rules for her.

'In the legend that has grown up around Virginia Woolf, Leonard features as a grim head nurse of a husband, ceaselessly gauging his wife's symptoms and doling out the amount of time she may spend chatting with visitors,' writes Daphne Merkin in the *New York Times*. But I am determined to defend Leonard on this, because it is clear that his actions worked: Virginia remained relatively stable throughout the rest of their marriage – up until the final tragedy of 1941.

How we view Leonard's attempts to control her life relates in part to how we view what Virginia went through. Some critics object to the focus on Virginia's madness: they argue that by doing so we imply female genius has to be seen through the lens of insanity and regarded as an aberration. After all, we can choose to remember Virginia attacking her nurse, or speaking a babble of dissociated words. Or we can remember her for being a prolific, groundbreaking writer: not only talented – indeed, a genius – but hard-working, regularly seeking to produce 1,250 words a day. Or we can remember her donning a fake moustache and beard, part of a group of friends who played the infamous Dreadnought Hoax, pretending to be the Emperor of Abyssinia and his posse, and hoodwinking the British Navy into giving them a tour of the Home Fleet.

It may be the case that we focus on the madness because we envy Virginia Woolf. We love to hear about writers suffering from madness as a penance for their creativity, a price they have paid for gifts that we covet. Perhaps we *are* afraid of

Virginia Woolf; a little afraid of her genius. After her suicide at the age of fifty-nine, she was publicly regarded as a frail, fragile woman who had been unable to cope with life. Later in the century she would be revered as a feminist icon who was ahead of her time. Now when people write about her madness, it is with caution, even anxiety. One biographer, for example, states rather uneasily that 'Virginia Woolf was a sane woman who had an illness. She was often a patient, but she was not a victim. She was not weak, or hysterical, or self-deluding, or guilty, or oppressed.'

Understandably, critics want to celebrate her strength, her genius, and fight back against the chauvinism that diminished her posthumous reputation. But to downplay her madness is dangerous too. Virginia *did* experience fits of insanity; and sometimes she did suffer from hysteria and self-delusion and guilt; yet throughout her life she too pondered on the question of whether her insanity improved or impeded her writing. As Woolf herself boldly declared: 'As an experience, madness is terrific I can assure you, and not to be sniffed at.' Virginia was both sane and insane, wise and eccentric, fragile and strong.

If we downplay Virginia's madness, then Leonard appears more villain than carer. If we acknowledge her madness, that there were times when she was fragile, when she did need help, then Leonard's actions are not just reasonable but responsible. Many commentators, even those who are sympathetic to Leonard, are critical of the rules and routines he imposed on Virginia and feel that he colluded with her doctors in being oppressive at times. Hermione Lee's epic biography of Virginia

Woolf beautifully captures the complexities of their marriage and is generous in its portrayal of Leonard. But she does argue that 'there is no doubt that after her suicide attempt he "made her into an invalid" in order to prevent a recurrence' (echoing Virginia's assertion herself in a letter to Violet Dickinson in 1912 that 'Leonard made me into a comatose invalid'). I disagree. From my own experiences at Summerfields, I have seen how stabilising a good routine can be for those suffering from psychosis. Proper sleep and a healthy diet are crucial components of good physical and mental health. The clockwork routine at Summerfields gave my father a structure, a scaffolding around him, enabling him to be free and peaceful without having to worry or plan the little things in life.

Psychiatric institutions have been accused of infantilising patients. Whilst this can be true, I would also argue that it is the illness itself which infantalises the patients. My father benefited from being treated like a child because his illness had rendered him as helpless as a child; he needed to be looked after in order to grow strong and become independent and adult again. The very automatism of a routine is a lullaby that soothes the mind and body. It seems dull and childlike to someone who is healthy because they have the energy and capacity for variety, but it is beneficial for someone in a vulnerable state – where day-to-day tasks such as planning a meal might become huge and wearying.

I don't want to deify Leonard either. There is no doubt that he had a tendency to micromanage (he was obsessed with noting down car mileage and expenditure, for example), but perhaps a micromanager, albeit a compassionate one, was just what Virginia needed. It was a co-dependent relationship that worked.

Though Virginia complained about Leonard's interference at times, she also recognised that he had stabilised her mental health problems. In 1935 she confided in Vanessa that 'she found Leonard absolutely dependable & like a rock which was what she badly wanted. She said she could never make up her own mind & must have someone to do it for her – which L no doubt does – & that he was also very unselfish – & always ready to plunge into any enterprise she suggested.' She frequently used the word 'vibrations' when she was describing her illness and once, on contemplating her marriage to him, she reflected that 'one's personality seems to echo out across space, when he's not there to enclose all one's vibrations', as if by enclosing her – by creating boundaries – he also created comfort and calm. As the years went by, Leonard managed to integrate his roles of carer and husband until they blurred into one. He looked after her when needed, but I don't think he patronised her or manipulated her; he stepped in and intervened when it was necessary. For the most part, they had a happy life together. In her last words, Virginia told him: 'I don't think two people could have been happier than we have been.' Unlike my parents, illness didn't create an increasing separation, a pane of glass between them. Leonard and Virginia were able to enjoy being husband and wife.

PART II

She rose to His Requirement—dropt
The Playthings of Her Life
To take the honorable Work
Of Woman, and of Wife—

If ought She missed in Her new Day,
Of Amplitude, or Awe—
Or first Prospective—Or the Gold
In using, wear away,

It lay unmentioned—as the Sea
Develop Pearl, and Weed,
But only to Himself—be known
The Fathoms they abide—

Emily Dickinson

14

At the bottom of my father's garden is a crab apple tree. I planted it in memory of my mother, Glesney. During her life, the garden had been a little oasis, lush and overgrowing, fences obscured. One of my grieving relatives had reacted to her death by chopping nearly everything down. The garden had been left a barren thing since she died. Just a stretch of grass with a few spindly plants. In retaliation, I had planted the crab apple. It had been the same height as me when it was delivered, with branches whispery in their delicacy. Now it was a foot taller, and developing hints of grandeur, branches kinking and reaching up in beautifully unexpected ways. I liked to walk by the tree and feel its tips shiver against me. It made me feel close to my mother.

When I was younger, my mother would often tell me about the baptism of fire that accompanies having a baby. After Mum's first baby was born, her mother visited her in hospital and warned: 'From now on, your life will never be the same again. You won't be able to think of yourself anymore – you must put your child first.' Childbirth and caring might seem to share a similar territory, both requiring love and patience and sacrifice. But raising a child usually has an upwards trajectory – the very word 'raising' suggests you bring the child up, up, up, nourishing and shaping their growth. When you're caring for a parent, however, you are trying to prevent them from slipping down, down, down; slow the inevitable, take arms against the Grim Reaper. Childbirth fires you up with fresh hormones. No such biological advantage accompanies caring. Child-rearing is generally a choice; caring chooses you.

I think (I hope) I've become a good carer to my father. But when I look back on 2010, the year my mother fell sick, I am still haunted by the worry that I was a bad carer to her. That said, the terms 'good' and 'bad' are ones that I feel ambivalent about. My mother was a 'good' carer in that she was prepared to sacrifice everything, but in the end I believe it destroyed her. I keep turning it over in my mind: did she do the right thing, or should she have been more selfish?

'The Gods … were taking us seriously.' That quote from Virginia Woolf, in reaction to all the tragedy and death that befell her as a teenager, resonates when I think of my mother.

I have a photo of her in her mid-thirties. She was a beautiful woman, with long, fine dark hair, but in this picture her face is taut with worry. Rewind to a photo of Glesney in her early twenties, perched on a motorbike, and you can see her sparky sense of her life ahead of her, her taste for adventure. I don't suppose she ever once considered, at that age, that she would devote much of her life to being a carer.

My mum once told me that when she was a little girl,

growing up in south London in the fifties, she and her neigh-bouring kids would play in a yard at the Elephant and Castle. It was filled with rubble from buildings bombed-out during the Second World War; there were most likely unexploded bombs amongst the debris, but nobody was fussed. She was an only child. Her dad worked as a printer on Fleet Street, though he also served in Egypt as a military policeman during the war. He was a jovial, light-hearted man before he went; when he returned, he rarely smiled. Her mother grew up on a farm in Wales. During the summer holidays they would return there; I have visions of Mum sitting by a cow in the mornings, working its udder as warm milk flowed out. She was smart at school. But, unlike us, her children, she didn't have a sheaf of certificates boasting good grades. 'I was top of my class in history,' she'd say to me, or 'My English teacher said I was really bright', in a taut tone, knowing she had only her word to prove it. There was hurt in her voice too. She had wanted to go to university. But this was the 1960s and there was still a lingering attitude that a woman's place was in the home. Her dad asserted that higher education was a waste of time for a woman. Why bother when she was only going to get married? And so he bullied her out of the idea.

Twenty-two years old: that's how old Mum was when she married. It seems so young to me, but she asserted it was the norm then. Men and women didn't tend to be friends the way they are now, she added: if you went out with a boy, it was A Date. She and my dad first met at a meeting for Young Conservatives, though neither of them were Tories. They went along with friends; I wonder if they both thought it might be a good opportunity to find a marriage partner.

My mum exuded glamour. She was working as a receptionist in Fleet Street, and she wore all the latest London fashions. Her dark hair was a bob, her lipstick a red slash, her skirt a mini in vibrant, screaming sixties colours. My dad wasn't the only one who tried to chat her up that night; there was a whole crowd of men offering to walk her home. Why did Dad stand out? Well, he was handsome, and had a sweet smile, and a decent job. 'He had great moral integrity,' Mum told me, which sounds an admirable if old-fashioned term. They married in a church, a traditional white wedding, my dad looking proud and puffed up to have won her.

My parents were poor when they moved into their first home, a maisonette in Morden. A year went by before they could afford proper furniture. But Glesney and Edward were sparkly with happiness and anticipation for the future, planning a large family. My mum used to tell me that other husbands of that era would carve a line between them and their wives, declaring that parenting was mothering. Not Dad. He would change nappies and take us to the park and give us piggybacks and help with shopping. Before he got ill, he was a keen father.

In the summer of 2010, my mum phoned me and asked if I'd like to go on a two-week holiday to Turkey with her. Mum and I often went on holiday together. I could hear the expectation in her voice that my reply would be an immediate yes.

So I felt ungrateful when I said, 'not really'. I was surrounded by boxes and attempting to downsize my book collection, having accumulated over two thousand books during the decade I lived in the north. My house had become too expensive to rent and now I had to move.

'It's for free,' she emphasised. 'Noah's paid for it. And now he can't come.'

'Mum, I have to move, my lease is up,' I replied. 'And I still haven't found a place to go next.' Pause. 'When is it?'

'July the first to the fifteenth,' she replied eagerly.

'So the day after we come back I'll have to move,' I objected.

I thought she would back down. I thought she'd resolve to take a friend from work. I was startled when she began to cajole and coerce me. Emotional blackmail or bullying was forbidden in her house – a backlash against the dominance of her father. She prided herself in letting us make our own choices instead of imposing them on us. In the end, as she mentioned Noah, Noah, Noah again and again, I relented. Noah: a man I had never met, a myth to me, a hero of so many stories.

On the flight out I felt as sulky as a teenager. Next to me, Mum was coughing. She'd been coughing for two months now, ever since she'd heard the bad news about Noah.

On our first evening in Istanbul we had dinner and then wandered out into the starry night. There was a vibrant energy on the streets; the shopkeepers (who all seemed to be men) would hail passing tourists to come inside and take a look.

We pottered down a cobbled side street and found ourselves lured into a shop which was lavish with large rugs, tasselled and patterned with exotic geometric shapes. The shopkeeper looked appreciatively at me, and then my mother. Though she was in her sixties, she could easily pass for mid-forties. Her dark hair, speckled with grey, was cut into a shiny bob.

'Can I buy your daughter?' he asked her. Mum pretended to haggle with him and we all had a good laugh, followed by some sweet, spiced appley tea that he served us in little crystal glasses. Suddenly I felt sheepish. I realised how unkind I was being, how immature, sulking my way through the holiday. Mum needed me to be a good friend to her as well as a daughter. I resolved to forget my housing woes and enjoy the holiday.

Istanbul was a good place for people-watching. My mother and I sat in cafes, watching the world go by.

People-watching was something we'd enjoyed when I was a child. I remember sitting on a park bench together, when I was about six or seven years old. 'The thing you have to learn about people is this,' she had advised, 'there's a gap between persona and what's inside and those two things are often opposites.' She pointed out an example: an old man who was buying fruit from a market stall. Time had puckered and spotted his face into a grumpy, rotten old apple, but when he passed over money for his bag of carrots, the smile in his eyes suggested a soft heart. I was fascinated. For an hour or so, we scrutinised people carefully, trying to look beyond hair

SAM MILLS

and smiles and facepaint for flashes of their inner selves. People are like fruit, I'd concluded then, with peel on the outside that hides what lies beneath.

There was a line of psychology textbooks on Mum's bedroom shelf; she was determined to become a therapist and repair the damage her father had done to her life. I used to read the sections on body language, learning that exposing wrists or crossing legs fireworked signals of seduction – all of which was helpful for attracting the type of boys my mum would disapprove of.

As a teenager, I would occasionally bring a boyfriend home and Mum would be pleasant to them while they were present, but a touch disdainful once they'd gone. You're going for pretty boys, she would complain, boys who look like film stars. She thought that I ought to make more effort to look beyond superficial sheen, and base romance on depth of character. But I was too young to appreciate her wisdom and I carried on falling for height and dark eyes and swoony smiles. The advice she gave me about people's personas later developed into: 'You can live with someone for many years and not really know them. People are tricky.'

For the second week of the holiday, we travelled to a small island and passed the time peacefully, swimming and reading and snoozing. When we ate our meals on the terrace, frogs croaked loudly as though suffering from burpy indigestion. My mother, I noticed, was still coughing. I felt anxious: was it a nervous condition? The GP whom she had recently seen had dismissed her as a hypochondriac, saying he'd 'got a cough too', before sending her away.

The place we were staying in had a little bookcase of well-thumbed paperbacks where travellers left their holiday reads in exchange for new ones. I spotted a slim volume of Emily Dickinson poems and savoured 'Because I could not stop for Death'. I glanced over at Mum: she was engrossed in a book too. This was one of the things I loved about being with her. We could both sit together for hours with a book in our hands, a solitary act made companionable, softly aware of each other's presence by the scratchy turn of a page. She had opted for a fantasy novel, her favourite genre. She loved being transported to another place; her own life was so constricted she craved worlds with magical possibilities.

That day we read together on our beds as a breeze came in and danced around the room, playing hide-and-seek with the curtains and caressing our hair, and the sun slowly moved its stripes across the floor. It felt like pure peace.

A memory of me, aged five: darting away from the living-room window and crying: 'Mum, there's someone at the door!' My mother got up from the sofa, her eyes red. I heard her footsteps as she went down the hallway, the creak of the door, her slow return. I thought she'd laugh at my prank. I'd hoped it might stop her crying; I felt crushed when she sat down on the sofa and carried on weeping. She whispered that my grandmother had passed away.

It all fell on her at once, in her early thirties: death, calamity, tragedy. Her story was supposed to have been a fairy tale. Society had told her that if she married a good man and stayed at home and had children, she would be happy, a myth her father had perpetuated. She had been willing to play the role; she had settled into being a homemaker and mother. And then her husband lost his job, had a breakdown, developed schizophrenia, and her father died at the age of sixty-five from lung cancer and her mother, unable to cope without him, developed dementia and ended up in an institution (Summerfields, by ironic coincidence) and died there and my mum's comfortable life dissolved into poverty. With three children to look after, a husband who had become a stranger, and a job to hold down, she was stretched thinly, with no time to care for herself. Putting herself last became a habit; and the danger of that is that you descend from carer to martyr. She became accustomed to the belief that life would deliver her bad luck and the gods would applaud it.

They had separate beds, my mother and father, and eventually, like Leonard and Virginia Woolf, separate rooms. As I grew up, Mum and I became closer, taking holidays together. She also went on trips abroad with her 'friend from work'. I pictured this friend as a woman who was very glamorous, with big earrings and a fat fur coat, who would cajole my mother into drinking cocktails. In my mother's dull grey life, these holidays ran like a stitch of gold thread. Morocco, Vienna, Canada – she would return from them with chocolate, post-cards, pictures, though, strangely, none of the photos ever contained a single shot of her companion.

And then one day on a trip to Kent, as we took a walk in a forest, my mum told me that her friend was not female but male. His name was Noah. And he was her boyfriend, she added delicately, as though I was the parent and she were a teen confessing her first love.

Over the years, I came to see that my mother was trapped in one of those situations in which an affair is the only thing that will hold a marriage together. It offered release, relief, escape; without it, the pressure cooker would have erupted. My mother had split her life in two, to allow a small part of herself happiness and fun. It was clear that she wasn't a mistress. She and Noah were best friends.

2008: we were on holiday in Switzerland, staying in a hotel that overlooked Lake Zug. I kept asking my mother what was wrong. Finally, she confessed that Noah had suddenly dumped her. After a decade of infidelity, in a fit of conscience, he'd confessed all to his wife and family. And now he had cut off all contact. She admired his moral integrity, she went on, with a brave smile. But I could see that she was broken.

Two years went by. Noah didn't get back in touch and my mother mourned his loss like a widow. And then, out of the blue, he left a message on her answerphone saying he wanted to leave her something in his will. When he'd told his wife, she had thrown him out of the family home. In the aftermath of stress and shock, he'd been diagnosed with cancer. Now he was living on his own in a flat in Epsom, with a few months left to live. The trip to Turkey had been a treat they had planned together, the last holiday they would ever share. But in the end Noah had been too sick and weak to go; his absence shadowed every moment.

On the last day of our holiday, we hired canoes and clashed on the high seas. Mum was very cautious; I was very adventurous. As a storm vivified the sky, she kept calling out that we should stay near to the shore, but I wanted to play in the deeper waves, savour the exhilaration of their foaming danger. I felt exasperated by her cries, experiencing flashes of what I'd suffered throughout the holiday: as though I were a teenager again, and she was my chaperone, cossetting me from the slightest interesting experience. It was the only disadvantage of our close relationship. Because of my father's illness, I had become everything to her – friend, sister, confidante. But her love could feel claustrophobic at times; I was complacent then of how precious it was.

Saturday morning: the day after we'd returned from holiday. I was munching marmalade on toast and still slightly jetlagged. It was early but Mum was up and dressed and ready to go out.

'I just need to go and see Noah,' she told me. 'He needs some company.'

Noah needed more than company. He needed a carer. He had hired a nurse to look after him at nights, when he sometimes suffered nightmares and epileptic fits, where he would end up on the floor, screaming. Now my mum was spending her weeks looking after Dad and her weekends looking after Noah. At his flat, she would hoover and wash up and cook for him. No wonder she looked so exhausted and hollowed out, despite our holiday. I hoped she wasn't overdoing it. I wondered if she ought to be more selfish.

I remember feeling that my mum was destined – or doomed, perhaps – to play the role of a carer. She had always been a very kind, compassionate woman; she never seemed bitter about the fate that had befallen her. Her friends adored her because she was such a good listener. You could tell her any problem and she'd respond with empathy and then give advice that didn't feel slanted by bias, just simple, clear, wise common sense. She was tender towards human nature. She didn't like to judge people. If someone was rude or unkind, she felt there must be a reason behind it, and wanted to know it so that she might help them.

I saw this tendency when we went to meditation retreats together. Most of the people there were much as to be expected: middle class, good jobs. But there were always one or two who stood out for their difference or vulnerability, such as the guy who had ME and wore sunglasses to protect his sensitive eyes and who would fuss about the light and his leaky flask and his strict gluten-free diet. In general, people were nice to him, but I did notice some avoiding him, and others clearly finding him tiresome to talk to, for he wasn't interested in discussing much beyond his health problems. That was the person my mum would gravitate towards. She'd be gentle with him, and soothing, and make an effort to make him feel included. There was a strong desire in her to bring those on the margins into the centre.

15

Two days after we got back from holiday, my mum booked an appointment with her GP to discuss her worsening cough. Meanwhile I wandered across Bloomsbury, carrying the opening first hundred pages of *The Quiddity of Will Self* in an A4 brown envelope. It was a novel I'd spent nine years on. Now my agent was trying to get a deal for it.

I had been feeling somewhat awkward about never having mentioned the book to the man himself. Everyone I knew had a different take on whether I should confess or not, and whether I'd get sued. In the end, my mother said it was only right and polite to inform him, and since she was a wise woman, I followed her advice.

On holiday, I'd received an email from Mr Self instructing me 'to send some sample material – a chapter, whatever – and we can take it from there'. Now I was sending him pages of the manuscript which included a scene where a ghost slithers into Self's body and dictates his prose as he hammers away on his Olivetti; a religious cult who worship him with bizarre orgiastic rites; and a murder mystery set in 2046 when his body, preserved in formaldehyde by a collector, is cut up and sold to fans. Legal action seemed inevitable.

I was writing the sort of book that I knew women weren't supposed to write. Whenever I browsed in bookshops I would notice that the cult fiction sections were ninety to a hundred per cent men, piled high with Burroughs, Bukowski, Paul Auster, Hunter S. Thompson, J. G. Ballard – and Will Self. The very term avant-garde is a military one, derived from the French for vanguard, suggesting masculine power and might in marching forward to smash the conventional boundaries of fiction. Those cult-fiction book tables seemed to imply that men ought to be out there fighting with their prose whilst women should stay at home and stick to the domestic. I wanted to flick a V-sign at all that.

What I didn't admit in my letter to Will Self was that the book was about my father as much as it was about him. The first section was narrated by a character who obsessively devours the novels of Will Self until Self's voice becomes a constant in his mind; I wanted to play with the idea of reading as an act of schizophrenia. My father's illness was a watermark on every page of the book.

I'd found it hard to find fiction that captured my father's condition. Once, I read a much-praised novel that was written from a schizophrenic's viewpoint but seemed unconvincing to me. Given that the illness fractures the self into voices and hallucinations, how can a coherent first-person voice narrating a classically structured story with a beginning, middle and end, make any sense? Will Self was different: he knew how to write about madness. He got it. It was the surreal, night-marish flavour of it that his stories captured, such as *The*

Quantity Theory of Insanity, which plays with the theory that sanity is a fixed quotient in society: if you cure an asylum of schizophrenics in London, then a group of sane and rational people in New York will go crazy. Schizophrenia is the most surreal of mental illnesses. I once encountered a schizophrenic who related that, while lying in bed in hospital during a psychotic episode, he had received all his visitors without speaking, a blissful smile on his face; he was living out reality in a Star Wars film, and each person who visited appeared as a hallucinated character from the film.

Simplistic tales about schizophrenia don't tend to resonate with me. Art that captures its surreal, smashed psyche are the ones where I have an intuitive feeling of 'Yes, that's it! That's what it's like!' *Alice in Wonderland*, with its strange dislocations of time and space and place – that is my dad's illness. The modernist fragments of T. S. Eliot's *The Waste Land* – 'These fragments I have shored against my ruins' – that is my dad's illness. And Self, writing about a man who seeks to find patterns of meaning in the graffiti on toilets across London – that is my dad's illness. I remember as a teenager sitting down and watching an episode of *Monty Python*, my mum laughing with me, my dad silent. The way it jumps from one mad scene to another, from a man holding a dead parrot, to the chorus of 'The Lumberjack Song', then back to something completely different – that is my dad's illness.

My mother must have witnessed his illness in a much rawer, more shocking state than we, her children, did. She saw him in the years before he was put on the right medication, and she witnessed his resistance to taking it. She would tell me fragments of story from time to time, such as the time he took his clothes off and wandered about naked, or the way he had a 'mad monk' phase and became so austere with his food that he would only eat tomatoes, as a kind of religious penance. Things eventually reached the point where she told him: take your medication, or I will leave you. He loved her, or needed her too much, and caved in, swallowing down his pills, his symptoms subdued into a sad, quiet existence. My mother was not a controlling person, so I know my father must have been in a very bad way for her to lay down an ultimatum. Whilst my mother experienced his Monty Python years, we mostly saw a quiet man in an armchair with an obsessive love of the Bible. Writing *Quiddity* was a way of trying to understand the wild incidents that accompanied his schizophrenia, of setting them down in the guise of fiction.

After dropping off the chunk of *Quiddity* at Will Self's literary agents, I wandered on across London. As I walked I exchanged text messages with Z. Five years we'd been connecting, five years of daily emails, meeting only once a year for a night of wild passion, in order that the chemistry between us would not diffuse, tame into domesticity. We danced an eternal courtship, always on the brink of a climax that never came; once he promised that he was going to chase me across the arc of a lifetime.

Arriving home, I saw that there was a job application form on the dining-room table. My mum had filled in her name and a few other details. My mother still hadn't managed to fulfil her teenage dreams. If she had become a therapist as she had hoped, she would have been a carer of a different sort – a type of middle-class caring that earned good money and carried prestige. Instead, every day throughout her thirties, forties, fifties, sixties, she went to work as a secretary. It was a job that was clearly wasted on her. She was bored by it and tired by it. Her frustrated talents were rotting inside her. During the evenings she studied for A levels in sociology and psychology. Then one day when I was a teenager, I had come home from school to find her sick in bed.

'Your dad's resigned from his job,' she said, savagely peeling an orange.

I knew Dad even having a job was a rare thing. He had been working for the last six months as a clerk. It was a step down from the managerial position he'd held before his breakdown, but at least it helped pay the bills.

'He asked them for a pay rise and when they didn't give it to him, he walked out. But it's not really about that. He can't cope with work, he's not strong enough.'

It seemed that even though my dad was now on medication, he wasn't really well: the meds might have repressed the most surreal symptoms, but the illness was still kinking up in unexpected ways.

I couldn't see it then but I can now: Mum was in a state of despair. It wasn't just the worry of money. She was surviving in the present because she had a dream for the future, and now it was sailing away like clouds tugged by the wind. She had to increase her hours at work. In some ways she and I were in parallel: we were both taking A levels, but mine were by day, in the luxury of lessons, and hers were learnt in the little scraps of time before bed, when she was dog tired, falling asleep over textbooks.

Mum often applied for new jobs, but backtracked at the last minute, failing to post the forms, or she would simply run out of time and energy. I think she knew it would only ever be a sidestep: going from one secretarial position to another, and once the novelty of a new boss and office had worn off, little in her life would have changed. Now, in 2010, she was ardently looking forward to her retirement: just a few more years to go.

I was at home the day she heard. I'd headed south to visit my parents for the weekend and had fallen unwell. I was lying in the room I'd grown up in as a child, the sunlight dancing on peeling wallpaper. I heard the slam of the front door below, then Mum and the coughing. Finally, rather begrudgingly, the GP had allowed her to have some tests. I was sick with worry; I wanted to be mothered; I went downstairs to see her.

She had a tumour, she said. She was sitting on the sofa and my dad was hovering nearby and she told us that she had a tumour in her kidney. Cancerous. I flung my arms around her and held her as though she was my child. Dad said nothing.

In the evening, I cooked her dinner and when she came down I saw that her eyes were sore and puffy from weeping. I had been crying too, though I was still too devastated by the news to fully digest it. Throughout my life, I had always seen

SAM MILLS

her death as something on the distant horizon, a tragedy that would strike when I was old and grey. My dad carved away at his food and a memory came back to me, of sitting at this same table as a teenager, doing my homework. Through the hatch that opened into the kitchen, like a window without glass, I could see my mum making some jam tarts. My dad suddenly entered, kissed her like some hero in a black and white film, and declared: 'You're the most wonderful wife and I love you.' She smiled, looked slightly embarrassed, and he left the room. Five minutes later, he was back. He kissed her once more, said the same thing, then left. And then – again, until my mum pushed him away, laughing and saying: 'You're just being silly now.' I watched, wide-eyed, trying to work out what emotion had overwhelmed my dad – whether it was love, or madness.

A few weeks later, I was back in Appley Bridge, still trying to pack up my things. I had agreed to move back to my parents' house; my cat had already gone ahead of me, transported on the back seat of a friend's car. For the first time in my life, I was about to become a carer.

Sifting through my books, I came across a collection of Emily Dickinson poems. I thought back to being on holiday with Mum, when I had read the poem about death, and shivered:

> Because I could not stop for Death –
> He kindly stopped for me –
> The Carriage held but just Ourselves –
> And Immortality.

It was painful to think the tumour had been growing in Mum's kidney all that time. The poem had carried more resonance than I'd realised – Death's Carriage had been sitting there outside all the while, whip poised. And we had been relaxing and laughing and reading, unknowing … though there had been that cough. That dry, wracking cough, which I now discovered was a symptom of the cancer snarling in her kidney. When I'd heard it, on some level I'd sensed that it was more than just a minor virus.

The carriage in the poem travels slowly, suggesting an illness that creeps up on you, gradual and insidious. And the play of those words at the start – the way we like to think we are in control of our lives, that we can stop for Death, whereas Death, in fact, stops us.

I got a call from my older brother. It was the first time he had phoned me in years.

'Mum's got … cancer,' he said. His voice was high, almost sounded cheerful, a front to cover his agony.

'I know.'

I pretended I'd only just found out. My mum had held off from telling my brothers because she hadn't wanted to spoil a birthday dinner we had all recently shared. I'd been conscious of shooting my mother nervous looks throughout the meal and her giving me reassuring smiles in return. The dinner had felt fractured. My brothers viewed me as my mother's favourite. We were a family of three tribes: me and Mum, my brothers, and Dad lost in his own isolation. Now, reluctantly, we were being bound together. As my friend had warned me: when one person in a family has cancer, everyone has cancer.

'So I think we should get Mum eating organic food,' I said to John. He wanted answers, and this was all I could come up with, after an extensive google search. 'Organic crops have got sixty per cent more antioxidants than conventional ones,' I parroted.

'Yes, that's a good idea,' he said breathlessly. 'Organic food. Right.'

My mum telephoned soon after to say that Stefan had reacted to the news by turning up at hers with a new HP printer and a huge box of chocolates. Meanwhile, John had started doing DIY on the house and tidying the garden. We weren't an expressive household, so now we were all trying to say I love you at a hysterical pitch through various acts of devotion, me with my lists of super-healthy foods, my older brother with his paintbrush, my younger with his credit card.

There was a day when I spent hours roaming across London in pursuit of an organic cauliflower. I suffered no delusions that it was going to cure Mum in any way, but I felt helpless, and I knew she loved my healthy cooking. The internet had misled me, told me that there was a branch of Planet Organic open in west London but when I got there, I found a computer shop, so presumably it had closed. So I went all the way to the Goodge St branch, by now quite exhausted from the other organic shopping I was carrying, and felt a surge of triumph as I picked up the vegetable, its limp green leaves flapping around its white heart. This vegetable ambrosia contained seventy-seven per cent of the recommended RDI of Vitamin C, was high in fibre and swirling with antioxidants. This was what I did the day after my mother received a new diagnosis, that the cancer had spread from her kidneys to her lungs. If it had only attacked one lung, it could have been removed by operation, but both lungs meant it was terminal.

16

My mum was in the living room, watching a horror film. It was called *Drag Me to Hell* and the noises alone – shrieks and screams that resembled drills and saws – were making me wince as I scooped a tablespoon of some purple Japanese seaweed powder into a glass and added water. It was meant to have all the vitamins and minerals anyone could ever need.

I dislike horror movies and refuse to watch them. For me, the fear they evoke is too extreme, too intense, reducing me to a childlike state. To my mind, they are modern-day explorations of what it's like to lose your sanity, dramatised in the most lurid and sensational way. Horror films are a harking back to medieval ideas of mental health, when a Christian Europe saw those who were mad as possessed by evil spirits; people were superstitious of having contact with them because spirits might fly from their bodies. The horror film uses various imaginative tropes to explore the same emotional experience: breakdown. The couple in the house who become nervous of creaking doors, hear voices, imbue dolls with sinister meaning – all seem symbolic of someone descending into paranoid schizophrenia, embodying our own terror as to what it feels like to lose a grip on reality. Such films almost always have a key scary scene, a denouement in an attic or basement, the very place that the mad were usually locked up in by their embarrassed families. The resolution of conflict is normally a kind of exorcism of the evil – a more dramatic finale than watching someone pop Chlorpromazine in Act 3.

Or: perhaps Mum's love of horror was because she did recognise the echoes and found catharsis in them. In any case, she was grinning away when I brought her the purple drink, which I proffered as though it was some elixir of eternal life. She sipped, winced, sipped some more, said it tasted better the more you drank of it and at least it made her hair shiny. She was now on a drug called Everolimus. Chemo isn't given for all kinds of lung cancer, and I think she was relieved because she hated the thought of hair loss and wither. She said she was feeling a lot better on her new super-healthy diet, but her hands, as they caressed the fur of my cat, looked frail and bony. Patients diagnosed with lung cancer have a life expectancy of one to five years. That was the verdict I'd read online.

One of my father's care co-ordinators once gave me a leaflet about being a carer. It described different ways of caring that ranged from emotional support to assisting with meals to just 'keeping an eye on them'. That final definition gave me a massive boost of confidence. I'd always seen caring as an extreme act, a twenty-four-hour, round-the-clock-nursing duty. It confirmed that caring can also take root in small gestures of the everyday that build up to a huge contribution in the end.

I could have done with that knowledge when I moved back in with my mum. In the first few months, I felt a little frustrated. I missed my friends in the north and the freedom of being in my own place. It felt small and cramped in my childhood bedroom; ancient *Narnia* novels were piled beneath my bed, pages stained yellow with age. At times I had a childlike wish to be able to push through the back of a wardrobe and wander into a parallel world of snow and magic, beauty and danger.

I was someone who liked to have goals. To be active. And my caring duties felt vague. Yes, there were certain things I could do, like carry her shopping because her arms were becoming too weak, or cook her lunch. But mostly I just needed to be there for her. Sometimes this made me feel slightly useless, as though I wasn't doing enough, for emotional support is harder to define than practical help – even though it can be equally, if not more, important.

As the months went by, I began to feel trapped by my caring role, elaborately so, like a rodent caught in one of those complex laboratory mazes that makes it scurry all over the place, duck and dive, ping against walls and doors. It was my worst fear: losing my freedom. My mother had hated her job, but it had given her a security she craved; whenever I had a job, I'd been fired within months for writing my books instead of working and for being too resistant to taking orders. Not having the peace or space to write was the hardest thing. It wasn't just my way of earning a living: it was my daily drug. Having written every day since the age of eleven, this was my first real hiatus. But writing is not a profession that is particularly compatible with caring, because it involves shutting the world out; writers are notorious for neglecting their loved ones.

Whenever I sat down and got a flow going, my mum would interrupt and I'd be half-chatting to her whilst part of me remained in my imagined world. She needed me to be present, on the surface, engaged with the minutiae of her daily decline and in sympathy with it. I could not fail her. But the house became thick with a fog of claustrophobic doom and some part of me was scurrying, scurrying, trying to find an escape.

Z was an escape. I emailed him my good news: I had finally got a deal for *The Quiddity of Will Self* and the man himself had written me a generous letter saying that he liked my writing and was happy for publication to go ahead. Z sent congratulations, and tender sympathies for my mother. I cherished our connection in that moment; our friendship was evolving beyond its endless tango of flirtation.

A few mornings later, my mum came downstairs looking sad. She had just woken from a dream about Noah, she said. They had been on a boat together, fighting rocky waves, when he'd hugged her and said he was going to have to say goodbye for a while. She had intuited the news even before she picked up her phone and saw the text from one of his daughters saying he'd just passed away.

It was like some domino chain of death, I thought. There are all sorts of causes for illness, of course, but I do believe that deep trauma can play a part. Noah tore his family apart and got cancer; my mum, I felt sure, had got cancer in reaction to Noah's cancer, and the strain of caring for Dad. But if Noah hadn't had the affair, he might well have left his wife anyway; and my mother would probably have left my dad and he would have died. My dad was a man in fragments and every day that she went to work and shared his home and kept his ring on her finger was a thin binding which just about held him together. Without her, I think his shattering might have taken the form of suicide, or else homelessness, despair, death. Basically, the Grim Reaper had a share majority in the situation; he was always going to have won one way or another.

17

March 2016: the moment I entered the house, I needed to know where my dad was.

A week had passed since his release from Summerfields. After waking at eight, I'd headed to the library for two hours of writing and editing. I'd been absorbed in ideas, my mind circling in a dreamlike meditative state; now I was back on the surface, alert and anxious. I called Dad's name. Ran upstairs. The bathroom door was locked. I heard the rush of running water.

I banged on the door: no answer.

He must be having a bath.

He must have fallen into a catatonic state. I pictured him lying stiff, water ebbing into his frozen mouth, helpless against its surge—

'DAD!' I banged again.

'I'm having a bath,' he called back.

Downstairs, it took some time for my heartbeat to calm.

Life was refusing to revert back to ordinary patterns; I suffered a perpetual sense of optimism and dread all at once. He had had two catatonic collapses in the last six months, what was to stop a third, a fourth, a fifth happening? The other morning I'd walked into the kitchen to find Dad eating his breakfast. He had cheerfully recounted how he'd come down in the night and set his dressing gown alight while brewing up some hot milk. He showed me where the evergreen towelling cloth was charred – eaten up by flames – before he'd thrust it under the tap.

Now I had visions of all the possible scenarios in which a collapse might occur. What if I awoke in the middle of the night to the smell of smoke, and found my dad in the kitchen, an upright zombie, flames raging around him?

Leonard Woolf wrote about this too: the uncertainty of it all. Virginia's illness was 'the menace . . . under which she always lived', like a storm cloud that might fracture into rain at any moment. When they went on holiday to Cornwall after her 1913 breakdown, Leonard found it 'nerve-wracking', anxious that the narrative of her illness was reaching a final act of stability and wellness. That is the stress of it: we want to feel that conflict and crisis will follow the rhythm of the story-telling that we grow up with in fairy tales and movies, stories that promise us Act 3 will conclude with progress and peace. But sometimes the end of the story, the finality of resolution, can be even worse than the constant anxiety of the present.

Monk's House, Rodmell. One o'clock in the afternoon, 28 March 1941. Leonard is in the garden when he hears Louie, the cook, ringing the bell for lunch. Inside, Leonard enters the sitting room to listen to the news – and stops short. Two letters are propped up on the table. One is addressed to him, the other to Vanessa. His is dated Tuesday. It reads:

Dearest,

I feel certain that I am going mad again. I feel we can't go through another of those terrible times. And I shan't recover this time. I begin to hear voices, and I can't concentrate. So I am doing what seems the best thing to do. You have given me the greatest possible happiness. You have been in every way all that anyone could be. I don't think two people could have been happier till this terrible disease came. I can't fight any longer. I know that I am spoiling your life, that without me you could work. And you will I know. You see I can't even write this properly. I can't read. What I want to say is I owe all the happiness of my life to you. You have been entirely patient with me and incredibly good. I want to say that – everyone knows it. If anybody could have saved me it would have been you. Everything has gone from me but the certainty of your goodness. I can't go on spoiling your life any longer.

I don't think two people could have been happier than we have been.

V.

The River Ouse is searched, the meadows are searched, a local ruin that Virginia likes to inhabit is searched. Nothing is found except her walking stick on the river bank. Leonard knows that he has lost her.

The following week, Leonard has lunch with his trusted

friend, Willie Robson. Leonard's eyes are 'red from weeping, his face haggard beyond description'. Leonard waits while the river is dragged. He notifies *The Times*. Letters of condolence pour in. Friends keep reminding him of how happy Virginia has been, how he has kept her alive for three decades. It is a reassurance that Leonard desperately needs.

Was Leonard less alert to Virginia in the months before her suicide? I know from my own experiences that being a carer is hard to sustain: the constant feeling that you are wearing an invisible uniform and carrying a clipboard, on watch for your loved one's symptoms. Over time, it is natural to slip back into the roles of family. Leonard became very busy with work, carrying heavy responsibilities as the editor of the *Political Quarterly*, as well as working for the Labour Party and keeping Hogarth Press going. He was also preoccupied with the outbreak of world war and the spread of Nazism. It overshadowed them both: the harshness of rationing; Monk's House cold and damp; a picture of the *Kristallnacht* that lingered in Leonard's nightmares, for it depicted a Jew with his fly torn open to show he was circumcised, being dragged out of a shop by stormtroopers, surrounded by mocking, laughing onlookers. He and Virginia made a pact: if the Nazis set foot on British soil, they would lock themselves in the garage with the car engine running and gas themselves. They weren't the only ones in the Bloomsbury set who regarded suicide as their best defence in the event of invasion – also prepared were Virginia's brother, Adrian, Vita Sackville-West and Harold Nicholson.

Leonard argues in his memoir that war had a paradoxical impact on them: 'If one is in the exact centre of a cyclone or tornado, one finds oneself in a deathly calm while all round one is the turmoil of roaring wind and wave. It seemed as if in Rodmell in those last months of 1940 we had suddenly entered into the silent, motionless centre of the hurricane of war.' For Leonard, Virginia's descent into depression and breakdown came on suddenly; he compares it to her 1915 mania when she woke up one morning and started to speak gibberish. He did not feel uneasy until the middle of January 1941. For him, 'The depression struck her like a sudden blow.'

But perhaps he did miss the signs. Virginia's diary reveals hints of depression in late 1940. The war changed the rhythm of their lives. They'd always alternated between the capital and the countryside, a fizzy social life and a quieter life of reading, walks and writing. The latter often worked as a therapy for Virginia's illness, but too much quiet had been damaging, leading to a deep introversion as they found themselves marooned in rural Rodmell. Their London properties were bombed. When Virginia came back from the capital she looked grey with melancholy, scribbling in her diary that she found herself 'in the desolate ruins of my old squares: gashed; dismantled; the old red bricks all white powder, something like a builder's yard'.

Virginia was working on a new novel, *Between the Acts*, and some memoir writing too. For her research, she had pored over old love letters between her father and mother. Traumas

SAM MILLS

of the past began to seep into the present: memories of George's abuse, her mother's death, her father's dominance. As her depression set in, she seemed tired of village life – 'Rodmell life is very small beer' – and clawed by a sense of unworthiness. Harpers rejected one of her short stories; she confided in Octavia Wilberforce, her present doctor, that she felt *Orlando* and her biography of Roger Fry were failures. Then, on 18 March – ten days before she left the suicide note – she turned up at home, drenched, looking shaken, saying she'd slipped into one of the dykes. It was like a dress rehearsal for the final act. Fearing tragedy, Leonard drove her to Dr Wilberforce for an examination. Virginia begged her not to prescribe a rest-cure; Leonard was also nervous of hiring nurses, fearing that Virginia might react violently against them, descend again into psychosis.

We can see how tough the decision was by the way Leonard repeats the predicament in his memoir. He keeps circling back to its awful catch-22:

> It was essential for her to resign herself to illness and the drastic regime which alone could starve off insanity. But she was on the brink of despair, insanity and suicide. I had to urge her to face the verge of disaster in order to get her to accept the misery of the only method of avoiding it, and I knew at the same time that a wrong word, a mere hint of pressure, even a statement of truth might be enough to drive her over the verge into suicide.

Arrangements were made for Dr Wilberforce to visit them at Rodmell in a few days' time. Meanwhile they would carry on as normal and hope Virginia got better. Then she left the note; and then she was gone.

On 18 April some teenagers picnicking by the Ouse threw stones at a 'log' in the water – discovering Virginia's dead body.

There were two elm trees at the back of their house, which the Woolfs always called Leonard and Virginia. Leonard buried her ashes at their roots.

He wrote: 'I know that V. will not come across the garden from the Lodge, and yet I look in that direction for her. I know that she is drowned and yet I listen for her to come in at the door. I know that it is the last page and yet I turn it over.'

Leonard's last conflict was that of a carer, caught between love and responsibility. Writing to Margaret Llewelyn Davies, he reflected that he might have called in nurses, but: 'I suppose I ought to say I was wrong not to have done so. I have been proved wrong and yet I know myself that I would do the same again. One had to make up one's mind which would do the greater harm – to insist, in which case I knew it would be a complete break down at once and attempt at suicide, or to run the risk and try to prevent the last symptoms coming on.' Perhaps he had also grown tired of years in which he had to exert control; in the depth of his love for her, he wanted to treat her as a wife rather than a patient.

Reading about Virginia's suicide brought tears to my eyes.

If I had lost my dad to catatonia, if it had descended at a fatal moment, it would have felt like part-accident, part-suicide to me, even though I knew he was helpless. The words of the Summerfields nurse sung sad inside me: *He doesn't want to be alive right now.* This had not been a medical opinion, just an intuitive response from her, but I'd felt the truth of those words. If there was a psychological element to his catatonia – and I felt sure there must be – then I needed to keep him happy. But how? '*I don't have moods,*' he'd told me firmly, as though happiness was out of the question.

The pill packets in white boxes: I checked them every day now, noting the ratio between pristine circles versus the ragged little holes of pills popped. I was becoming familiar with the names: twelve drugs in all, many fighting the side effects of his anti-psychotic medicines.

I cooked Dad meals. I watched for signs of slowing down and drumming fingers. I asked him if he slept well and encouraged him to develop his love of classical music. I remembered that when I was a teenager, he had a collection of tapes which he kept in a black briefcase. Now he bought storage boxes, made handwritten lists of his music, built up a stock of over fifty CDs. His favourites were Handel's *Messiah* and Mozart's symphonies and Vivaldi's *Four Seasons*. Often in the evenings he'd sit in his armchair, CD player on his lap, a look on his face of being transported. It reminded me of how I'd read books as a child and been taken to other countries, other worlds. Once at lunch he tickled me by saying that smoking in his twenties had turned his hair prematurely grey, as though his hair had been stained by it. I giggled and my dad smiled, but he was firm in his belief. I loved his flashes of eccentricity.

After Dad had been home for a week, we went back to Summerfields for a final official discharge with his doctor and their team. It was a warm, friendly, positive meeting: they'd told me to make sure he took a laxative (a powder poured into water, which fizzed into a fruity drink) every day. They were still wondering whether his delirium might have been caused by constipation. The *might* was a word that niggled. I suppose that, like Leonard Woolf, I wanted to exert control. I couldn't bear for history to repeat, but all I could do was press a laxative packet into my father's hand each day. It didn't seem like a particularly powerful weapon.

Once on a train from London to home, I suddenly turned and gazed at a stranger in horror. He jumped and I shook my head, apologising. He had been drumming his fingers on the plastic tray in front of him, and the noise had tapped into my panic response. My father's fingers were still now but I shivered at the thought of them trembling. When I arrived home, I saw that a letter had arrived, setting a date for the delayed operation on his aneurysm.

For weeks I felt on edge, as if there were a Damoclean sword hanging over us – and then my fear faded as I accepted that I could not sustain being on vigil 24/7. There was little I could do but watch out for the signs of danger, and hope I was there at the right time – so many *ifs* that I had to surrender to the unknown.

18

May 2011. About seven months after my mum had first received her diagnosis, there came a turning point in our relationship. She called me into the kitchen, frowned fiercely at the kitchen surface and pointed – 'Crumbs!' I had cut some bread and forgotten to wipe them away. This was typical of me. I was habitually messy and known in the family for being the least domesticated of us all. Normally my mother would have reprimanded me with affection and I couldn't understand why she was making such a big deal out of a tiny offence. A little voice in my head argued back: *but I'm sacrificing my life to be down here, I've left a house I love and a city I'm at home in, and I'm cooking for you and looking after you every day and now you have a go at me.*

But her fits of temper continued. She was cross because I'd used up the last of the pasta and hadn't yet bought a replacement bag. Because I plugged the hoover into a socket and swivelled it into the next room and the lead was being stretched. Then she declared that if I only hoovered once a day, it wasn't enough to pick up all the cat hair – I should vacuum, two, three, four times if necessary. As a lifelong cat lover, she'd never been bothered by this before. Her outbursts lacerated me and I felt I could never reply back. I would stare at her in bewilderment, as though she were a woman possessed, wondering where my real mother had gone. Often, I would attempt to appease her with small gifts, which she would regard with unimpressed grimaces.

My upset was exacerbated by the occasions when her friends came to visit. Then she would revert back to her old self. I'd hear them in the living room, drinking tea and gossiping; my mother, cheered up, would be warm and kind and laugh and joke. I'd always been her favourite child, yet now I was the one person who had to endure her meanness and her moods. Being a carer to my dad in the years that followed would create intimacy; being a carer to my mum was creating distance between us.

One night we were watching TV when *Little Britain* came on, David Walliams dressed in a shabby cardigan, pushing Matt Lucas around in a wheelchair, carer and cared for. Matt Lucas's character, Andy Pipkin, makes outrageous demands and requests for his carer to fulfil (seeing the opera, going to Helsinki) and then responds with the bored, flat line: 'I don't like it.' I'd always found this comic routine outrageously funny, but now I was biting my lip, finding too much truth in it. Being a carer can sometimes mean that you end up being an emotional punchbag. You have to remind yourself that it's often your loved one's illness speaking, not them.

It is disconcerting to see someone you love change through illness, to see personality twisted by the denigration of the body, particularly as I tend to be focused on the mind and forgetful of the body. When I cook I have a tendency to burn food whilst being distracted by a good book idea; a day might easily pass when I realise I have neglected to brush my hair. I plot characters for my novels, plucking characteristics from real life people, blending shades: flaws, hopes, fears, likes, but rarely depict illness as something that shapes character. In her 1926 essay *On Being Ill*, Virginia Woolf writes about this problem, musing that illness ought to take its place alongside love, battle and jealousy as a primary theme, but 'literature does its best to maintain that its concern is with the mind; that the body is a sheet of plain glass through which the soul looks straight and clear'.

Yet it was not just a matter of her illness playing ventriloquist. I'd been wrong: my mother, I realised, *was* bitter. Her compassion, kindness, sweetness – these qualities were not persona sheen. They were a sincere reflection of her heart. But she'd had to stamp down on a whole load of desires and swallow back her frustrations year upon year and decade upon decade. Whilst she had managed to get a couple of A levels, she had had to give up halfway through her degree course, too exhausted from the demands of work and caring to see it through. She'd believed that the day would finally arrive when she would get to enjoy life. Now it was too late. There would be no retirement, no holiday, no degree, no rest after her decades of devotion. Life was not operating according to some principle of the scales of justice. No wonder she was mightily pissed off.

* * *

This will make her happy, I thought. Mum was in hospital, having an operation to remove her kidney. It wouldn't cure her, not now that her lungs were pitted with cancerous lesions; I pictured them like a poison ivy, clinging and burrowing into her organs. But it would give her more time.

Dad and I were moving everything out of her bedroom. We hauled out books. We unscrewed her bed and took it to pieces. We struggled to squeeze the mattress out through the door. When she returned home, she would see a revamped bedroom and new carpet, a replacement for the rather tatty thing that was currently on her floor.

We went to visit her in hospital. It meant travelling on the tube, something that my father had probably done about twice in the last decade. He looked anxious as we bought the tickets. Throughout her illness, he had been silent as always; I was too preoccupied with my own devastation to ponder what this meant.

The tube doors swished shut behind us; with the pressure of crowds, we had to move down the carriage.

'Oh!' an elderly woman screamed.

'Dad!' I cried. He had forgotten to hold onto the pole and had gone flying on top of a lady with coiffured grey hair and a fur coat. She appeared to think she was being assaulted. For a moment he flailed on top of her, and I struggled to tug him back to his feet. 'I'm really sorry,' I said to her. 'He's not trying to … he's just ill …'

An awkwardness hung jagged in the carriage. Someone else stood up and graciously gave my dad a seat. He sat down, looking like a terrified boy. I said sorry again and then – a terrible habit I have when I am under deep stress – I started to laugh. Hysterical bubbles kept flying up from my chest and I had to force my mouth into a straight line for the rest of the journey. When we got off the train, I burst into giggles. We were social outcasts again, just as we had been when I was a kid and he was sick and walking around with no clothes on. Laughter was a defence, a shield, an oh-well-everyone-thinks-we're-loonies-but-never-mind.

When my mum returned from hospital, she was much weaker, thinner. I took her upstairs to show her the new carpet. It was beautiful: glossy, thick, royal blue, soft underfoot. It's okay, she said in a vague tone, and then lay down on her bed to rest.

19

That July, I decided to go away on holiday. Looking back, the thought of spending a week away from my mother, when we had so little time left, disturbs me. But there's an anecdote in Christopher Bollas's *When the Sun Bursts* that resonates. Bollas describes how he looked after children who had autism and schizophrenia during the late sixties. He relates how major tragic events – the assassinations of Kennedy and Martin Luther King – would worry them because they'd think *they* were responsible (I wondered if was this because of their paranoia, or because society was already training them to be scapegoats). He notes that they were unable to cushion themselves by constructing the usual illusions that make reality bearable. They would question their teachers as to why such tragedies occurred: '…we often found ourselves helpless to provide a rational answer for the madness of the so-called normal world beyond its walls …'. Bollas concludes: 'the state of normality rests largely upon the capacity for denial. To live in our world we have to deny its reality.' Working with these children became trying, distressing, not because of their conditions 'but because of how they deconstruct the defenses crucial to our own peace of mind'.

Fiction can tell greater truths than non-fiction, yet story-telling can also be deployed as a weapon against reality: our own internal feed of fake news. This is why global warming, a slow slide into horror, is inevitable; we are conditioned to shut out the bigger picture; it is how we survive, day by day. An online search had informed me that my mother had a life expectancy of between one and five years, which in my mind meant five, which would probably stretch to seven, and because she looked young and healthy, then surely she'd live a decade. At least. I believed in this myth most days, otherwise I would not have been able to cook and shop and eat with her. But every so often brutal truth pierced reality – or else, I allowed a little fragment of brutal truth to come in.

I emailed Z for advice on where I should go. We debated exotic locations, but in the end, it could only be Switzerland. I knew some friends who owned a hotel there. Nothing else was affordable and even a cheap trip seemed a little reckless, but I booked it all the same.

Switzerland was a place I'd visited time after time with Mum. The journey there was the most harrowing I'd ever been on, despite the pleasant staff, and trains that ran on time, and a bus that curved with confidence up the winding mountain paths fringed with pine trees. The singularity of myself kept punching me. Me in a single seat on the plane with a stranger next to me; me choosing a cream cake without her beside me, laughing and groaning at the calories. The thought came: *when she's gone, who will love me with the depth she does? No man I've ever met, no friend.*

My friends' hotel overlooked Lake Zug. The view from my room – the blue of lake, the soft mists hanging over it, the sighs and slopes of mountains – was so exquisite it looked unreal; I was half-convinced that if I reached out of the window I'd touch oil and canvas. When I lay down for a nap, I could hear goats roaming nearby, the bells tinkling like something from a childhood dream. I'd craved nothing more than being away from the weight of caring; now I wanted nothing more than to be back home. Mum and I exchanged texts and I told her about every detail of the trip, so that she could share it with me in her imagination. Here was the paradox: now that I was away from her, from the fog of her cancer and its moods, I felt close to her again.

At meal times, I would eat with my friends, a warm and welcoming couple. The guests were a wonderful range of nationalities, which meant that I picked up numerous scraps of language, custom, anecdote. One man stood out. He was very tall and slender and had a look of Daniel Day-Lewis about him, a debonair face framed by dark hair. His name was Antonio, he said, and he was staying for a week. One day he sat down opposite me at the lunch table and we found ourselves talking a lot and eating very slowly. I discovered he was Spanish and in his forties. Our lunch stretched out.

Outside, the lake looked like a colour that had been invented to express the purest shade of happiness. We walked in the pine forests; we began to tease each other. I asked him to teach me Spanish and he enjoyed correcting me, sighing and being stern over each syllable. We came to a clearing that looked out over the mountains. In the distance, one line of peaks still had snow on them. He gently put his hand on my wrist whilst telling me that the Spanish word for intimacy was *intimidad*. I looked at the faraway mountain and thought how eerie it seemed, on this bright day, like some sort of Narnia of eternal cold; I pictured statues of people frozen life-in-death tucked beneath evergreens, mouths in Os of silent screams.

Coming home: I could not stop grinning. The capital seemed ugly after the colour-rush of Switzerland, the sky a swirl of dirty water after its clean blue. I was so pleased to be back. My week's break had reset our relationship: we were mum and daughter again.

We sat and ate biscuits whilst I told her, a little shyly, that I'd met a tall, dark, handsome man. I dreaded Mum's frown, but she smiled approval. I gave her some general details, then sank into reverie, reliving moments from my last evening with Antonio, when he had snuck into my room and we'd made love through all the hues of night. It had been so euphoric, I'd been uncharacteristically reckless; now his sperm were still swimming inside me. This brought faint panic; the urge to laugh; and then pleasure at the memory of his kisses and caresses.

I suddenly became aware of Mum's voice trying to tell me something. I sat up. She hadn't wanted to text me the news whilst I was away, she said, for fear it would wreck my holiday: the Everolimus drug she was taking had stopped working. The tumours in her lungs were no longer shrinking, they were spreading. The holiday had blossomed in my mind like a flower with spread petals; now they curled up in instant withering. It was over, a dream I'd woken from, and I was back in the cruelty of the present, losing the person I loved most in the world to cancer's slow grind.

The next day I saw that Antonio had emailed. I had wondered if our love affair had meant nothing more than a holiday romance, and my heart leapt at his suggestion that he might fly to England to visit me.

My mother had no future anymore, nothing to plan for, nothing to hope for. She was living in the past, raking over it, regretting, angry, regretting. I was in a pattern, I realised, of living for the future. My daily anticipation had always been shaped by books I might finish and deals I might get. Without writing, without a job, my income was dwindling, my ambitions on pause. The emails from Antonio gave my life a sense of shape again.

Oddly, it felt more acceptable to be distracted by love than work. Work was a cynical thing; love a helpless indulgence. He wrote to me in poor English and I attempted to reply in Spanish, claiming that I was now fluent in his language (joking that no, no way, I never heard of such a thing as Google Translate). He was often stern and often teasing. He told me off for signing my emails with 'x's which he said made me sound like an illiterate; instead, he asserted that we ought to sign off with *beso*. As we emailed back and forth, I felt as though I was escaping into a world I had once entered through writing.

On Antonio's first night in England, I collected him from the train station. He had a tired, slightly bemused air, as though he were wondering how he had come to be magicked into this sleepy little place of stone cottages and sloping fields in the north of England. I felt the pinch of having given up renting my own house, for it would have been lovely to have a place to ourselves. Instead I had managed to wrangle a double room in a friend's house, leaving my mum for the weekend. I attempted to cook him dinner and he kept interfering, fussing over water, spices, cooking times. Once he'd eaten, he looked a little happier. After we made love, a smile softened his eyes. He told me that he loved me, and I said I loved him.

The next day, we went for a woodland walk, with the sun smiling over us and the birds hyper in the trees above, and as he helped me over a stile, he cried: 'I'm so happy that you are my girlfriend now.'

I was drunk on illusions and euphoria but even so, the *now* hurt. There had been a girlfriend. He'd mentioned her the first night we'd got together in Switzerland, after we'd made love. I had whitewashed this detail away when I had told my mother and my friends about him. I pictured a plump Spanish woman in some very remote village in the southernmost end of the country whom he hardly ever saw and did not care for. And if I was the *now*, then she was most definitely *past*.

On the last day of our holiday, after days of walking and having sex and eating and confiding and sharing stories of our pasts, our exes, our families, we lay on the bed checking our emails. Something snagged my attention. He noticed me noticing it: the number of emails in his inbox from a girl called Carlotta. 'Oh, she's the one who was my girlfriend,' he said.

The icy shock of it: *Carlotta had been there.* I remembered her from the hotel in Switzerland. She had been working there; she must have been the reason he'd visited Zug in the first place. I rewound our courtship and realised that she shadowed every frame. We had been the ones behaving like a couple and she had seemed like a vague friend. She had been eating dinner with him when he had smiled, called out to me, flirted. She had sat behind us one night when we'd attended a concert. On that last night, she'd been sleeping in the room below mine whilst I had been in Antonio's arms.

After Antonio had gone, I returned to London to cook and care for Mum again. We went to the cinema frequently and each time we got the train into Wimbledon, passengers would watch us in surprise as we grappled with the gap between platform and carriage: I would physically *yank* Mum up whilst she clung to the train's safety bars. Her legs were losing muscle, wasting away, her skintight jeans now baggy. We went to a cafe and I assured her that I'd had a lovely time with Antonio, stung once more by the memory of Carlotta, and the guilt of being his girlfriend *now*, and having stolen someone's boyfriend right in front of them without even knowing it. It was like one of those stories from a crime scene where everyone remembers a series of events differently, and subjectivity is shown to be skewed.

My mum had arranged to have a break too. The plan was that we would both go to Appley Bridge for a few weeks. On the way home, I mentioned Antonio. He would like to return to England, I explained, and if he visited they could meet each other.

'That's nice,' my mother replied, then fell into a silence for the rest of the journey.

At home, Mum ran a bath and retreated into its bubbles and steam, looking crushed. I hovered outside the bathroom door, feeling panicked. Did she feel I was deserting her? I hadn't meant it to seem that way, but it was true that a trip with both of them present would mean I would be splitting my energies between being a carer/daughter and being a girlfriend.

The trouble is, I needed accommodation. My mother had sorted hers, but I had run out of money to book anywhere. Antonio had generously offered to pay. It was a strange scenario for me: I'd always been so independent, had never relied on a man's income before. I wasn't sure if I liked it. It felt so vulgar and mean to start discussing money with Mum – because then what? If I was going to earn, then I'd have to start neglecting her, and that would only upset her even more. I knew that if she'd been healthy and well, she would have intuited the problem immediately, but she was too sick to perceive it, too lost in the battle to survive.

A day after Mum and I arrived in Appley Bridge, Antonio joined us. We all shared a stiff lunch together, during which everyone was very polite.

There were emails on his computer. It seemed as though our love affair was one narrative and his inbox told another, wove an insidious subplot. Antonio had already explained about the emails from the Norwegian woman. She was a woman he'd had a fling with a year ago, but they still emailed every few days; he was happy to show them to me. I pointed out that by flirting, he was leading her on. He looked surprised, as though he hadn't stopped to consider this; he'd been enjoying her attention and hadn't thought of her expectations. There were also a lot more from his 'ex' Carlotta. One day, when Antonio went out for a jog, I did the unforgiveable. I read his emails. I kept having to cut and paste phrases into Google translate. As I did so, as I pieced together the real narrative, a growing horror came over me.

I put on a brave smile and went to see Mum. She had been catching up with friends and seemed happy. I'd bumped into one of them and they'd marvelled to me: 'Your Mum's so calm, given what she's facing …' I wasn't sure what to make of this, whether the calm was pure persona, or whether a part of her had found acceptance. In any case, she was never calm with me anymore. I might have been alarmed if she had been – it would have been far too Stepford wife. She was upset because she'd bought a bottle of orange juice and the makers had screwed the lid on far too tight. I felt embarrassed as I took it from her and undid it with ease. Her wrists were so thin, I noticed. Everything was hard for her, doors heavy, suitcases made of lead, jars stubborn. The world was becoming an obstacle course.

I asked what she thought of Antonio and she replied that he seemed great. Oh yes, I agreed, he's great.

Later that evening, I confronted Antonio. I had an *intuition*, I said, that his Spanish girlfriend was not past but present. He seemed relieved to come clean. He confessed that he hadn't quite broken up with her. It seemed that their romantic past was messy. They often took other lovers whilst they were dating. And yes, he admitted, they were planning a trip to South America together in the autumn.

'So you've got two girlfriends,' I said.

'I've had two before,' he said, smiling, 'and I've found it's worked quite well.'

20

We were in France and Antonio was not in a good mood. We had been wandering down a pretty, cobbled street in a town near Valréas. Antonio was peering into a bin, into which I had thrown the remains of a pear. In his eyes, this was a travesty, for I had left too much fruit dangling on the stalk, a sin he would never, ever dream of committing, and it might be some time before he forgave me. He had other gripes, too, besides the Pear Sin: that I complained too much about his other girlfriend, that my long hair was annoying him (the hairs kept turning up in the sheets, in the bath), my breasts were too small, and I kissed him too much. I alternated between being loving and prickly, between showering him with affectionate kisses, then making sarcastic comments about the fact that he had *two* girlfriends and how utterly farcical the situation was. Both only served to incite his cruelty and thicken its poison.

He's tired, I told myself. His eyes looked hollowed out, his features gaunt; he was working over here for a friend. On our last night, we camped out in sleeping bags under the stars, surrounded by a rustling percussion of insects. I thought of a recurrent nightmare Antonio had told me he suffered, in which he found himself back at school, struggling with an exam, panicking about failure. When I pictured him as a boy, I still saw a possible future, our own child with my blue eyes and his dark hair. We still weren't using protection: all part of the farce.

The next day we set off in a van, hired to transport some goods for his employer from Valréas to Marseille. The sun burned its white heat through the windows, drilling my temples. I put on sunglasses, draped my cardigan around my forehead, but it failed to appease the bleached feeling in my body. I asked him to stop by the side of the road, but he refused.

In the end I had to resort to a plastic bag. Vomiting was a relief, but only for a short while, before the churning in my guts resumed. I thought of the floral lavender water Antonio had passed me to drink just before we'd set off; it was meant to be healthy to drink, a tonic. Or was this sickness emotional, a horrific venting up of anguish and horror at the way our romance had descended from declarations of love to some kind of polyamorous hell, whilst I was trapped in this hot, claustrophobic van with a man who appeared to hate me, hundreds of miles away from my mother who was at home missing my company, and how could I be here when I could be there, spending every last minute with her?

I threw up again. And again. By now we'd run out of plastic bags. They sat by my feet, the used ones, like animals that had been killed and packaged for consumption. Antonio pulled over by a verge. I threw up in the grass, drowned insects, ruined flowers, and found a bin to dump the bags in. All the while, Antonio looked on with mild disgust.

Later in the hotel, I asked him why he was being so unpleasant and he said he was taking 'revenge'. He added something about a past failed marriage; now, clearly, all women had to pay for it.

The next day, for the first time in our relationship, he was physically violent. The crimes I had committed were a refusal to sit in the exact spot he wanted me to sit, and opening a free hotel soap when one was already in use. The hotel room had small windows, little light, and in the aftermath of the violence, we sat in this shadowy cell, saying nothing.

That evening, it was such a sweet relief to emerge from a London taxi, step through the threshold of home, and pass my mum a gift – a large, painted seashell with a mermaid dancing in the waves, which she unwrapped with an uncertain smile. I went into the kitchen to make her a cup of tea. I knew I wouldn't be seeing Antonio again.

A few weeks later, I sobered up: *what the fuck was that all about?* It had all been a kind of madness. I was more puzzled by my own behaviour than his. I had met plenty of men like Antonio in my life. But I'd never dated one. This was because I wasn't a masochist. I'd always steered clear of the type who want to treat you mean to keep you keen, control you, inflict wounds, fragment you. I had always felt I deserved to be treated well and opted for men who agreed with this idea.

It had been one of my most fictional relationships. I had superimposed a narrative onto the romance, ignoring the widening gap as fantasy and reality diverged, desperately clinging to the idea of a Fairy Tale Happy Ending. My mother's death had been looming, like a motif in a movie where the road suddenly becomes rough and rocky and a sign appears warning 'ENDS HERE' and the jagged plunge of a cliff face. I'd been desperate to construct a bridge across it to a life beyond.

The eve of funerals are a popular night for conception: the instinct to fight death's spectre by creating new life. I've known various friends and family who were languid about marriage and kids up until the death of a parent; and then the next time I saw them, were married, mortgaged and surrounded by a screaming brood, and looking, if not entirely happy, then at least relieved. I'd attempted to do the same, but perhaps deep down I hadn't been entirely convinced I did want to forge this path, given that I'd chosen someone so unlikely for the role.

I've heard so many other stories over the years, first-hand and second, of how friends or strangers have reacted to parental illness or death with madness in their love life. One friend told me of a woman who found out that her mother was terminally ill. She was in a four-year relationship with a guy, they'd been living together in contentment – and she decided she had to end it. She felt that if they cared for her mother together, to the point of witnessing her death, it would be a bonding experience so intense that their relationship would be changed forever. They would end up marrying. And she didn't feel he was the one, or she didn't love him deeply enough for such a conclusion. Once they'd spilt up, she became a carer and her love life became wild. She took solace in flings with unsuitable men – addicts, married men seeking affairs.

Another friend of mine said that a fortnight after her mother died, she booked a flight from London to North Carolina. She had been chatting to a random guy online and decided to spend a week with him. This was completely out of her nature; she was prone to sensible decisions rather than whimsy or adventure. She desperately needed to escape the unbearable weight of her sadness. It turned out that the man she met with was even more miserable than her. He wasn't grieving; he was just in hate with life. She said she hadn't thought it was possible to come home feeling worse, but she did. When we are vulnerable, it's easy to make bad choices, to become someone's prey.

Perhaps I had chosen Antonio because I was playing out an adult version of me bringing home a dark, handsome teenage boy and waiting to be told off, because being told off would indicate that someone was still looking out for me.

Victoria Glendinning has speculated that Leonard Woolf may have had an affair when Virginia was suffering her breakdown in 1915. If he did, it is unlikely it would have been with another member of the Bloomsbury group; up until Virginia's death, he seemed like their most chaste member. 'If Leonard were to seek sexual solace with anyone,' Glendinning muses, 'it would be with someone like Lily [their maid in Hogarth House], or one of the working girls he met on his Co-operation tours in the north of England.' Lily, a young woman from Sussex, had previously given birth to an illegitimate child who was then cared for by nuns. Leonard does devote a surprising number of pages in his memoir to Lily – he calls her 'psychologically fascinating' and describes how 'she found it almost impossible to refuse anyone anything'. However, he may have just felt a great affection for a maid who helped out during a difficult and vulnerable time in his life.

After Virginia's suicide, Leonard fell in love again, with a painter called Trekkie Parsons. She was married to Ian, a director at Chatto & Windus. Their arrangement is intriguing, for Leonard ended up buying a house next door to the couple in London; eventually they bought a property close to Rodmell. Trekkie would go on holiday with her husband, and then again with Leonard. They also became entangled in business: Ian ended up becoming a partner in Hogarth Press. But this wasn't a ménage à trois of great passion. It seemed to be one based more on love, affection and companionship, for Leonard and Trekkie behaved like lovers but never slept together. Leonard was a man with a lust for life and a lust for women but, by all accounts, he ended up in two monogamous, sexless relationships.

I only ever saw a few photos of my mother's lover, Noah. They had a rule that they should never be photographed together, so I found separate pictures of them standing against the same backdrop, as though one photo has been sliced in half. Noah didn't look like the dashing suitor I'd expected. He looked warm-hearted and gentle and kind. Their relationship, I suspected, had been like Leonard and Trekkie's – one of companionship and emotional sweetness.

21

April 2016: I was sitting at the dining table, typing out editorial notes on a novel, when my fingers slowed on the keyboard at the sound of the doorbell. I listened to my father's footsteps, the creak of the front door opening.

A murmur of voices: my father was speaking to a man and woman. One of them was saying: 'When we came last time, we discussed what happens when you die. We said we'd come back for more discussion.' (*Last time?*) 'Do you have your Bible to hand?'

I heard my father go into the living room to collect his Bible and reading glasses. I thought of how, on Sunday mornings, he always left at nine to go to his local Catholic church for the service. I was glad that he'd kept up this routine, for it was one of the few instances where he seemed able to participate in a group activity, even if he did set off early before each service to get his favourite seat, shyly tucking himself away in a corner at the back. He was no longer the fanatic of teen years; now his faith stabilised him.

'So if you turn to *Revelations* …' a male voice instructed.

As I went into the hallway, words were forming in my mind: 'He's schizophrenic … I don't think it's appropriate that you try to convert him … it might confuse him …' But then I saw my father standing there, Bible in hand, engaged and interested, making a rare connection with strangers. It felt wrong to pin a label on him and shut the door, as though he were a madman to be tucked away in the attic; at the same time, the idea of my father as a Jehovah's Witness was a worrying prospect.

The couple standing at the door were young. Though they were ardent evangelists, there was a sincerity in their smiles, a warmth in their energy. 'D'you mind if I talk to my dad for a minute?' I asked them. 'You see, I'm his carer.'

All of a sudden, that dreaded word had become potent. It implied that my father was vulnerable, without restricting his identity. They digested it at once, nodding obediently.

In the living room, I whispered to Dad: 'You're a Catholic, you have your own faith. You don't have to listen to them. We can tell them to go?'

But he insisted that he was fine and wanted to speak to them.

Back in the dining room, I heard them asking my father to read out dystopian biblical passages. My dad informed them, in his quiet way, that actually when a soul died they would be judged and then go to heaven or hell. They accepted the stalemate. Before going, the woman said: 'Was that your daughter? If she's your carer, she must love you very much.' I was still cynical that they might be trying to manipulate Dad, but even so, I felt a glow. Carer: it was a word I was beginning to get used to.

* * *

But the glow soon faded into resentment. My hope of heading north to see Thom was abandoned when my dad exhibited a few warning signs of catatonia.

My workload was also growing. 'Dodo' had once referred to the pet joke I shared with Thom, but had now become a business venture. Thom and I, together with my friend Alex Spears, had set up an indie press called Dodo Ink, partly inspired by the iconic indies of the past – including Hogarth Press, which Virginia and Leonard Woolf had established in 1917. Originally, it had been a hobby to help Virginia stay grounded and prevent her from 'brooding'; it went on to publish T.S. Eliot's *The Waste Land* and the first English translation of Freud, as well as Woolf's greats *Mrs Dalloway*, *Orlando* and *To The Lighthouse*.

Hogarth Press did not quite bring the stabilising calm that the Woolfs had hoped for. Their first editorial assistant, Alix Sargant-Florence, only lasted a day. I laughed when I read Hermione Lee's observation that 'It was a well-known joke among their friends that working at the Hogarth Press drove you mad'. We were suffering similar anxieties, overwhelmed by a heavy workload, a lack of money (the kickstarter we ran was quickly swallowed up by printing and covers) and three novels to publish in 2016. The emails I exchanged with Thom were shifting from the personal to the professional, from discussions of my dad and his daughter to contracts and covers.

Caring for my dad was seeping into my daily life. It had not been a conscious decision, but something that had crept up on me; when I researched the history of carers, I felt a chill of recognition. Studies show that women 'most frequently become snared in the role because caring is often a gradual responsibility'. Families rarely have group discussions in advance to plan what will happen if a parent becomes ill; women tend to start helping out vulnerable relatives with small chores that increase incrementally until they cross the line to become full-time carers. There is often an unspoken family assumption that caregiving is expected of them, whereas when a man cares it is regarded as a heroic act. The gender imbalance in caring is sometimes backed up by the clichéd biological argument that women are more naturally nurturing and empathic than men. Yet research has shown that when men care for children, their testosterone levels fall by around a third. Sympathy, patience and kindness evolve from caring, regardless of one's gender. It is more likely that women end up caring because girls are brought up to be more compliant.

Hence, a set of statistics that look grim: in the UK, women have a fifty-fifty chance of becoming a carer by the time they are fifty-nine; men have the same odds by the time they are seventy-five years old. In the US, women are twice as likely to end up in the role. Women are four times more likely to reduce their working hours than men due to multiple caring responsibilities. That said, for elderly carers, the figures shift – carers over the age of eighty-five are more likely to be men. Men do make their contribution and they make it well: forty-two per cent of informal carers are male. As the nation prepares for Brexit, there are worries about a big reduction in

EU care workers; one dossier released by the Department of Health fretted that there would be a 'decrease of labour market participation levels, especially among women'.

Indeed, the carers' rights movement in the UK was founded by a woman. Reverend Mary Webster gave up work in 1954 to look after her parents. After nearly a decade of caring she wrote a furious letter to the newspapers comparing her situation as akin to being 'under house arrest', arguing passionately that carers needed more support. She received a flood of responses from those in a similar situation. This paved the way for welfare support such as Carer's Allowance, introduced in the 1970s.

A century earlier, Florence Nightingale had been celebrated as an icon of courageous caring. Victorian women were defined by their roles as wives, mothers, sisters, nurses, housekeepers and governesses. They were the caregivers and they were expected to be selfless. Life was one of constriction, from the imprisonment of domesticity, to the crinoline hoop-shaped dresses that were so physically restrictive they made travel difficult. Middle-class women were expected to be well educated but not too clever; a woman who read too much might be deemed a blue stocking, put off potential suitors and end up a spinster. Nightingale, born into an upper-middle-class family, found herself infuriated by her oppressive upbringing, her brilliant mind unsatisfied by the tedium of daily life for women of her era. She described how, after days spent doing activities such as worsted work, reading out loud, and taking drives in the carriage, at night, 'the accumulation of nervous energy ... makes them feel ... when they go to bed, as if they were going mad'. This quote comes from *Cassandra*, an essay she wrote later in life, which Virginia Woolf thought read more like screaming than writing, so furious was her prose. It would be a major influence on Woolf's essay, *A Room of One's Own*, where she declared that women needed space, money and time to be creative.

Florence Nightingale's family initially thwarted her ambition to be a nurse, though they softened when she began to achieve fame. She was deified as the ultimate carer – the woman who went out to the Crimean War to treat wounded soldiers, the sweet and gentle 'Lady of the Lamp'. Her public persona was far more feminised than her reality. She was a brilliant health-care reformist, fighting to establish a hygienic and integrated healthcare system, decades before Nye Bevan. She pioneered the use of statistics and their visual presentation (pie charts, graphs etc) and later dismissed her feminine celebrity as 'all that ministering angel nonsense'.

Back then, you were not called a carer. You were simply a family member doing your expected duty for a sibling or parent or relative you loved. It is only contemporary society that has given the role a tag, a way of imposing responsibility but also recognising that we, the carers, are people who might need support. Emily Dickinson, whose poem about death had resonated so strongly with me, was also a carer. After her father died, Dickinson's mother had a stroke, broke her hip and became bedridden. Emily washed her, fed her, told her stories. She cared for her alongside her sister and the family maid.

But even with a ratio of three caring for one, she found the responsibility a strain. A family friend, Judge Lord, came to visit the house and noted 'how wearing ... the incessant cares and the anxious necessities of your situation are', concerned that Emily was so unselfish she might get ill. Her caring duties went on for seven years.

Becoming a carer at that time in history was something that was far more likely to happen to you at a younger age; the safety nets of modern medicine were absent and Death was far more strident. Women would be expected to step in if Mother – the Queen of Caring – was unable to fulfil this duty in some way. Emily Dickinson would have grown up seeing the pattern. When she was at school her friend Emily Fowler was pulled out of lessons when her mother died. At the age of eighteen, Fowler found herself in charge of the house and replacing her parent. Emily, writing to another school friend, referred ironically to the baby daughters of two women: 'I don't doubt if they live they will be ornaments to society. I think they are both to be considered as embryos of future usefulness.' Another poet of the era, Edward Lear, was the twentieth in a family of twenty-one children. With a mother too exhausted to love him and a father suffering financial ruin, he ended up being cared for by his sister, Ann, who encouraged his passion for drawing and painting.

Often women who struggled with the domestic, with being the selfless angel in the house, coped by doing as my mother did – by splitting themselves up; they would consciously play up feminine personas to please society in order to veil their private selves. Take Charlotte Brontë. Famously, she wrote to the poet Robert Southey at the age of fifteen, asking for advice about her writing ambitions. His chauvinistic response was deeply patronising, advising that: 'Literature cannot be the business of a woman's life.' In her reply, Charlotte was quick to reassure him that she was devoted to her job as a governess. 'In the evenings, I confess, I do think, but I never trouble anyone else with my thoughts. I carefully avoid any appearance of pre-occupation and eccentricity, which might lead those I live amongst to suspect the nature of my pursuits,' she wrote. 'I have endeavoured not only attentively to observe all the duties a woman ought to fulfil, but to feel deeply interested in them. I don't always succeed, for sometimes when I'm teaching or sewing I would rather be reading or writing ...' A poker face, then, kept Charlotte from alarming others that she might be having profound thoughts – and therefore seem eccentric, unbalanced even. Fragmentation became a strategy for survival.

There was a line in Bollas that I kept turning over in my mind: schizophrenia turns a sufferer into someone unfamiliar and '*we feel that our presence is negated*'. *Our* was the word that jolted me: the paradox of absence as an active rejection.

My mother experienced an echoing problem with a dominating father and a remote husband: her father had denied her an education, via bullying and control, and her husband, through absence, had inadvertently steered her into the role of a carer, causing the negation of her own growth and desires.

Of course, my father could not help the fact I had now taken on that role: I would never blame him for his illness. I accepted his limitations; I didn't feel negated by his lack of support and praise, or his failure to ask how I was or what I'd been doing.

However, it was also true that being a carer narrowed my self down into one dimension. One of the best things about being with a lover is that they allow you to be complex. Our enemies caricature us, put us in the strait-jacket of sex, race and class, refuse to allow us contradictions and complexities. With Thom, I could be all shades of myself, eccentric, silly, serious, erudite, dumb, playful, warm, pensive, quiet, noisy. As a carer, I had to exist as one shade, so that the other hues of my nature were erased,

I was learning to see that what Dad needed from me, every day, was to translate the world for him, give subtle shape to his being in a way that was not intrusive but suggested how he might live life. I would start each morning by asking how he'd slept; what he was reading in the papers; I would look over his post with him, discuss bills and letters. I suggested what time we ate lunch; I asked what his plan for the day was. These are all questions one might normally ask of a loved one, but I injected a force, an enthusiasm into my voice, noting that he responded to it, as though it persuaded him that life was not only worth living but enjoying. Within his body politic I was becoming his spine. It made him happy.

My sympathy for my mum was deepening by the day. I could see why she had needed Noah, so that she could experience a fullness of being. Out in the garden I brushed my hands over the crab apple tree, ice creamy with spring blossom. I thought of Thom, how he had once told me that he wanted to grow old with me. But how could anything *grow* when we couldn't see each other? *Soon*, I emailed him, *I want to see you soon.*

22

It was November 2011 and St Pancras Station was bright with decorations; two enormous Christmas trees twinkled in its arcade. I was returning from the north, where I'd accepted an award for a novel I'd written called *Blackout*. The moment I stepped into the house, my glow dissipated.

Mum was sitting up in bed. She looked wan and said she was having such trouble breathing that getting up and going to the toilet left her gasping. Then, sounding cross, she added that she hadn't been fed. Apparently Dad was supposed to have made her lunch but he'd forgotten. He'd remembered to feed the cat but not her, she added with a bitter laugh. Horrified, I hurried downstairs and got her some crackers and cheese, which was all she could stomach. I wondered if I should abandon my evening plans. I was meant to be presenting an award for new authors, and it seemed too late to cancel. The bursary had been set up in honour of Luke Bitmead, an author who had committed suicide, so it felt important to be there – but they say that charity begins at home and it's often easier to do good deeds in the abstract than personal. In the end, Mum pushed me to go and I impressed upon my father that he must, must cook her some dinner.

Outside it was only five in the afternoon and the sky was already frowning with night. My breath made mist-dragons in the air. It was the time of year that I usually associated with anticipation and celebrations. It was my birthday in a few days' time and Mum and I had worked out a solution for my presents: I would buy them for her to give to me. On the tube, I scribbled out my speech for the winner. With this and the prize and the proof copy of *The Quiddity of Will Self* that had arrived earlier, it seemed as though my career, withering over the past few years, was finally sprouting new buds – just when I couldn't care less. Or, if I did care, I wasn't able to keep my attention on it.

I knew that whatever success I had was all down to my mother, anyway. When at the age of eight I told her I wanted to be a writer, she had encouraged me so sweetly. I'd written my first novel when I was eleven, bashing it out on a second-hand typewriter that she must have scrimped and saved to acquire. Mum had helped me to submit it to a publisher too, and beamed with a kind of pride when I received my first rejection letter. I had been so lucky to have had a mother as nurturing as she was.

Later that evening, after I presented the award, someone asked me about my background – when I'd first started writing, how I'd broken in. It had reminded me that every time I looked back at the past I could always see two selves, two possibilities: the life I had lived, and a shadow life, one in which I could so easily have ended up like my father, had it not been for my mother's influence.

Aged fifteen: I stood in the hallway of my parents' house, enchanted. Through the slit in the doorway, I watched my dad, sitting in the living room, fingers trembling on his armchair as if the chair were an instrument he was learning to play. It had been a year since his illness had been explained to me. He slotted a Vivaldi tape into the cassette player and I imagined the Voice in his head being crowded out by the beauty of the *Four Seasons*, kicking off with violins so strident they sounded like string trumpets. Summer bled into my skin in flourishes of green and bright flowers, and then the tune softened, quietened, as Autumn seeped in, down-strokes of damp earth and brown smoke and dying leaves. A solo violin circled in notes of piercing sadness. My edges dissolved; I felt myself becoming abstract. I was a wind of violin notes, I was a cello with its baritone voice, I was Vivaldi himself, the lines of the wallpaper were disappearing, the house becoming air—

I hurried upstairs to my room, touching the wall, needing to feel the solid edges of my fingers. There were tears in my eyes and my heart was still beating with the after-colours of the music. I opened the window, breathing in the night air, hoping it might rinse away the sensation. Opening a book, I sat down to read, but it took some hours to feel myself again.

A few days later, in our English GCSE class, I pulled my finished essay from my rucksack with care, ready to hand it in. Between the final two pages was a small, jagged note. It had been torn from the corner of a page of my diary. It described, in fragments, how I felt death was approaching. I had wanted the note to fall out when the teacher was at home; she would read it and be puzzled and ask me what was wrong, and finally someone would see what was happening to me. I couldn't tell anyone because I couldn't translate the feelings into words. I needed someone to start asking questions.

But in the here and now, it seemed a bad idea. I'd just look crazy. So I extracted the confession and my essay remained just an essay which I handed in, and was folded into the white Pisa of paper.

How had it begun – this strange hue my life had taken on? I'd spent the last four years, aged eleven to fifteen, enjoying school. My grades were good. My wrist was thick with a rainbow of friendship bracelets. But a darkness had slowly seeped into my mind, at first in small inky droplets, and then blotches, and now it was threatening to fill me up with night.

I was at a party and I was Queen of the Bathroom. The door was locked, and teenage couples who wanted to snog, and those who wanted to pee, had to use the downstairs loo. Every so often someone would bang an impatient fist on the door. My friend Lucy played guard for me. I had drunk a ridiculous number of beers; it had been a way of trying to dilute this feeling inside me. And now I could barely stand up.

'God, she's so pathetic,' I heard a voice out in the hallway and even in my blurry state something inside me tightened up and cringed. *The voice belonged to a boy I liked.*

'Don't be horrible, her parents are getting divorced,' Lucy defended me furiously.

'Okay, yeah, that's heavy,' he muttered.

Splat! I vomited once more into the toilet bowl and sat back, shakily wiping my lips with a sliver of toilet paper. The line about my parents getting a divorce wasn't true, of course. I'd had to create a grand reason – to feel this bad without any explanation made no sense to me. Divorce was a story that made sense.

Dad drove over at 11.30 to pick me up. I got into the car, and rolled down the window, lamp posts blurring past into an orange comet. I was starting to sober up; I felt hollow. Dad remained silent as always; he seemed barely to notice that I was unusually reticent.

Back home, I waited in my room until my parents had gone to bed. Then I crept downstairs, filled a glass with water and opened the medicine cabinet. There were plenty of paracetamols in there. Upstairs in my room, I pulled out a bag from the back of the wardrobe, in which I'd been secretly stashing pills. When I added them all together, I had at least sixty. That ought to be enough.

The notes to all my friends took a long time to write. When I laid all the pills out on some sheets of A4 paper, they looked like some Warhol art piece. I swallowed two, then another two.

Another two—

A sound; a door opening. I was sitting in the dark but my door was slightly ajar. I quickly pulled my duvet over the pills, for I could tell from the sound of footsteps that my mother had got up to go to the toilet. The thought of her rising in the morning to find me sprawled out in bed, like Ophelia in her river, was romantic. But it also cut me, the thought of her losing me, and as I shifted, some of the pills slipped away and went down the side of my bed. I put the notes into a tin, reassuring myself that I'd do it another day – death like money in the bank, something to be drawn upon later, a future which made the now just about bearable.

Mum saw more than I realised. The next morning, she surprised me. She came into my bedroom and said: 'You have to start your meditation again. You really need to do it.' I replied yes, without much enthusiasm.

I had first felt the pull to learn Transcendental Meditation when I was seven or eight years old. I'd seen my mother disappear into her bedroom and when she came out, her energy was different, as though a light had been switched on inside her. I'd begged and begged to learn and finally, when I was fourteen, she took me to the TM Centre in Wimbledon. There, at the introductory talk, I learnt that Transcendental Meditation was an effortless technique, not one of concentration or controlling the mind; you were given a particular mantra to repeat and you let it work its magic. I remember enjoying my first experience, the softening and slowing of my breath, only aware of how much tension there had been in my body as it began to melt, my limbs becoming liquid. My mind seemed to sigh into a place of exquisite stillness and peace.

But I'd slipped out of the habit and the months had gone by, and now I had no inclination to pick it up again. For a while I'd enjoyed certain benefits. My thinking had been sharper and clearer; I'd noticed that I was speeding through my homework more quickly and getting better marks. And there had been a lovely period around Christmas when I had suddenly gone into a rarefied state, my mind pristine, everything effortless.

Now I was trying to remedy my despair by studying Nietzsche.

'We can go for a group meditation,' my mum went on.

'Great,' I replied in a pale voice, and went back to reading *Beyond Good and Evil.*

There was a week to go until the group meditation. During the days that passed, I suffered another night where I did not go to sleep but counted pills in the dark, rewrote goodbye letters, and contemplated to be or not to be. I only got as far as taking eight. By day, at school, I would put on a smile, do my homework, hand in essays, and engage in discussions about my A levels.

The meditation was held in Croydon, in a pokey house, in a living room decorated with an array of insipid cactuses. I slumped onto a sofa and surveyed the rest of the group – about six other people, all decades older than me, with whom I had nothing in common. Then the meditation began. As I repeated the mantra, I felt my breath soften, the buzz in my brain grow quiet, and my whole body felt as though it exhaled in peaceful release. Then it came, a sensation of swooping downwards, as though I had dipped into a sea of bliss. It was such a shock to my system, this sensation of exquisite happiness after so many months of darkness, that it stunned me. *This is what life is*, I thought, *this is what life could be.* The meditation finished and as I looked up at my mother's face, she smiled down at me and her face mirrored the radiance I felt. On the train home, the sunset fractured through the leaves of trees and patterned its light over us, and I made a silent promise that I would do my meditation every morning and evening, without fail.

A year after adopting this routine, I felt a little better: my meditations dissolved away the worst stresses of the day. It had cured the dramatic storms of emotion, the highs and the lows, but I was still in neutral and life was often grey.

Another year passed.

It was the summer before the final year of sixth form. Walking through the neon lights of a nightclub, I joined my friends on the dancefloor and felt happiness glitter through me. It was happening to me on a daily basis now, this appreciation of life. The music pumped joy through me; the lights were as exquisite as stained glass. I was almost religious in my gratitude, aware that I had swerved away from some terrible

fate, and only by a matter of degrees. I still had no understanding of what I had suffered in those years past; nor did
it occur to me to connect it to genes or my father. Only now
do I realise that some of my experiences in that dark period
matched up with the early symptoms of schizophrenia. All I
knew was that in the centre of my heart was a place of silence
and peace, which grew stronger with each meditation.

An old friend approached me and we hugged in excitement.
It had been a year since we had last seen each other and I
could tell that she was surprised by the difference in me. She
had, after all, once witnessed me sobbing in a lunch break,
emitting high-pitched, thin screams of despair while a friend
stroked my hair.

'I'm going for Oxford,' I said, 'even though my teachers
have said I probably won't get in.'

She laughed, chinked her glass against mine and said: 'Good
luck!'

My teachers had warned me that the odds were against me,
but I'd had a good feeling ever since the prospectus had come
through. My redemption had been such a wild piece of good
fortune that I felt as though I'd caught luck, like a positive
illness. And when, later that year, the acceptance letter came
through from Oxford – and I ran upstairs to be alone and
open it, and then ran down to tell everyone I'd got in, I
became quite drunk on it, this feeling that life had blessed
me. I remember the lift it gave my mother too; it completely
redefined the story of our family, which had been nothing but
bad luck and tragedy for years. Finally, something good had

happened to us. It was also a sign that we had not entirely failed at becoming middle class: this was a victory for aspiration.

It served to create a sensation of invincibility, and for some years I naively believed that nothing could ever go wrong. During my twenties, I sometimes tried to explain to my friends that I had once suffered from depression. And I could see they couldn't get their head around the idea. They couldn't connect the present version of me – strong and happy – with the one I was describing. So I gave up talking about my past.

I lived carefully, though. I treated my body with love; I slept well; ate well. I tried to live a good life.

I was aware that I owed my mother everything. She had got me a good education, a good start in life, saved my sanity. She was my hero.

Eleven o'clock: speech delivered, awards night done, back home. I entered the living room to find both my parents asleep in armchairs, heads slumped forwards. Mum woke up and I was briefly, selfishly disappointed that she didn't ask about the awards ceremony, as she would have done in the past; I felt I could no longer make her proud of me. Looking anxious, she said she needed to get upstairs to bed. I woke up Dad and asked if he'd help me.

Dad and I supported her from each side. I was shocked at how frail she was. She seemed to have deteriorated so much over the last few days, as though her bones were made of twigs. Halfway up, where the stairs narrowed into a corner, the three of us couldn't fit. My mum started laughing at the farce of it and I joined in nervously. Finally, somehow, we got her to the landing, where she sat on the top step, gasping for breath. She said the easiest way to get to her bedroom was to crawl. I helped her climb into bed and tucked her in.

The next evening, Mum reminded me that we were supposed to be going to the cinema. It was a birthday ritual. But she felt in too much pain. She reached down by the bed for her handbag and drew out a twenty-pound note, saying: 'Go on – let me treat you. You go for both of us.'

I studied the posters in the local Curzon. The choice was *We Need to Talk About Kevin* or Andrea Arnold's *Wuthering Heights*. In the end, I chose the latter. I felt weird buying a ticket for one, as though I was advertising a 'no-friends' status. There were only about two other people in the screening and I sat as far away from them as possible.

Roman Polanski says that 'the cinema should make you forget you are sitting in a theatre'. Normally I loved that loss of self, that immersion. But I was more aware of the theatre than the film. The empty seat beside me: an omen for the future. I was glad of the dark because I spent two hours crying and by the time the lights came up, I was dry-eyed and able to return home and tell Mum how much I'd enjoyed the film.

The next morning, I called 999 for her. Mum's breathing was becoming too shallow; the situation was unsustainable. An ambulance came and I travelled with her to St Helier hospital, holding her hand, her face obscured by an oxygen mask.

Mum had been in hospital two weeks when the nurse told me that we had a choice. My mother could stay in hospital over Christmas, or she could come home to us, and we could take care of her. Mum looked cross when the nurse took me aside to ask me if I was happy with this. Perhaps it made her feel like a child. I said, of course we want Mum to come home for Christmas. The nurse looked me straight in the eye and advised us to celebrate Christmas early.

23

But there was no way we were celebrating Christmas early. It was 15 December. How could Mum possibly leave us within the next ten days? I busied myself decorating the tree, wrapping it in hugs of tinsel, stringing up decorations, buying large boxes of chocolates, Pringles, nuts, crackers – all the things my mum would normally have done. Christmas had always been her favourite time of year. She was delightfully uncynical about the commercialism of it. She loved the lights in the town, the sparkle, the shopping; she loved buying new decorations for the tree, coming home and unwrapping gauzy angels, reindeer and Father Christmases with great excitement.

The doorbell shrilled. The ambulance had arrived. As two men wheeled Mum into the dining room, she beamed, lifted her oxygen mask and said: 'Good job, Sam!' For her homecoming I had converted the room into a bedroom, shoved the dining table against the wall, stacked up the chairs, hoovered every corner, decorated the oil paintings on the walls with loops of tinsel. Leo, the cat, emerged, her ears pricked and swivelling, curiously sniffing the large oxygen machines installed in the hallway. Their fat coils meant the dining-room door would have to be kept open.

I had been given a bag of mum's medicines and a Macmillan nurse went through the list with me, citing dosages and times to dispense. My older brother grinned when he saw me and called me 'Nurse Sam'. I think he was nervous of a nursing role, of its intimacy and intensity, and was relieved that I had taken it on. His job was to find a lawyer, for my mum had not yet drawn up her will. I envied him: he'd been given a whole month of paid compassionate leave from work. My bank balance was empty and I desperately wanted to buy Mum the best Christmas presents I'd ever bought her, so I was still accepting freelance work, which I squeezed in between dispensing squirts of morphine.

This is how it went on for a week: every morning I would rise and tumble-hurry down the stairs and find Mum sleeping or sometimes crying out for help because she'd slipped down the bed and had twisted into an uncomfortable position. She said that the mask made her feel as though she was permanently underwater and her emaciated body seemed increasingly amphibian, her legs morphing into a mermaid's tail. I would cook breakfast, wash up, dispense medicines, squirt morphine into the back of her mouth, which was furred white with candida; cook lunch; give her a steamer, which created vapour to help loosen up her weak, clogged lungs; sit with her whilst she slept; dispense morphine – cook – morphine – cook – morphine. My brothers visited every day, as did Mum's friends, and Dad said very little to her or indeed any of us. Being a full-time carer made me feel close to my mum again; it closed the rift that had opened up at the start of her illness.

By day seven, I could feel my exhaustion translating into illness, a scraping feeling at the back of my throat, a heat behind my eyes. I was terrified that if I got flu, I would pass it on and it would kill her. So I drank hot water, knocked back ginger and lemon and told myself fiercely: *stay well, stay well, stay well.*

Mum's will had not been drawn up yet. A lawyer had been called and then cancelled; Mum had waved a hand airily and said she'd do it some time in the new year. The fat rainbow files containing her accounts sat there on the table, making us feel fretful, guilty, ashamed. It wouldn't have mattered if she was just leaving us a few hundred, but we'd all been amazed to discover that our mother was a brilliant investor and had, over the years, built up a small fortune. She was a woman who had gone to work each day to do a hated job she felt trapped in, yet she had been sitting on a sum that would have kept her in a life of leisure for two decades. I confided to the Macmillan nurses that I was worried my mother was in denial. They had a little chat with her, and she nodded agreement that yes, she understood the situation was very serious.

As soon as they'd gone, however, she told me she wanted to make some mince pies, a favourite ritual. I agreed to help her get up so that I could carry her to the kitchen, set her on a stool and hold her upright whilst she mixed butter and flour and rolled out the dough. Somewhere in the midst of this plan, it all went wrong. I had managed to get her sitting on the edge of the bed without dislodging the little yellow bag that collected her urine, when a panic attack set in. Remember that game you play as a teenager, when your friend stands behind you and as you fall back into their arms, your stomach screams with the horror that they might not catch you? This is how it must have felt to her, without the familiar solid safety of the bed, and the air swirling around her, and a body that no longer did as she commanded, and which might collapse at any moment and in any direction. 'I've got you, I've got you,' I kept crying, but I wasn't sure I had. I yelled out for Dad and he came rushing in. We eased her back so she was lying down. My father looked red-faced, exhilarated; I realised it was probably the first time in a long while that he'd been able to help his wife.

Having calmed down, Mum suggested we might try making mince pies again another day. I wondered: is she truly in denial, or is she maintaining an act for our benefit, because she can't face seeing us facing her end?

Day nine. I was sitting in a chair wedged by Mum's bed, my laptop perched on the dining-room table/medicine unit, my fingers speeding over the keys. I had an editorial report to write which had to be finished by 5 p.m. Mum was sitting in her web of machines, drowsy, the mask clamped to her face.

Tears were welling up in my eyes. I was thinking of how she never had got her degree. Of all the lottery tickets she'd bought, of how keenly she had checked them each and every Saturday. She had wanted the gods to take her seriously. I suppose she must have felt that if they could throw down curses, they might also toss sudden bolts of good luck. Most of the time she was a very practical woman, but she had consulted an astrologer (who had promised she would live until she was eighty) and seen the odd psychic. I realised that becoming a carer had made her feel entirely trampled; she had lost all sense of having free will. To feel your life is governed by fate is a form of depression; a helplessness. No wonder she was bitter.

And yet – she'd had the money. Sitting there, all the time. She'd been so locked into the mentality of poverty, of having to scrimp and save, that she'd been unable to digest the fact that she was actually quite rich.

'I want my steamer,' she suddenly burst out.

'Okay, Mum,' I said, quickly concealing my tears. 'I just have to finish my report. Just give me a few minutes.'

'I want it now!' she cried.

'But I'll get into trouble, the agency won't send me any more work ...' *and I'm nearly bankrupt as it is*, I thought.

'I want it now, give it to me now.'

'Are you having a bad day, Mum?' I said.

She looked taken aback by the question. She crumpled, her anger dissipated. 'I'm always having a bad day,' she said sadly.

I leant over and gave her a hug, murmuring, *'Poor Mum.'* She looked shocked. I gave her the steamer. Then I went into the kitchen because I was welling up again. She remained quiet.

Later in the afternoon, the will was done (a tall, charming man with a briefcase had swished into the house and left an hour later) and there was a sense of relief. The uncertainty had felt painful for all of us, not knowing whether to cajole her to complete it or let go, not wanting money to become tangled up in precious memories. My mother seemed in a more cheerful mood. I was going out for dinner with a friend, Lola, to have a brief break, and as I left I heard Mum sharing her viewpoint with my older brother about how important it was never to talk about people behind their backs. She said these words with such love and compassion; she was her old self again.

When I got home that night, Mum was sleeping peacefully, muttering strange word fragments in her dreams. I tiptoed to the living room, pulled out my copy of George Eliot's *Middlemarch* and read those final words: 'But the effect of her being on those around her was incalculably diffusive: for the growing good of the world is partly dependent on unhistoric acts; and that things are not so ill with you and me as they might have been, is half owing to the number who lived faithfully a hidden life, and rest in unvisited tombs.'

Christmas Eve: everyone was fraying. The three of us – my brothers and I – were crammed into the dining room with Mum. Dad was doing the washing up. John had set up a slideshow of family photos from the eighties on the computer. We were enjoying it, but I suddenly noticed that Mum wasn't. For her, it was probably too close to seeing your life flash before you when you pass. She asked us to leave her in peace. Next door, subdued, we sat on the carpet in a circle and played rummy. It was a family tradition that we played card games at Christmas; it was as though we were kids again. I could hear the distant, haunting notes of 'Silent Night' from carollers on the street, their singing glittering with snow and stars, and the lights from the Christmas tree cast magical colours over the huge stack of presents we'd bought for my mother. It was very strange for her not to be sitting on the sofa with a glass of wine, chuckling away at some Christmas special sitcom on TV.

My brothers were tired and I was sick. Flu was creeping into my body, and my limbs felt as though they'd been boiled white. When I retired to bed, I couldn't sleep. I got up and went downstairs and sat next to my mum. She woke up briefly, but as I held her hand and meditated, she soon drifted off again.

The meditation calmed me down. When I opened my eyes, I gazed at her, her face tinted by the light from the hall reflecting on the tinsel, green and red streaks on her hollowed eyes. Yesterday I'd caught her taking off her oxygen mask for bursts of ten minutes. I'd chided her and she'd insisted she needed to practise surviving without it. Looking back, I'm sure she was speeding things up, sick of her imprisonment – as Woolf says, illness makes the mind a slave to the body – and she was craving freedom's soar. I thought of Noah's family, alone on Christmas Eve for the first time, no doubt equally raw with the absence of father and husband. What a mess. Those lines from Martin Amis's *Money: A Suicide Note*, came to mind, so perfect on the tangle of existence: 'Each life is a game of chess that went to hell on the seventh move, and now the flukey play is cramped and slow, a dream of constraint and cross-purpose, with each move forced, all pieces pinned and skewered and zugzwanged.' Then I thought of what Noah had told Mum, the year before he'd died, which she had repeated to me: 'I'm going to find you, in the next life. We've got it wrong this time round, but I'm going to come and find you and we'll do it properly next time.' Would there be a next time? It was something my mother believed in. I hoped so.

'Happy Christmas!' I greeted her the next morning.

'I'm still here!' she cried. 'I made it to Christmas!'

I gave Mum her presents, unwrapping each one for her, as her hands were too weak and frail. There was a terrible moment where I half tore the paper off a DVD we'd bought months ago, with the horrifically inappropriate title *Before the Devil Knows You're Dead*. As I hastily rewrapped it and tucked it away, laughing nervously, Mum smiled. Then she seized my hand with a sudden burst of pain. On and on, it kept coming, waves and waves, her breathing becoming thinner and thinner, as though water was rising around her, stealing her breath, and she kept saying to me, over and over: 'What am I going to do with myself, what am I going to do with myself?' I rang the Macmillan nurses, begging for help – and as I was speaking to them, I saw her head tip forward and I suddenly realised – *oh my God, it's happening*.

An hour later, she lay there, looking so serene, a smile on her lips, as though in her passing a great care had been lifted from her.

All around her lay her presents, a desperate mass of them, twice as many as we'd usually buy her, gifts she would never see, never read, never enjoy.

Our forgotten Christmas turkey sat in the oven, cooking to black cinders, setting off the fire alarm with tendrils of smoke. My brothers were weeping. I suffered a panic attack and shook violently; Stefan thrust a bottle of vodka into my hand and ordered me to swig.

As flu descended, I attempted to nap and woke up gasping for air, as though I was echoing the trauma of my mother's last minutes.

'Are you okay?' we kept asking Dad, puzzled by his blankness.

'I'm fine.' He acted as though we'd had asked whether he might be upset by a bad weather forecast.

I had held her hand when she died. It felt as though we'd walked into the valley of death together. I saw it as a place of withered black trees, a barren landscape, shadowed by mountains. In the days that passed I felt as though she had gone to a heavenly realm, but I was still wandering in its shadows, trying to find a horizon, a slit of light.

24

No matter how much time you spend with a loved one before they die, it is never enough. Regret conflates the memory of times spent apart and salts them raw. After the loss of her father – with whom she did not have the best relationship – Virginia Woolf felt wretched, lamenting: 'I never did enough for him.' I had spent the last year living with my mum and in the last ten days, in the intensity of caring, I had lost all sense of self, felt as mechanical as the oxygen machines that hissed in the hall, that I functioned merely to keep her alive. Yet I still regretted those four weeks that I wasted on Antonio; regretted those times when I had needed a psychological distance.

One of her friends called me. Mum had asked her to phone after she'd gone, to make sure we were holding up. She confided that my mum hadn't liked Antonio at all; she'd thought he looked 'shifty' and had been very worried about my poor choice. She hadn't said anything for fear of offending me. I smiled when she told me that.

There is a busy period after death when you are snagged in the bureaucracy of the Grim Reaper, in the banality of ticking boxes on a list: *get death certificate, close bank account, take clothes to charity shop, organise vicar, see lawyer re: will, send invites, write eulogy.* I noticed that the relationship between me and my brothers changed dramatically. Age had never been a defining factor when my mother was alive. Now the hierarchy sharpened up, with my older brother taking charge and becoming the dominant male, and me playing a substitute mother, and my younger brother more relaxed and playful. My father continued to be a mystery, a man who might or might not have been grieving, who slept a good deal, and ghosted his way through the house. We had all feared he might have a breakdown and were slightly baffled by the fact that none of us had even seen him shed a tear.

Then, after the funeral, as the last guest left, there was a sense of anti-catharsis, that its cleansing had been too slight, and we were left with a house of empty cups and dirty plates and chairs to stack away, and my mother was now dust, buried under a thin new rose bush in a crematorium, where worms and beetles would be wriggling through the parts of her that had once been heart and lips and lungs and love.

After the funeral, the paperwork ends, the sympathy cards cease, and habitual greetings of 'How are you coping?' gradually slip back to the monotony of a daily 'How are you?' There is a sense that the world is moving on, that life is stitching together the gap left behind, that you should take a step forwards towards a new life. But you feel out of sync, wanting to press the pause button a while longer.

What to do; how to live? I had a book out soon; I received an email from my publishers: *would you like to film a video, which we can put up on YouTube, of you talking about* The Quiddity of Will Self? I declined. Instead, I took a trip back to Switzerland. I walked amongst mountains that were austere with snow and gazed at distant peaks, shrouded with clouds, and wished I had died with my mother.

One evening, I went into her old hotmail account and read through her emails. They were lovely. She spoke of how quiet the house was in the periods when I was away with Antonio and how she missed me. One tickled me: *Sam is constantly buying all this organic food and it costs so much and doesn't really taste any different – why does she bother?* I thought of that epic odyssey I'd made across London to get her puritanically pesticide-free cauliflower. I burst into laughter and felt as if she was laughing with me.

I was travelling back to my dad's house from London one evening when I saw a homeless woman sitting on the edge of a brick wall outside Waterloo Station. She was calling out for change, her voice thin with hysteria, violently waving a polystyrene cup with a jagged rim, and commuters were flooding past her, collecting copies of the *Evening Standard*, which had details of a homeless appeal: much easier to give to a cause without getting emotionally involved in the messy realities of it. I sat down next to her and gave her some money. I put my arm around her and held her tight. This wasn't something I'd ever done with a homeless person before; I too had often been guilty of drifting past in indifference. Afterwards, I realised that I had seen in her face an echo of my mother, sitting on her bed, in pain and wanting to be relieved from it. No longer able to care for her, I wanted to care for someone, anyone, to fill the void. I felt something similar when I saw mothers and daughters out shopping together, discussing the purchases of clothes or books or food. I would feel a slash of raw envy followed by sadness.

I headed north. Still lacking my own place, I stayed with a friend called Jenny.

Jenny was one of the kindest people I'd ever met. In her spare time, she voluntarily cared for elderly people who needed help and lacked family support. She was a Catholic and there was a quote on her wall from Mother Teresa that I found very moving: 'You can do what I cannot do. I can do what you cannot do. Together we can do great things.'

An email came through from my agent: 'buy the *Sunday Times*'. I went to a newsagent and flicked through it, found a review of *The Quiddity of Will Self*. Jenny was peering over my shoulder and exclaiming how exciting it was. *Was it?* I thought dully. And then, reading it, savouring the reviewer's enthusiasm, I thought for the first time that I might leave the valley of death.

The opening story in Will Self's collection *The Quantity Theory of Insanity* captures the loss of a parent beautifully. The narrator loses his mother to cancer, which 'tore through her body as if it were late for an important meeting with a lot of other successful diseases'; he finds that suddenly 'gusts of air seemed personalised' and the ghost of his mother invades his dreams.

Atheism becomes a hard position to sustain once you suffer a bereavement. There were times when I was convinced I had not been fully abandoned. Once, I was walking through a supermarket when I perceived my mother was there by my side, smiling with me; and then there were dreams of her that felt too vivid to be just dreams. I even prayed to her once, in an emergency, and in that moment I made her a deity, looking over me in protection. At other times, I accepted that this might well be illusion; my belief in her watching over me flitted between hope and cynicism, like one of those Catholic holographic cards that show Jesus on one slant, and the Virgin Mary the next. A friend of mine passed on some advice a Carmelite nun had given her: 'After death, you still have a relationship with your mother, it's just changed to a different form.' And I realised that this could be true whether or not it was mystical; whether you believed in a soul or you were a solid atheist – those we lose live on in our memory and our connection with them does not end.

Autumn 2012. I was taking tentative steps towards a new caring role. It was becoming a routine: whilst staying with Jenny I rang Dad every night before I went to bed. I found the calls a struggle. My eyes would often stray to the clock on my phone, and I'd think: *okay, I've managed five minutes – is that enough?* I'd ask him questions like:

'Did you eat lunch? What did you have?'

'Did you sleep well?'

'Did you go out today?'

'Did you read anything interesting in the papers?'

And, if I was getting desperate:

'What's the weather been like down there?'

The last question was often more satisfying than the others; he would describe stages of sun and cloud pattern in more detail than his minimalist descriptions of food and sleep.

I remember phoning him that October and saying to him in a voice tight with excitement: 'I'm going to meet Will Self tomorrow.'

'Oh, right.' Pause. 'Who's he?'

'He's the one I wrote the book about. He writes books too.' Pause – my dad didn't read novels, only the Bible. With his stupefying meds, he didn't have sufficient concentration for them. He'd never even read one of my own books. 'And he's on TV, on *Newsnight* sometimes, and *Have I Got News for You* and other political shows ...' Pause – my father no longer watched TV. 'Well, I wrote that book about him and I'm going to meet him.'

My father found Self as hard to grasp as a character in a book he'd never read, but he picked up on my excitement. 'That's good.'

'Okay, I'd better go to bed now. Bye Dad.' My eyes on the clock: *six minutes.* That was a record.

I lay back on my bed, fretting. Was it a good idea to meet Will Self? The only reason we were having lunch was because I'd had a go at him. I'd suffered the agony of 'Oh God, why did I press send' the moment that I'd seen the email compress, like a speeded-up plane taking flight and schooming into the digital distance. Self had been rude about me in an interview and I had complained, referring to the letter he'd first sent me upon reading extracts of *Quiddity*, in which he had praised the book. His reply was quick and as kind as a hug. He assured me that he'd been misquoted. If anything, he seemed pleased and amused that I'd berated him, and advised me it took time to get used to public and *ad hominem* criticism – 'I've been at it for a while now, both pitching and catching'. As a peace offering, he'd suggested lunch.

I felt afraid of gaps. The gap between the Self I'd been emailed and the Self whose novels I'd loved and the Self I saw on *Newsnight* savaging politicians. Which self of Self was I about to meet? And then there was the gap between my persona and my prose. All year I had come to feel like a book with a misleading cover, finding that people who had read *Quiddity* were taken aback by my appearance. They expected some kind of flame-haired, chain-smoking drug-addicted-nymphomaniac. Invariably, they were disappointed. I couldn't take drugs; there was too much risk that I would end up like my dad; my imagination was already like someone on acid. My schizophrenic imagination: an inheritance from my father.

The following evening, I phoned my dad again. We discussed sleep, food, weather, and then, to my surprise, he said: 'Did you like meeting Will Self?'

Wow, I thought, feeling touched. Usually there was no continuity in our calls from one day to the next; they were self-contained. The words hovered in my throat. I wanted to tell him everything: how I had sat on the train into Manchester, frayed with nerves and groggy from insomnia, thinking of lines I'd penned in *The Watermark*, my novel-in-progress, where I had written about a hero who goes to meet his literary idol:

Augustus Fate wanted to talk and me to listen; he wanted to be the guru and I his disciple. I felt a sense of disappointment grey over me. We seek out our idols not for themselves, but in the hope that they, with their rarefied consciousness, will elevate us to their level, burrow into our souls and see something special in us. They, however, need confirmation that they are worthy of worship. That was why meeting an idol invariably involves an inevitable crash, as the concrete splats into grey shit around their pedestal.

'It didn't go that well at first,' I replied. 'It was a bit awkward.'

We had drifted into a random restaurant which Self observed was suffering from a gastronomic identity crisis. He gave the menu a rather withering look, as though it was a bad novel he'd picked up in a bookshop that would cement the death of fiction, and concluded: 'I don't do food.' My soup and fries arrived. My soup chinked uneasily as he watched me sip and slurp. The conversation sparked a few times, died a few times, and then there were the charred remains of silence.

'Oh, right,' my dad said.

'And then it got better.'

All of a sudden, I had blurted out to Self that my mother had recently died.

It wasn't something I had confessed to anyone that year unless they were a close friend. As I said the words, I regretted them. But his demeanour changed into one of shocked compassion; he understood immediately where I was at. He had lost his mother back in 1988 and said he'd felt like an orphan ever since. And then we began to talk more easily, about my father's illness and how I loved his books because he was better at writing about madness and schizophrenia than any other living novelist I'd come across …

A day later, I sent him an email saying: 'I'm sorry if I was a boring cunt during our lunch' – I only ever swore with people I felt affection for. He replied: 'No, no, boring cunt you weren't – or at least, if you were, I'm guilty of being a didactic prick. Loss of parents is a Big One.' I felt then that we had bonded in some sort of way.

I wanted to tell my dad all these details, but it would have felt weird, supplying a monologue down the phone, wondering if he was even digesting my words.

'So, in general, it went okay,' I summed up, checking the clock: *six minutes*. Then I said goodnight and he said goodnight and we hung up.

The reviews for *Quiddity* had called the book mad but they had also praised it. There was catharsis in this for me, even though I had not been conscious of it during all those years of writing. Middle-class publications and Radio 4 were endorsing a novel infused with my father's insanity; it was as though I was attempting to correct my childhood trauma, to alchemise stigma into art.

I told my Will Self lunch anecdote to Thom the second time we ever met, when we arranged to go for a drink near Manchester Piccadilly. He arrived looking like a World War I poet, and revealed that he was growing a moustache for charity. I had warned him that he would recognise me by the turbulence of my eyebrows and he commended me on their expressiveness. When Thom told me how much he liked the crazy moments in *Quiddity* – especially the orgiastic ceremony in Self's honour – I smiled warmly. We sat close together in a bar by Oxford Road Station, knees touching, and his hand brushed mine. It was getting late; we were reaching that Cinderella moment when the last train would depart. Thom offered to let me stay at his and I grinned a thank you.

The next morning, I woke up in Thom's bed and told him: 'It's my birthday.' On our way back into Manchester, he bought me a birthday coffee. I'd been dreading the day, the first without my mother, but now I felt as though I might get through it after all.

I don't do flings, Thom told me on our next date. If we were going to do this, it had to be a serious relationship. Immediately, I felt the kick of my commitment-phobia; heard the echo of a previous boyfriend who had complained to me that I didn't let people in very easily. Antonio had been my grieving exception. Usually I erected barriers. I was addicted to writing and, though men who were highly creative often seemed to attract muses, it was rare that men ever wanted to be the muse. Besides, I had Z.

But I was beginning to realise that Z wasn't enough anymore. I was tired of being his temptress. It was a role I had once loved to play, but now I found myself wanting an intimacy that bled into every area of my life.

There came a moment in our relationship where Thom and I realised how lucky we were. We'd been dating a few months. We were sitting in a cafe in Manchester, side by side, reading books and sipping drinks. Every so often our eyes would drift from the page and connect and spontaneous smiles would break out on our faces. 'I'm so happy,' Thom burst out, voicing my heart. We could enjoy spending hours together doing simple things. Both of us had experienced relationships in which communication existed through friction and argument; by contrast, we never rowed; we were kind and tender with each other. When times were hard, when Thom was made redundant, or I went through a long era of being out of contract and publisher-less, we looked after each other.

Three years on, Thom and I were still together.

And we might have gone on being happy for many more years, if it hadn't been for my father's illness.

PART III

Carers make an invaluable contribution to society by selflessly caring for friends and family and we recognise this must not come at the expense of their own health, wellbeing or employment.

Department of Health
and Social Care spokesperson, 8 March 2019

It's worse always on the people who care than the person who's ill.

Zelda Fitzgerald, writing to her editor Maxwell Perkins,
on news that his son is ill, *c.*19 May 1932

25

'Dear Mr Rose,' I began. My pen hovered. I was writing my goodbye on the back of a postcard of a Tyrannosaurus rex.

What to say?

I watched Thom scribbling away at his postcard. We were sitting in a cafe at London Victoria Station, acting out our usual goodbye ritual, having spent two days together. My pen felt spineless. I found myself writing what I ought to say rather than what I felt.

We swapped postcards with a sense of sadness. In the past, we'd idealised our adventures to reflect their euphoria; to exaggerate felt more honest. Now we were using hyperbole to hide the gap between past and present, creating myth instead of story.

At Victoria Coach Station, we hugged and kissed and waved goodbyes. I headed back to the train station. There's a line of ancient trees alongside Buckingham Palace Road that I love: tall and greenly avuncular. Normally I'd walk down that row with a giddy smile stretched across my face, but today, even minutes after parting, I felt lonely. Thom's stay hadn't been the honeymoon I'd anticipated. I'd been tired, not quite able to give, hollowed of energy.

It hadn't helped that we'd had little time for fun. No parks, no ice cream, no lazing and reading, no flirting and insulting each other. On top of my caring for Dad, I was working long hours on our indie press, and Thom and I had had to use our stay in London for meetings. We'd met with Alex, our co-director. We'd planned our budget (we had no money). We'd looked over our Arts Council funding application. We'd met with an agent. Our time had been slight and there had been a lack of intimacy, a sense of the connection thinning between us.

A friend of mine was suffering a dilemma: should she put her mother, who had Alzheimer's, into a care home? She spoke anxiously, as though she were making a decision about whether or not to imprison her mother – even if that prison was going to be a pastel-coloured one, with tea and biscuits served every day. She said it made her feel old, having to put her mother away, and there was a strange sense of regression, of having to restrict her space, like a parent who has to confine a child to a cot. At the same time, it was necessary: Alzheimer's is a condition that requires specialist care. My friend was learning all the ins and outs of funding, that any assets or funds her mother had over £23,250 would be used to fund her care.

And then there was the worry of finding a good enough place: the fear of putting her somewhere like Mossley Manor, a care home in Liverpool which was eventually closed down and branded by a judge a 'lack-of-care-home': a tip that smelt of urine, where some patients were not properly washed in four weeks. There is a regulatory body called the CQC (Care

Quality Commission) that checks out care homes, rates them, keeps them in line. Whilst only three per cent of care homes are rated outstanding, seventeen per cent have been given a rating that they could do better. One might imagine that this evolves from carelessness, capitalists setting up homes to make a profit and spending as little as possible, but to be fair, it isn't easy for those running homes even to get enough staff in to cover all their patients; there are currently 100,000 unfilled jobs in social care. Retaining staff is also a problem, for 360,000 social care employees leave their job every year, tiring of low pay and zero hour contracts.

In the end, my friend found her relationship with her mother improved significantly after she went into a home. Freed from caring, she could be her mother's daughter once again. I felt a little jealous of her. She had decided that she would visit her mother once a week; her caring was neat and compartmental-ised, whereas mine was threatening to devour me.

Was it a warning? I was alert to the signs now, for I knew they could be subtle. There was a look in my dad's eyes, a flitting of his pupils, that made me uneasy. He was sitting in his armchair, drumming his fingers very lightly, a whisper that I knew could become a shout, could eventually evolve into fists pounding away at a hospital bed.

He'd been weird at lunch, too. My dad's conversation was typically unpredictable and peppered with non sequiturs, but they were usually charming ones. He'd suddenly blurted out: 'Do you know about Hiroshima?' I said I did, but he proceeded to tell me about it anyway. 'It's so terrible,' he concluded, and a look of profound sadness came over his face at the knowledge that such things could happen in the world. It reminded me of how I had felt when I'd found out about the Holocaust as a teenager; that moment we all go through when we learn of the great evil that mankind can do; the moment where shades of the prison house begin to fall. If catatonia was a cliff face, then he was standing on the edge, swaying, and the wind was picking up and starting to whistle. My dad had been home for six weeks and we did not want him to fall again. So my younger brother and I called a psychiatrist and asked him to come for an emergency visit.

Dad was in his bedroom when the doctor arrived. He was sitting up in bed in his pyjamas, the curtains drawn, the spring light sickly and pale.

'How are you feeling?' the doctor asked.

My father proceeded to put on the most spectacular act. He became a man who was coherent and intelligent, who had been feeling a little under the weather today, whose children had misunderstood him, and who was in no need of any further help – all of this was conveyed with charm and smiles. My brother and I tried to protest, but we felt a little mean. Dad continued to weave his web around the psychiatrist and he left soon after, assuring us there was nothing to worry about. As I closed the door on him, I realised that my dad had developed survival strategies over the years. He might not be able to make everyday chit-chat or develop friendships, but he knew how to skilfully manipulate a professional. It was almost funny, if we hadn't been so worried about him.

That evening, my dad took an hour to eat a boiled egg. He seemed to be in some twilight place between waking and dreaming. I ate my dinner and then opened my laptop across the table from him. Every ten minutes or so I gently interrupted his vagueness, and suggested he eat a little bit more, a little bit more. His spoon carved slices from the cold, hardening yolk in slow motion. I was reminded of Leonard Woolf, the way he had to coax Virginia to eat during her depressive phases. Finally, Dad abandoned his meal and said he needed the toilet.

I proceeded to hammer away at emails. Yawns were circling up my throat, wanting to fly out like birds. I didn't normally work this late at night, but there was so much to do on Dodo Ink, with books needing editing and contracts needing finalising, and working with Alex on the fine details of covers.

A clash of senses. My eyes looked out at a clear evening sky through the window; my ears told me that it was raining. I carried on working, shaking myself, as the noise became more vehement – was this unseen storm tropical? I hurried up the stairs, noting that the drumming sounded like a watery version of Dad's fists.

He was standing in front of the sink, frozen. He'd been washing his hands when the catatonia descended. Water was flowing across the blue lino, soaking his shoes, seeping into the hall carpet.

As I reached across him to turn off the taps, I became alarmed by what-ifs – what if I'd decided I needed a brief break this evening? If I'd gone for a walk? Seen a friend? Then the whole house would have been flooded. My poor father would have been left standing there, helpless, water slowly rising from his ankles to his shins.

And yet: he could walk, just about – if I assisted him. His eyes were closed but if I guided him, shaky step by shaky step, he was able to cross the hallway. In the doorway to his bedroom he stood and swayed. I coaxed him forward just one more step; helped him on to the bed, where he lay on his back. When I called my brother, we debated and fretted: should we call the ambulance now and face being stuck in A&E until 3 or 4 a.m., or let Dad sleep and see if he might wake up feeling better? He had made it to his bedroom, after all. And I could already hear him snoring gently.

We decided to leave him for the night. I pulled a blanket over him. Every hour or so I woke up and anxiously checked him. His snores rumbled out, deep and sonorous; when I was a kid, I thought his snores sounded like the sounds mountains might make if they were dreaming. Morning came and I sat on the edge of his bed, trying to wake him. No response. He was breathing and alert, but it seemed as though catatonia had formed a sarcophagus around him.

Then I realised that the bed beneath me was wet. Whilst waiting for the ambulance, I peeled back the covers, took off his trousers and slowly cleaned him up.

* * *

Dad's got ill again

I deleted the text to Thom and tried again:

I'm sorry but Dad has gone into a bad state and–

Perhaps I should just avoid the subject altogether:

The Dodo has been using absinthe for mouthwash again & his nest smells like an opium den.

No: I had to be honest.

On the way to A&E, I sat next to Dad, laid out on a stretcher in the back of the ambulance. I had managed to send the text before we left home. I imagined Thom reading it, the knowledge sinking in that I couldn't come up north next week as planned, and probably not the week after, nor the month after. I knew that he had used up nearly all his leave from work for his last visit. Now I feared this would be the final blow to our relationship.

And so the cycle began all over again: a message left on my mobile phone by a woman with a brusque Scottish accent, telling me that Dad had been sectioned for twenty-eight days under the Mental Health Act; his transfer to Summerfields once more; and those daily visits. As I travelled there, I noticed trees that had been sharp in winter were now soft with blossom, and austere flowerbeds ebullient with flowers. I felt glum, wondering whether the catatonic attacks might get worse as he suffered them, until perhaps a day might come when he didn't recover at all. A friend of mine had warned me that when you go into a psychiatric ward, the chances that you will return become much higher. Would life always be like this from now on? I thought wearily.

I went out for a drink with a group of friends. Normally I didn't drink much and got by on alcoholic appropriation. But this evening I felt I needed a drink, a G&T for starters, and more on top. Thom had been sympathetic about my situation, of course. He was a kind and caring man. But he'd also asked if my brothers could take over, do more of the visits, and I hadn't been sure how to reply.

It felt difficult to integrate with my friends, at first. Aside from my melancholy over Thom, I had found that being a carer made socialising weird sometimes; you become so rusty at good conversation. I was habituated to delivering short, simple questions in an optimistic tone of voice, in order to try to coax my dad back to good health. Everyone around me seemed so eloquent, their speech so complex! As the evening went by, however, I began to shed my carer persona and remember who I was.

As the landlord rang the bell for closing time, I looked around at people swaying and shouting, at the fight breaking out at the table in the corner, where several men were slurring their insults. It all looked like a youthful simulacrum of the psychiatric ward. Two of my friends had been eagerly discussing taking LSD during the course of the evening, a drug which can produce the same kind of mindset as schizophrenia. The brain imaging of a schizophrenic, for example, shows that the networks involved in introspection and external attention bleed into each other – which are just how psychedelics influence the brain. How ironic, I thought, that people will pay good money to flirt with the same brain chemistry that afflicts my father.

They talked about the aftermath of drug-taking too, the lows that followed the zing of cocaine – and it all sounded like a compressed cycle of manic depression. My friend explained to me that he needed to indulge once a fortnight, going out with friends and taking drugs in a group, in order to blow off steam. Perhaps we all crave moments of insanity, though we only want to experience it in a controlled way, a kind of madness with a safety valve, a Jekyll and Hyde experience where we can flip back and forth at will, and because any craziness that does come out can then be blamed on the drug and drinks rather than ourselves. So, it's a kind of purging of uncivilised, crazy urges; a way of being able to stay sane and conform to civilised values the rest of the time. It seemed sad and strange, though, that those I'd seen on the ward wanted so much to be normal, to be able to drink in a pub like this, and those in the pub wanted a taste of the mental collapse of those in the ward.

On the way home, I texted Thom, waited for a reply – but no doubt he had already gone to bed. I thought fondly of our usual bedtime routine when we stayed in his flat. I would tell him that I was about to put my ear-plugs in; he would say, 'Goodnight, you appalling cunt', I would pull them out and ask what he'd said, he'd feign ignorance; I'd insult him back and then we'd say *I love you*s and *goodnight*s.

Blurry with drink, I wandered into the back garden. The darkness was pastel-coloured, a consequence of light pollution from our town; no stars, just pale clouds and a fleeting moon. I brushed my fingers over the leaves of my crab apple, the tree I'd planted for my mother. When I'd first planted it, it had been the same height as me. Now I could stand under it, its branches an umbrella that kissed the top of my head.

I thought about Thom's plea: *can't your brothers do more of the caring?* John lived too far away to visit Dad often. Stefan didn't get back from his job in the City until eight, nine o'clock at night, often too late to make Summerfields's visiting hours – though he was currently leaving work early to see Dad, two, sometimes three times a week. Once or twice, he 'lent' me money for my travel fares for visiting the ward, a loan he never called in.

I couldn't see either of them resigning from their jobs. I thought of my mother and how bitter she had been, right up to the moment of death. I didn't want my history to rhyme with hers, to die having lived a life of regret and sacrifice. And then I recalled my birthday dinner in 2010.

We'd gone to our favourite Italian restaurant. Mum had just had her cancer diagnosis but, in a daze, we ordered pastas and drinks and chatted about the film we might see later as though it were just another birthday. A silence fell between us, an awareness of death and time and the future to come. I peered at my reflection in my fork, my features made funhouse grotesque.

'I'm worried about Dad,' she said, 'and how he's going to cope after … after I'm not around.'

I had been wondering if she still loved Dad, given her relationship with Noah, but I could see in her eyes that she did, very much, and this was why she had sacrificed her life for him, never deserted him. Did I love my dad? Only in a theoretical, general 'he's my dad' sense; I could barely have a conversation with him. So my reply was more inspired by my love for my mother, my desire to keep her happy.

I watched my reflection open its wobbly mouth and say: 'Don't worry, I'll look after Dad.'

She looked relieved then, and we went back to discussing movies. Despite the brevity of the discussion, I never forgot its importance. I had made a promise to her, and it was one that I was determined to keep.

26

'I keep seeing you, day after day,' the guy in the newsagent said. 'Have you just moved to the area?'

He was an Indian man, middle-aged, with a sweep of dark hair, and a lovely smile. I smiled back as I passed over the coins for my bottle of Volvic: 'I'm visiting my dad.' I explained that he was in Summerfields and that was why I passed through most days; I held up a bag that was fat with my dad's clothes.

He looked amazed. 'It's very unusual for people in the West to care for their parents. Normally they just stick them in homes.' He went on to tell me that in India, children were diligent in caring for their parents hands-on.

I pondered his words as I walked down to Summerfields.

I've heard various stories since about caring traditions in India; once, on a trip to Kerala, I was told that the second eldest son is responsible for looking after the elderly, and in return he inherits the family home. And whilst I admired the tradition the newsagent had described, it wasn't entirely true of all countries in the East. In China, for instance, they had brought in a law in 2013 called the Elderly Rights Law. With a huge elderly population set to double by 2030, one often afflicted by loneliness, it had been made mandatory for their children to visit them 'often' or face jail. The Chinese had been joking about it on Twitter and indeed, it was a surreal image: imagining someone in a cell with some murderer, saying they'd been banged up because they didn't have time to see their Alzheimer's-affected parent. I'd been reading that schizophrenics had a much better chance of recovery in developing countries; I wondered if this tied in to what my newsagent friend had said about a stronger sense of family ties and support.

Increasingly, I was feeling confused by the very term *schizophrenia* as a blanket label. Before my dad had fallen sick, he was the only schizophrenic I'd ever met; but the more I encountered, the more I noticed how different they all were, and how few of them seemed to fit the textbook definitions. As I entered the ward, there was a new patient present: a small Greek woman with short grey hair. She walked around weeping cacophonously, wringing her hands and addressing people in Greek, as though begging for a *deus ex machina* to descend and end her suffering.

I went over to my dad. My hope was crushed when I saw that his recovery this time was no quicker than before. He had been here three days: he still couldn't eat, or talk, or move; his eyes were closed, his mouth an O of bewilderment. As I fed him his drink, the weeping woman came over. There was almost a grandeur to her pathos, as though she were on stage in a Greek tragedy, or playing an elderly Ophelia. I looked at the tears glistening on her cheeks and thought of the tears I was holding back. Perhaps the only difference between us was that I was repressing and she was expressing; I was obeying social convention and she couldn't do that anymore.

What trauma had cracked her apart? It was as if a dreadful accident had happened, and she was begging people for help, and nobody would listen.

I turned back to Dad. I patted his arm and felt a flicker of guilt, because for all the praise the newsagent had given me, I was starting to feel that I couldn't cope anymore. It was the grind and monotony of a whole year of visiting wards, the exhausting repetition of it: fretting over his third catatonic collapse whilst already anticipating the fourth, the fifth. The future seemed without hope.

The words of the newsagent were echoed in newspaper headlines. David Mowat, a Tory health minister, declared that we ought to look after our parents with the same dedication we do our kids. So we've reached a complete reversal from the early Victorian era, when Philippe Pinel decreed that the sick and elderly must be cared for by the state, back to the state saying that only families can do the best job. Of course, it all relates to the rising demands for and costs of social care, and the care homes that are going bankrupt year in year out, and the government's reluctance to increase spending or raise taxes.

The Victorians' wild optimism about the incarceration of the mentally ill, their belief that they would be entirely cured by asylums, gradually diminished in the face of reality. They downgraded their expectations and shifted their focus to cleanliness and comfort. In 1855, at the Geel lunatic colony in Belgium, an asylum superintendent called John Galt argued that lunatics should be spared the daily routine of the asylum, which proceeded 'with the inexorable, monotonous motion of a machine'. He felt that whilst patients being cut off from society was unhealthy, it was equally the case that a return to their family home might set them back. The solution, he argued, was for lunatics to be allowed to live in the community under some degree of supervision.

His proposals were met with outrage. His colleagues were hostile and derided the idea. But Galt was ahead of his time. He foresaw the introduction of 'care in the community', which began to sweep Europe and the US over a century later in the 1980s.

Care in the community represented a seismic change in the history of mental health care. Its aim was to remove the stigma of mental illness and give patients more dignity, by treating them at home rather than institutionalising them. On a more cynical note, it was also a way of saving governments considerable sums of money. In the mid-fifties, there were over 150,000 patients in England and Wales in psychiatric wards; by 1975, this figure had dropped to 80,000. If my father's breakdown had occurred during the 1950s, he would probably have spent much of his life in a place like Summerfields, and my childhood memory of visiting him would have been a regular habit. Instead, my mother (then me) became his carer, our fates influenced by government policy as much as personal choice.

By the second half of the twentieth century, psychiatry had come to be regarded with suspicion and was often seen as an instrument of social control. *One Flew Over the Cuckoo's Nest*, set in an oppressive Oregon psychiatric ward, was a tale that captured the mood of the era. In the early decades of that century, numerous people were swept into institutions for dubious reasons – single women who had fallen pregnant, or wives of whom their husbands had grown tired – from T. S. Eliot locking up his spouse Vivienne, to Mussolini, who got rid of his mistress Ida Dalser by having her incarcerated in the San Clemente asylum. As society loosened its corset in the sixties, psychiatry was used to stall social change – black men fighting for their rights were given lobotomies; women who resisted the restrictions of domesticity and were developing feminist leanings were prescribed Valium; homosexuals were given electroshock therapy in the hope it might 'cure' them. In the USSR, the psychiatric hospital replaced the Gulag. Dissidents who rebelled against the regime were diagnosed as suffering from 'sluggish schizophrenia'. So by the time Enoch Powell – dubbed the father of care in the community – announced 'the elimination of by far the greater part of the country's mental hospitals' in a speech in 1961, his view that asylums were effectively prisons was one that was shared by many.

As the backlash against psychiatry and asylums was being felt, doctors at the vanguard of the anti-psychiatry movements became counter-culture celebrities. Thomas Szasz wrote the classic *The Myth of Mental Illness*, declaring: 'In the animal kingdom, the rule is, eat or be eaten; in the human kingdom, define or be defined.' Most diagnoses, he declared, were not medical but moral judgements on those who had failed to conform to society's norms. He was dubious about the way schizophrenia was classified, pointing out: 'If you talk to God, you are praying; if God talks to you, you have schizophrenia.' For Szasz, mental illness was not a disease but a reflection of 'problems with living'. But he was not entirely against psychiatry – he simply felt that it was too coercive and should be replaced with trust and consent, adhering to the Hippocratic injunction to 'do no harm'.

Care in the community was made possible by the introduction of new anti-psychotic drugs such as Chlorpromazine. These provoked the same kind of wild optimism in politicians that the building of new asylums had in the Victorian era. Sir Keith Joseph, the Secretary of State for Social Services in Margaret Thatcher's government, introduced a White Paper with the confident claim that: 'People go into hospital with mental disorders and they are cured.' As the first long-term patients were released into the community, de-institutionalisation got off to a shaky start, for they were frequently relocated to seedy bedsits and B&Bs which were located in the poorest parts of towns and cities, creating psychiatric ghettos; or private residential homes, which often lacked proper regulation. In the UK, Sir Roy Griffiths produced a Green Paper on the 'no-man's land' of community care, describing it as 'everybody's distant cousin but nobody's baby'. And in the States, where de-institutionalisation was also being lauded, the sociologist

Andrew Scull notes that in Nebraska, 'in a splendidly original variation on the ancient practice of treating the mad like cattle, it placed the licensing and inspection of homes for the mentally ill in the hands of its state department of agriculture. When scandals erupted, it removed the licenses – but not the patients – from 320 of these homes, and abandoned the inmates to their fate.' For many 'inmates' across the US and Europe without family support, their fate was homelessness or jail. In US jails, a 2006 report showed that 24 per cent of patients met the criteria for a psychiatric disorder.

In the UK during the 1980s, the weaknesses of community care filtered into public consciousness. Murders by schizophrenics – vulnerable patients who had clearly been left without adequate support – hit the headlines. As a result of this outcry, the Community Care Act was introduced in 1990. It established the rule that any patient being discharged from a psychiatric hospital should have a care plan and continuing support and aftercare at home.

I can see similar patterns occurring with the social care crisis today: whilst I'm not suggesting that thousands of homes will be shut down and the elderly dispersed, there is a growing emphasis on alternative care projects that take place in the community. There is the CareRooms scheme, for example, which has been dubbed the 'Airbnb for social care', set up in response to bed-blocking rates in the NHS reaching record levels: old people stuck in beds and recuperating, with nobody to look after them at home, and no package from their council. The scheme basically means that patients would be moved into the spare rooms in people's houses with hosts receiving around £50 a night. Unsurprisingly, it has attracted controversy, for fear that the vulnerable could easily be abused.

On the flipside of this, substitute nurses or carers can also be open to abuse. The Homeshare network, for example, was set up in 2015. It sounds wonderful in theory: someone with a housing need – a young person for example – can rent a room for a low sum from someone who needs help to live independently; they must spend at least ten hours per week supporting them. But I read about one case where a young woman studying for an MA was treated like a housekeeper by the elderly woman she lived with. Soon she was doing far more than ten hours a week, especially when her host became sick. Effectively, she ended up *paying* to be a carer.

Indeed, the relationship between carer and patient can develop into a power struggle, a game of wits – as was the case with Zelda and Scott Fitzgerald, another literary couple who held a growing fascination for me as I struggled on in my role as Dad's carer.

27

Now that my dad was back in Summerfields, I was back to pondering *why*: what were the roots of his catatonia? The questions I hadn't resolved before, which had softened over the last few months and become lost in the business of everyday life, were now sharp in my mind again. If we could find out why he kept going back to the ward, then perhaps we could break the cycle of eternal return. If I could find out why his schizophrenia had descended in the first place, then maybe we could solve the riddle of his illness, bring him back to stability.

The why that troubled me was also the why that haunted F. Scott Fitzgerald in 1930. The world economy had crashed, the Great Depression had begun, and his wife had entered a psychiatric clinic in Switzerland. Zelda, like my father, was hearing voices. She had been afflicted by paranoia and was suffering hallucinations. Dr Forel, the well-respected psychiatrist in charge of her care at the Prangins clinic in Geneva, promised that psychotherapy would cure her.

Judging from his letters at the time, it's clear that Scott felt that her family must be to blame. His relationship with them was never an easy one; they exasperated him because they never seemed to approve of him, to feel he was good enough for Zelda.

Once upon a time, Scott hadn't felt he was good enough for Zelda either. They had first met in 1918, at a dance in the Country Club of Montgomery, on a 'firefly' evening, a band playing in the background. He was an army officer, his unit posted to a nearby camp. And Zelda Sayre: she was the belle of the ball. Men lined up to dance with her. She was drunk when Scott met her; she was wild. Scott liked to drink too; Zelda's father would later complain that he had never seen him sober. Her parents were middle class, her father a judge, her mother a housewife. They thought that Zelda needed a husband to calm her down rather than a man who would become her partner in crime. When they were first engaged, Scott was working as a copywriter for an advertising agency in New York, having been discharged from the army in early 1919. He lacked money; he lacked success. Zelda broke it off.

But he won her back. He wrote a novel, *This Side of Paradise*. It was about him and it was about Zelda. He was Amory Blaine, she was Rosalind. It made Zelda a legend, celebrated and defined her; she became the heroine who inspired him. He called the book 'a novel about Flappers for Philosophers'. It was picked up by a young editor, Max Perkins, published by Scribner's, and it became *the* book of the Jazz Age, the book that everyone was reading (49,000 copies sold in its first year!) and discussing. Scott and Zelda became the literary darlings of New York. She was twenty, he twenty-four. They hardly knew who they were, or what they were, but they had created personas and in turn their personas created them. 'Sometimes I don't know whether Zelda and I are real or whether we are characters in one of my novels,' Scott mused. They stayed in plush hotels, they drank champagne and Scott strutted about with a spray of hundred-dollar bills folded into the breast-pocket of his suit like a peacock's tail in miniature.

Now, with Zelda in the Swiss clinic, Scott is confident that he has always looked after his wife well. They have a nine-year-old daughter, Scottie, and Scott has ensured they are provided for, that they have had the best lifestyle, servants, a nanny and a fur coat for Zelda. But still her family feel that he is a bad husband. Her sister, Rosalind, writes to him with stinging words: 'I would almost rather she die now than escape only to go back to the mad world you and she have created for yourselves.' Indignant, he writes to Zelda's parents emphasising that Zelda is in a very expensive clinic, 'the best in Europe'.

Prangins sits on the shore of Lake Geneva. It is lavish as a country club and patients are known as 'guests'. The cost is a staggering $1,000 a month. Scott is working hard, churning out short stories for newspapers and magazines, though he would much prefer to be honing his novel.

Is Zelda's illness the result of nature or nurture? There is a history of madness in her family. Her father is periodically afflicted by severe depression. Her grandmother and aunt committed suicide; her sister Marjorie suffers from anxiety.

Yet, when Zelda's doctors write and ask the Sayres about this genetic aberration, this zigzag in their family history, they feign innocence and reply evasively. Perhaps they are too ashamed to admit it: in the Deep South, these things are not spoken of.

Scott argues that nurture is to blame: he feels that they brought Zelda up to end this way. She was always a spoilt, wild child, always indulged. Once, when she was ten years old, she rang the fire brigade, pretending there was a child stranded on the roof of the Sayres' home, then sat on the roof and kicked away the ladder, waiting for them to rescue her. Zelda's mental collapse, Scott believes, is due to her mother coddling her too much when she was little, resulting in 'the necessity of an arbitrary and unmotivated, often *an even undesired self-assertion* – the contrast between which, and a rationality acquired by her father was later to drive her mad'.

I feel a certain sympathy for Scott for getting caught up in the blame game. I don't think it's uncommon; it stems from the chaos and bewilderment that accompanies a diagnosis. You have to rewrite your loved one's history and suddenly there are gaps in the narrative and it's easy to start seeking a villain. Maybe people are easier to blame than incidents or the weave of a family tree – people are more solid, concrete. When Dad first fell ill, my mum heard that his mother was blaming her. She found this out on the grapevine; casual gossip that burnt her.

Social attitudes at the time were not on the side of women.

During the 1960s and '70s, families were often blamed for schizophrenia, particularly 'the schizophrenogenic mother' – a term coined by the German psychiatrist Frieda Fromm-Reichmann, which depicted the negative stereotype of a dominant and overprotective but rejecting mother. Mothers of schizophrenic children were given personality tests so that doctors might work out which undesirable traits were causing the illness. Perhaps my grandmother, eager to avoid blame, quickly flung it elsewhere.

I don't think my mother and her mother-in-law ever confronted each other. My grandma still visited from time to time and smiles were on display. But I do think it exacerbated my mother's sense of isolation and loneliness. She wanted sympathy and support and instead she was cast as the evil wife. So I can understand Scott's indignation, even if his confidence that an expensive clinic would make everything fine was misplaced – one of many examples from their marriage in which money became a substitute for his own care, for love.

The blame battle did not only play out between Scott and her family, but between Scott and Zelda themselves. He was not allowed to see her when she first entered Prangins. He checked into a local hotel and wrote her letter after letter, receiving letter after letter. They circled their history like vultures fighting for scraps and spoils, tearing at their relationship, feeding off misery and memory. Sometimes they struck out, blamed each other; sometimes they backed down, admitted guilt, expressed remorse. They each had their own version of events and it became important to see who was going to win, who would dictate the narrative. In an echo of Thomas Szasz, it was a war between who would define and who would be defined.

In 1930, Scott was already ahead: Zelda had been labelled and the doctors were calling it schizophrenia. Nobody had yet put a label on him, though he was unsettled by an undertone that suggested they might.

In 1929 Scott and Zelda are still living in Paris. 'My latest tendency is to collapse about 11.00,' Scott writes to Ernest Hemingway, 'and with the tears flowing from my eyes or the gin rising to their level and leaking over, + tell interested friends or acquaintances that I havn't a friend in the world and likewise care for nobody, generally including Zelda ...'

Scott often goes drinking alone in the evenings, ends up bonding with strangers. Once, Zelda used to join him. In New York, in those early days of their marriage, they would drink and party and sit up in hotel rooms, talking and talking for hour upon hour. Drink made them laugh and it unlocked them and it bound them together. Drink made them crazy and alive, like the time Scott stripped off at George White's *Scandals*, or when Zelda dived into the Washington Square fountain and somersaulted down Prospect Avenue at Princeton. And people caught their energy and they wanted more of it. Dorothy Parker said that they looked as though they had stepped out of the sun. The gossip columns loved them, recorded their every prank. Scott has a dreamlike ache for that era, when Zelda was proud to be Mrs Fitzgerald, when she cheered the publication of a new book. Now she seems intent on being Zelda.

Scott has been working on early drafts of his fourth novel, whilst Zelda is determined to become a professional dancer. Taking ballet lessons in the mornings and afternoons, she has been pushing herself to a pitch of exhaustion, working through bronchitis and a high fever. Her husband is not entirely supportive, asking her: 'Are you under the illusion that you'll ever be any good at this stuff?' He confides in a friend that Zelda desires to 'replace Isadora Duncan now that she was dead and outshine me at the same time'. Yet Scott is not as dynamic as his wife. Days can easily drift by where he has written very little; he recalls that the previous year, 1928, was the first where 'he needed to drink in order to write'. They row a lot; they flirt with other people; they are growing apart.

Then there is a series of incidents that suggest Zelda may be in need of help. She becomes paranoid that people are criticising her. In a florists she tells Scott that she can hear the lilies talking to her. When Scott is driving along the Grande Corniche – the lethal French Riviera coast road that would later claim the life of Grace Kelly – Zelda seizes control of the steering wheel and attempts to send them both plunging over the cliff, with the words 'I think I'll turn off here.'

She checks into a clinic in Malmaison, just outside Paris, but it is not enough. Ten days pass, she leaves against the advice of her doctors, and she is no better. She imagines corpses in the house, suffers thoughts of parricide, tries to kill herself.

So Scott imposes his will. He breaks her down. She is admitted to the Valmont Clinic in Lausanne, then transferred to Prangins.

Dr Forel, Zelda's psychiatrist, writes to Scott, who is staying in a hotel near Prangins. Forel is concerned that Scott's drinking might be one of the causes of Zelda's illness. The letter is a shock. Scott responds furiously: she clearly has been bad-mouthing him, trying to swerve her doctors away from dealing with her own faults, her manic egotism, her ridiculous ambition.

Sitting down, he begins his rebuttal:

'<u>During my young manhood for seven years I worked extremely hard</u>, in six years bringing myself by tireless literary self discipline to a position of unquestioned preeminence among younger American writers ...'

And:

'We went on hard drinking parties together sometimes but the regular use of wine and apperatives was something that I dreaded but she encouraged because she found I was more cheerful then and allowed her to drink more. <u>The ballet idea was something I inaugurated in 1927 to stop her idle drinking ...</u>'

And Scott must not give up drinking, because:

'Would that not <u>justify her</u> conduct completely to herself and prove to <u>her relatives, and our friends that it was my drinking</u> <u>that had caused this calamity, and that I thereby admitted it?</u>'

This is what they need to understand: it is not *his* fault.

Scott, it could be argued, has also been acting strangely over the last few years. In 1928, after messing up a speech he was supposed to make at the Princeton University Cottage Club dinner, he flew back home and fought with Zelda in front of their guests, smashing one of her favourite blue vases in the fireplace and hitting her across the face. His drinking has led to him being put in jail several times in Paris and being beaten up by the police in Rome in 1924 after punching a plainclothes policeman. He has repeatedly upset their close friends with his drunken aggression: at a dinner party held by the Murphys, their wealthy expatriate American friends, he threw ashtrays at tables because he was jealous that Hemingway was getting more attention from the guests.

Both Scott and Zelda's outlandish behaviour was celebrated as daring in the Jazz Age, but now, as time has gone on, and in the sober light of day, it appears more akin to the symptoms of a severe mental illness.

Yet it is Zelda who becomes the patient and her husband who helps to supervise her recovery. Scott writes to her saying that he keeps looking at a passport photo of her – 'the face I knew and loved'. When he visits, he is saddened by the metamorphosis of his wife: there are bandages around her face.

Once she was beautiful; now her skin is pitted with eczema. The outbreak occurred in mid-June, after Scott brought their daughter to see Zelda for the first time.

Zelda looks frail, beaten down. She was sedated recently, after trying to run away; she was given morphine and bromides, inserted rectally to induce a state of narcosis.

Scott consults again with Dr Forel, who assures him that Zelda's competitive streak is a symptom of her schizophrenia. So is her 'lack of domesticity' and her recent tendencies towards homosexuality (not long ago she was flirting with Oscar Wilde's niece, Dolly, and she has confessed attraction to her ballet teacher, Madame Lubov Egorova). Her ferocious ambitions for ballet have exhausted her, but with their 're-education programme' she will change. She will stop being competitive. She will become a good wife.

Zelda cannot write to her family, since her letters are censored. She is forcibly restrained too: sometimes just her hands, and sometimes her hands and feet (and her hands are bound also when she is caught masturbating). She is injected with morphine, belladonna, administered endocrine treatments using dried thyroid gland powder and ovarian extracts and given insulin shock treatment. This involves injecting the patient with a high dose of insulin so that their glucose is lowered sufficiently to produce a coma. The side effects are serious, for it is likely that the procedure may have a tranquilising effect on patients because it induces brain damage by depriving the brain cells of glucose.

Scott reads medical textbooks, writes to Forel, offers his

opinion. He grows closer to the doctor. He does not relent when Zelda sends him a begging letter: '*Please* help me. Every day more of me dies with this bitter and incessant beating I'm taking,' and cajoling him: 'You can choose the conditions of our life.' Zelda is forced to undergo a metamorphosis, to let go of her career ambitions, to become the subservient wife of Mr F. Scott Fitzgerald.

F. Scott Fitzgerald is a man who stands in contrast to Leonard Woolf – a carer who, in my view, succeeded. Leonard might have struggled with his burden, but he is to be admired for the responsibility he rose to. Scott and Zelda were beautiful, talented, fragile: people who both lacked the capacity to look after others and needed looking after themselves. As she descended into madness, he descended into alcoholism: both dragged each other down, both drowned.

Virginia's illness exhausted Leonard and brought him to despair at times, but he was determined, in the fog of it, to find his wife and heal her so that her genius could flourish; he might have sometimes restricted her food, her rest and her routine, but he did not want to compromise her character and her gifts. Leonard was resistant to her having psychotherapy – even though it might have made life easier for him – for fear it might damage her genius. Scott, on the other hand, always had a strong desire to control others, and when Zelda became unwell, this tendency became manic, perhaps because her illness made him feel confused and helpless. His chauvinism was also a reflection of his era; it is Leonard, who was more feminist in his outlook, who was the exception.

I suspect my mother married my father – a man who was kind and easy-going – because her own father had been the domineering, controlling type. But I don't think she enjoyed having to control my dad. She told me that she would have stopped her affair with Noah if Dad had got well again, as though she were always secretly waiting for him to come back to himself. Like Scott, Mum was nostalgic for the past and their lost Edenic years. She also gave my father the freedom to live as he pleased, provided that he took his medicines.

Zelda, in comparison, was trapped. Before she entered the clinic, she considered divorcing Scott, but she lacked financial independence; this in part fuelled her desire to succeed in writing or dance. And so she had to relent, bend and break, and become a more docile woman – or at least create a persona that convinced the doctors and her husband she was the good wife they wanted her to be. Scott was relieved when she was released from Prangins seemingly meek and supposedly healed, but, of course, it did not last.

The Fitzgeralds fascinate me because they embody a question that has dogged me for the last few years: what impact does it have on you if you cannot rise to the challenge of caring? What happens if your loved one shatters and you lack the strength to bind them back together?

28

Here is F. Scott Fitzgerald on the insomnia that afflicted him as Zelda's illness took its toll: 'Now the standard cure for one who is sunk is to consider those in actual destitution or physical suffering – this is an all-weather beatitude for gloom in general and fairly salutary daytime advice for everyone. But at three o'clock in the morning, a forgotten package has the same tragic importance as a death sentence, and the cure doesn't work – and in a real dark night of the soul it is always three o'clock in the morning...'

I tossed onto my front. I buried my face in my pillow. Then onto my back, staring up at the murky ceiling. Then onto my right side, my left and my front again.

My mind was stuck in overdrive from the day, like a computer that wouldn't shut down, still drafting lines of prose and answering emails and playing out imaginary conversations with my dad's doctor. I tried to visualise a fortress. *There's a big white wall around the room,* I told myself. *And all the problems, of money, and Thom, and Dad, and Dodo, and Summerfields, are outside it.* My limbs softened as I sank down, safe in my fortress, and then all of a sudden, just in that gap between waking and dream, an image leapt into my mind: tendrils were shooting through the cracks in the wall, wrapping over me, a suffocating bindweed, and my eyes flew open.

Only sitting up and meditating for ten minutes worked, my body sighing with the dissolution of stress, and finally, around midnight, I fell asleep. But at four I was awake again, my covers a rumple of toss-turn creases. Finally, at seven, I rose and went to a cafe to write and have breakfast.

Coffee wasn't something I usually needed. Normally my morning meditation gave me both peace and a lovely zing of creative energy. But on four hours' sleep, I needed a latte to jumpstart my sluggish system.

Five nights in a row, I thought. Five nights where, instead of my usual eight hours which left me feeling refreshed and sharp and ready to have a great day, I had only managed a few hours and had woken up gritty and muzzy and bleurgh.

On my way back from the cafe, I stopped at a health food shop and stocked up on valerian and a few other herbal sleeping remedies. Normally my body was sensitive and reacted promptly to any form of medication. Night came, and I took a double dose of the remedies, and still the tendrils came, shooting through my fortress, sheathing me in worry.

In a cafe near Charing Cross, Thom and I were sitting oppo-site a bookseller from Foyles. He was looking slightly bemused. Our meeting was a discussion about Dodo Ink, over tea. We weren't chatting as a trio; Thom and I would take it in turns to talk to him; we were running two parallel conversations, until our desire for his attention became competitive. At one point, Thom stood up to go to the toilet and the bookseller gave me an enquiring glance. I returned a beaming smile, as though everything was fine.

And then the next day: 'I want to break up with you.'

Thom had sat me down for a talk in the dining room at Dad's house, fingered his collar nervously, then blurted out the words.

It was such a relief for both of us that we laughed. We'd both been sharing the same fear for weeks, afraid to break up in case we wrecked our fledging company. We agreed we would stay friends and run our business in a professional manner. That afternoon, we drifted into London bookshops together, and it felt easy, soft between us, on the surface. Yet there was still history between, unresolved, unspoken: weeks of poor communication, cross purposes and sadnesses lying strewn and rotting between us.

I felt that our break-up was the right thing. In recent weeks I had grown resigned to the death of our relationship. I had not consciously made a decision; but by staying south instead of heading north, by visiting Summerfields day in, day out, instead of visiting Thom, I had sacrificed my boyfriend for the sake of my father.

Yet my body seemed to suggest a self-deception. For five days after our split I suffered strange symptoms: a racing heart, a dry mouth, waking at four in the morning, unable to return to sleep – classic signs of depression. But I felt no urge to cry. In the intensity of my workload and worry for my father, perhaps there was no room left in me to process grief; it had to be put into storage.

A breakthrough: my dad has started talking again.

I was sitting in the common room in Summerfields and, on autopilot, I'd composed the text for Thom. And then I remembered that we'd broken up. We were no longer responsible for looking after each other's happiness. It had only been three days and we were in that uneasy, liminal state where our relationship might or might not become friendship. So the text remained on my phone, unsent. I felt the loneliness of the moment, then forced a smile and pulled out a newspaper from my bag, showing it to Dad.

I was so relieved that he was speaking again. This promised recovery; though discharge was still a long way off. Dad and I went through the newspaper together. There were more debates about the care system, about how much people ought to pay and whether they should have to sell their houses to cover the cost. Why should the system be weighted so unfairly, people were arguing, that if you get cancer, your hospital bill will be paid for in its entirety, but if you get dementia, you have to pick up the bill? The result would mean that families end up hoping for a quick death for their parent, because a long, drawn-out decline would become a crippling expense.

Back home, my exhausted body craved bed, but I ended up sending Dodo Ink emails until the early hours of the morning. Setting up a new business is one of the biggest challenges you can take on – and it might have been enjoyable had it not coincided with my father's illness. I kept thinking, if only *one* of these responsibilities had fallen upon me, I'd be able to cope. But life doesn't always measure out our tragedies and trials with an even hand; sometimes it flings them all in at once. I was caring for everyone but myself.

Pressure was something I'd always relished. I'd loved taking my finals at university, hadn't shed a sweat-drop of stress. Challenges gave me adrenaline. And if anything ever became too much, I would simply do extra meditation, which soothed me back to normal. But now I had no time for those; in fact, I'd cut back my meditation to once a day. Now I felt what F. Scott Fitzgerald described as 'a call upon physical resources that I did not command, like a man overdrawing at his bank'. It was a new sensation for me: this feeling that I couldn't cope, that I might shatter like a plate.

I studied a photograph of my mother – taken when she was in her mid-thirties, her self-negation becoming self-destruction – and suffered an uneasy recognition when I looked in the mirror, her face ghosting onto mine. I started to develop a weird daily habit of taking selfies. I obsessively examined the deepening bags, my eyes becoming smaller, my skin paler. I was charting my decline. I think it was a way of recording, and perhaps trying to control, this descent; one day I would look so dreadful the picture would symbolise a full stop, a moment when this all had to end.

The fragments of my days: wake up. Tired. Want more sleep. Body rigid, unyielding. Dodo emails. Coffee. Dodo cover. Tweet from Dodo. Joke about avians. Send twenty emails. Write a thousand words. Speak to Dad's doctors. Hoover. Eat. Do own tweet. To post or not to post. Post it. Editing. Emails. Write addresses on twenty envelopes. Meet Alex. Discuss finances. Retweets. What was the tweet but a sham? An avatar of a better Sam, a healthier, happier Sam. Consider deleting. Leave it. Tube train. Buy sandwich. Trail cheese and tomato down the road. Buy a drink for Dad. Summerfields. Twilight. See Dad. Give him drink. Smile. Chat. Witness two patients striking each other. Leave. Fearful. Home. Stroke cat. Emails. Valerian. Turn in bed. Sleep splinters, nightmare fragments. Yawns. Eye bags. Selfie. An email: a friend has died. Won't tweet today. Plan to visit Dad. Delayed: Dodo crisis. Friend of twenty years dies of heart attack while feeding cat. Funeral soon. Leo seems off. Take her to vet. She has six months to live. The gods are taking me seriously now. Emails edits writing envelopes post office literary talk. Repressing yawns, red-faced. Hard to speak. Mind feels like a broken limb. If only sleep would wrap around it like a bandage and heal me ...

29

Five months. That's how much time Scott has set aside to work on his novel. It's called *The Drunkard's Holiday* (it will eventually become *Tender Is the Night*) and he's been grappling with it through various drafts and incarnations. It has been seven years since *The Great Gatsby* was published, to disappointing sales. Scott desperately needs a success. For months, he has been churning out short stories for the *Saturday Evening Post* and various magazines in order to save up a fund to sustain him. He writes to his editor Max Perkins that this is 'the first time in two years + 1/2' that he will have enough space to write.

It is January 1932. After spending several years abroad, Scott and Zelda are back in America. Back in Zelda's hometown, Montgomery, Alabama. When they first arrived, it felt like a fresh start away from Europe, for Scott believed the continent was 'for Americans a place of dissipation'. But life is rhyming again: Zelda is falling away from him. In November 1931, he had to head out to Hollywood, for MGM hired him for a six-week writing job on a screenplay. He left Zelda missing him ardently and feeling lost without him; her father died later that month, but she put on a brave face and sent Scott a telegram saying *do not worry about us*, attending the funeral without him.

Scott takes Zelda for a holiday in Florida. A few spots of eczema appear on her neck; she begins to unravel. A few days later, she has to enter a psychiatric clinic – only five months after her release from Prangins.

The new clinic is called Phipps. It is situated in the Johns Hopkins Hospital in Baltimore and is yet another lavish place; the doctor there, Dr Meyer, is one of the world's experts in schizophrenia.

It is also very expensive.

Before he left for Hollywood, Scott approached Zelda's father on his sickbed. He asked for his blessing and received the succinct reply: 'I think you'll always pay your bills, Scott.' The words reassure him, remind him that he is doing his duty. But the bills are a strain. When Zelda first entered Prangins, he'd had to go begging to his publisher to borrow money. Zelda's stays in clinics have often plunged him into debt; now this incarceration threatens to wash his savings clean away, along with his dream of ever completing his novel. Writing to Dr Forel, Scott tells him that *Tender* is a book upon which 'my whole fortune depends'. Meanwhile at Phipps, Zelda will be able to indulge in writing and painting. Scott feels deep resentment at the situation: 'she has come to regard me as the work horse and herself as the artist'.

Money problems are common for carers. Almost one in three providing substantial care have seen a drop of £20,000 or more a year in their household income as a result of caring. The combination of higher costs and lower incomes can push families into financial crisis; almost half end up cutting back on essentials such as food and heating. The longer you care, the more likely you are to get into debt.

My inheritance had lasted a few years after my mother's death, but now I was back to being broke again, and Dodo was increasingly cutting into my freelancing work. When I had been caring for my mum in 2010, I'd looked into applying for Carer's Allowance, the benefit offered by the government to full-time caregivers. At that point, I was caring around fifteen hours a day and over a hundred hours a week. But I wasn't eligible. You don't qualify if you earn over £123 in any given week, and there had been odd weeks where I had squeezed in some freelancing. The allowance is only £66.15 a week (at the time of writing), which means that if you are caring for the minimum of thirty-five hours a week, you'll received £1.89 an hour – that's around a quarter of the minimum wage for my age group. I had to earn, for the allowance was too low for me to live on, not with my debts, and a cat to feed, and bills to pay. The government praised carers, said how important they were and how much money they saved the economy, but these words did not translate into real financial support.

I knew that it was crucial for me to visit my dad each day and lift him up with warmth and optimism, that without me poised for his return, he would probably have been stuck in Summerfields until his dying days, at huge cost to the state.

But how can you quantify love, and put a price tag on its nourishment? I was spending twenty-five hours a week helping to care for him, visiting him, washing his clothes and looking after his house, but I had to concede this was a liminal amount. I was not a full-time carer, yet my caring made my full-time work hard to sustain. As I juggled freelancing and writing and Dodo and my visits, I lost my evenings and weekends, took no time off, and found my income dwindling to a worrying degree. It wasn't just a matter of lost hours, but the impact on my productivity too: in a haze of worry, I found myself writing chapters that had to be discarded, book outlines that made no sense, freelancing work that took twice as long as usual.

I found a grant I could apply for: a contingency grant, offered by the Society of Authors, for writers who suddenly fall into financial difficulty, especially if there is illness in the family. I thought a little wryly of how, when Virginia was ill in 1915, the Woolfs struggled with the cost of hiring private nurses and ended up selling some of her jewellery and securities. Alas, I had no jewellery to sell. In order to apply, there were no pernickety forms. I just had to write a letter detailing my literary credentials and my situation. I decided I had just enough time to write a page before setting off to visit Dad.

I began with a formal, business-like tone. A few paragraphs later I found the words gushing out in a torrent of emotion. I filled one page, then another. It was cathartic, like a diary confession, but it also struck me how much I had been holding back, that I hadn't even written an email to a friend saying just how bad I felt, I was so intent on putting on a brave face all the time. Recently someone had told me that I came across as a superwoman, running a business, writing, looking after my dad, and I had smiled nonchalantly. In echo of my mother's stiff upper lip and my father's respectable suits, I had inherited a family tendency to craft a persona that concealed vulnerability. The more I looked into caring, the more I found I was not alone in this; I read confessions of loneliness, isolation and problems communicating their situation to friends, colleagues and unsympathetic bosses.

The letter written, I scrawled the address on the envelope, feeling subdued. It was unlikely I would get it: I never seemed to have much luck with grants. I posted it on my way to visiting Dad and within a few minutes, as I became lost in the usual clouds of worry, it was forgotten.

I asked the chemist for a sleeping remedy: one of those behind-the-counter packets they store in Boots. She passed it over, warning that I shouldn't take it for too many days. I barely listened. I'd tried so many herbal remedies that I had lost faith in anything delivering the blackout I craved.

Alone at home, I had my first evening off in weeks. I ended up watching *Cinderella*. I hadn't seen a Disney movie since I was a child. Towards the end, its sentimentality brought tears to my eyes. Emotions that had been knotted in my heart began to unravel. How exhausted I felt, torn in all directions, not wanting to let anyone down – trying to keep up with visiting Dad; my finances getting more and more painful; struggling with Dodo Ink and all the books and quills and other crazy rewards we'd come up with for our original kickstarter supporters when high with gratitude and now had no idea how to source. I found that I couldn't stop crying. I felt utterly beaten down.

I had been worried that I might end up like my mother; now I was despairing that I'd end up like my father. When I'd first started caring for Dad in the autumn of 2015, one friend gave me a stern lecture that I should put my father before everything. I think they sensed my struggle with my newfound responsibility and feared I might desert him; their admonition made me feel sheepish, immature. But my friend had never been a carer himself. His advice was purely theoretical.

Over the last few days, I'd turned to guides about being a carer. I found one, written by a man with experience, which suggested the reverse. Look after yourself, it advised: always put yourself first. This maxim made sense, to a degree. In order to give, you need to be strong; tiredness is the enemy of the carer. But I felt vexed too. The idea that you should entirely put yourself first is impossible – because if you followed it, you wouldn't be a carer in the first place. Caring will always involve some degree of self-sacrifice, force you to reorganise your life, drain you, stretch your limits.

I could see that a balance needed to be struck between selflessness and selfishness, between nurturing your loved one and nurturing yourself. But how could I achieve this? I felt utterly trapped. There was nothing I could do but wait it out. The question was: would I be strong enough to last?

Before bed, I took the Sominex. It was 10 p.m. and I turned out the light, dreading another night of being turned over and over on the hot spit of insomnia.

When I woke the next morning, fumbling for the metal coil of watch that sat by my bed, I saw that it was eight o'clock. *I'd slept for ten hours!* I lay back with a grin as Leo jumped up and turned into a purring feather boa across my neck. I could have kissed the packet of pills; instead I kissed her paw. Last night's sorrows seemed distant. With my newfound energy, everything seemed so much more manageable. Optimism was bright inside me like a sunflower. And the day went gloriously: I tackled over a hundred emails, wrote several thousand words, visited Dad, and had a drink with Alex, our Dodo author Seraphina and her agent.

On the tube home, I thought: these pills will solve everything. I'll carry on taking them every night. Sod the chemist's advice – I'm sure they can't do me any harm. According to Google, they weren't addictive.

It was now June. My father's doctor at Summerfields phoned me for a discussion. My father was walking in a funny way, he said. He would walk a few feet down the ward, stop, pause for a little while, and walk some more, then stop again.

I recognised the stop-start quirk he was describing: I'd noticed it happening to my dad in the weeks building up to his last catatonia.

'It's his schizophrenia,' the doctor said, and then went on to say that he was going to reintroduce one of the drugs Dad had stopped taking a year ago, an anti-psychotic called Amisulpride.

I replied yes, that was a good idea, but I knew my voice sounded flat. Exhaustion was killing my faith in anyone finding a successful treatment for my father.

'Maybe we should just put Dad into a home,' I heard myself saying. It didn't even make sense: he was already, in effect, in a home. The words felt like a betrayal. What I was really saying was: *I need a break, a rest – desperately.*

'In a home?' he said, sounding surprised, though he was too kind a man to judge me. 'Well, I think he's improving. I think he's nearly ready to come home, and he's been looking forward to your brother's wedding …'

I cheered a little. Yes, the wedding was important: my dad had to be there.

'And your dad isn't like many of the other schizophrenics I treat,' he added. 'He hasn't lost his compassion, his warmth.'

'That's lovely to hear,' I said, my voice lifting.

I put down the phone. I remembered the promise I'd made to my mother, but my sense of duty was being slowly eroded by my exhaustion. I was on the verge of losing the will to keep going. The flaws we see in others often mirror our own shortcomings. Perhaps I saw in Scott Fitzgerald my own potential to become a poor carer.

I bumped into one of my neighbours. Her mother had been in a home. 'Make sure he gets a care package,' she

exhorted me. 'They're not allowed to let him out without one.'
A care package? Another new piece of terminology.

I discovered it meant a schedule for carers to come to the house and visit on a daily basis, paid for by the local council. I managed to get this implemented and on Dad's first day back home from Summerfields, a woman turned up at lunch-time. She was extremely friendly and pleasant, but all she ended up doing was watching my dad shuffle around the kitchen as he cooked his lunch. It was a waste of the council's time and money: my dad needed emotional support more than practical help. So I rang our care co-ordinator and explained that we had no need of her. Effectively, I thought, as I put down the phone, *I* was my father's care package.

30

It was the morning of my brother John's wedding. The dawn air was crisp as apples. My younger brother, my dad and I met at our local station, looking bleary but excited. Dad was in a lovely suit and I was in a purple, floaty dress that was a size too small for me, because it was years old, and yesterday, at the last minute, I'd purchased an awful jacket with sleeves that were rolled up a few inches and sewn that way. I'd been so busy, there'd been no time for the luxury of seeking out a good dress. If Mum had been alive she would never have let me go to the wedding in this. She would have dragged me around the shops, insisted we look amazing, made us splash out on elegant hats.

Dad started to drum his fingers lightly on his knees; Stefan and I exchanged nervous glances. It still seemed absurd to me that such a minor gesture could be so significant a danger sign.

I knew that trains were a frightening challenge for Dad. I thought back to three years ago, when he'd had that stint of not taking his medicine and had been more lively. We'd agreed to go to the cinema. It was something I had never done with my father before. The train journey there was only ten minutes, but two stops in, he'd freaked out. Two stops for him were like two continents. So we'd had to return home, the cinema plan aborted.

The journey ahead of us stretched out. Two hours, thirty-six minutes; three trains. Was my dad going to manage?

At Farringdon we stepped off the train into the busy bustle, taking the lift because the stairs were too tiring for him. A brief moment of relief: we'd made it this far and Dad was still standing.

From there, we took the tube to London Paddington. The next and final train was the longest part of the journey. It would take just over an hour.

We took our seats.

Dad's fingers were drumming again.

I pictured a worst-case scenario: a catatonic slump; having to pull the passenger alarm; the train stopping; an ambulance; Dad carted off the train on a stretcher; calling my brother and telling him that his family wouldn't be there for the most special day of his life.

Ealing Broadway Station. Ten more stations to go. We had run out of conversation. We were too tired.

'Why don't you have a nap, Dad?' I suggested. 'Just have a rest.'

'That's a good idea,' he said, but not long after he'd closed his eyes, he opened them again.

His fingers ceased. And then started up again.

This was the final verdict the doctor had given us: that his hospitalisation had been caused by the reduction in his meds. Now that he was back up to a proper dose again, he was stable. So my mum had been right, all those years, to lay down an ultimatum, to insist that he took them: they were necessary for him to live a normal life.

West Drayton Station. I thought it might be a good idea to distract Dad and rather randomly pointed out an attractive tree.

'Very nice,' he said, smiling and nodding, his fingers pausing for a minute or so.

Why had he had his meds reduced back in 2015? We had pulled out the psychiatric review from the folder where we kept his medical reports. He never saw the same psychiatrist from one year to the next, that was the problem: there was a constant rotation, which meant he never had time to build a relationship with one doctor who could perceive patterns, intuit danger. The psychiatrist who had seen him back then had written in his report: *Edward seems happy and cheerful … smiling … see no harm in reducing his medicines.*

Iver Station.

I thought about my own grief over my mother's death. It had followed a pattern that seems to be quite common. The second and third years are harder than the first. In the first, slapped awake, aware of your mortality, you suffer a tendency to change your life, leave the job you always hated, or plunge into a new relationship and make it work with a dedication you might not have had before. This can create a feeling of drunken exhilaration, a sense that you can survive without them, you can make your own way in the world. But in the second year, you sober up. They've gone. You loved them. You are surviving and maybe you have a new life – if only they were around to meet your new love interest, hold your new baby. The grief is quieter, stiller, and you realise that it has, over time, been pushing down unseen roots, deeper and deeper, until the cracks of psychic subsidence begin to show. You slowly realise how many of your actions are reactions. For me, there was an eerie sensation that I had lost my free will (or, at least, the illusion of it). Grief seemed to be in the driving seat, pushing me into strange new directions. At the start of each year, I vehemently reassured myself – I'm getting back to my old self, I'm making good decisions again, I'm in control.

What if my father's grief had been repressed, had manifested through a physical reaction other than tears?

Slough.

'*I don't have moods,*' my dad had said, words that still haunted me.

When Zelda looked back on her time in one of the clinics she was moved to after Phipps, the Highland in North Carolina, she wrote: 'Friendship, conviviality, the right of choice, the right of resentment, anger, impetuosities; all these are as much a part of life as obedience, submission, obligation and necessity.' At the Highland, 'these manifestations of the human temperament are subject to reprimand and regarded as illness. Knowing this, patients (mostly) suppress themselves as much as possible, endure, and hope to get out.'

If you spend years being told that you are crazy, and you

become afraid to exhibit any sort of extreme emotion, because it is seen as an act of transgression, a possible prelude to incarceration, then how do you manage when you lose your wife? Maybe the urge to cry and scream is there, muffled by the meds. But perhaps there is a fear: are you allowed to express it? So the grief just sits there, a hard lump inside you, and there is no release, and one day it becomes too heavy, your body too tired of carrying it about, and so it just presses the off switch and caves in. After all, you might expect a widower to shut off or lose interest in food. These were the same symptoms that catatonia had inflicted on my father.

Maidenhead. The drumming was increasing, becoming more intense.

Maybe it was the only way he was allowed to mourn. Maybe it felt dangerous to break down in a supposedly civilised world; maybe the psychiatric ward felt like a safe space, for all around him people were fighting and crying and screaming and he wasn't going to look any different.

Reading.

And maybe it was also a test. A way of seeing if life *could* be sustained without his carer, the woman who had stood by his side all his life. Of seeing if there was a life that could be lived without her, if it was worth getting up in the mornings and taking pills and living a half-life, a quiet life, a life in the shadows. Of seeing whether other people would catch him and help him through his grief and back to reality

Tilehurst.

Just one more station to go. I had the camera with me and

I asked Dad to smile so I could take his photo. His everyday smile was warm and gentle, but in front of a camera, he struggled terribly, screwing up his face, his lips plunging downwards, a picture of anguish.

Pangbourne.

We stood by the doors. The button flashed green. I pressed it and we stepped off into the cold air. At a nearby cafe, we ordered some teas and I noticed that my dad had stopped drumming. We had made it. We had made it! I felt as though I had been carrying a heavy weight above my head for a long time and now I had been able to put it down, but despite the relief, I was the one who was trembling.

That afternoon, in the pretty, wood-panelled registry office, I watched my proud father going up to sign the book, and my heart swelled. John and his wife were radiant.

'You look well,' one of my aunts kept saying to my younger brother. She gave me a sterner look. I knew what she was thinking. I'd already been to the toilets and cringed at what my make-up couldn't hide, my squinty, hollowed-out eyes and haggard look. The sleeping pills, which had worked so well at first, had started to lose their magic, like those in Sylvia Plath's 'Insomniac': 'Now the pills are worn-out and silly, like classical gods / Their poppy-sleepy colors do him no good.' My aunt sensed that I ought to be taking better care of myself.

The wedding reception was held in a lovely country pub. I ate cake and drank champagne and enjoyed myself. At one point, I sat next to my dad's sister; she told me a story about him. When they were children, my father around eight years old and she around five, he had woken her very early one morning. Their parents, their siblings, were still asleep. *Come outside*, he'd said, *it's magical.* He had taken her hand and guided her out onto the street, into the beauty of a twilight breaking into dawn: the sky delicate as a good dream, cobwebs jewelled with dew, birdsong tender. It was a poignant glimpse into the man he'd been before he became sick – someone sensitive, alert to the natural world, with a capacity for loving life.

On the train home, my father was stable. Better than that: he was happy. I could see it in his eyes, in the stillness of his hands in his lap. I thought of Septimus in *Mrs Dalloway*, of those shell-shocked soldiers who returned from the war, and were punished for exhibiting tremors and tears, deemed hysterics, court-martialled. Men who were not allowed to grieve; who were deemed mad for their sane response to war. I thought of those *Bang! Bang! Bang!*s my father had made in the hospital as he hammered his fists on the bed, the tears that slid from his eyes as he reassured me it was just a cold. And I wondered whether his catatonia had not been a curious regression to infanthood, but an attempt to beat away his repressed fury and sadness that the woman he had always loved was no longer in the world.

31

'PLEASE DO NOT JUDGE OR IF ALREADY DONE EVEN CONSIDER ZELDAS BOOK UNTIL YOU GET REVISED VERSION LETTER FOLLOWS.'

Scott pounds out his emotion into the telegram; its necessary concision captures the intensity of his fury. He sends it to Max Perkins. It is March 1932 and Zelda is still in the Phipps clinic.

There is a younger female psychiatrist at the clinic called Dr Mildred Squires, who encourages Zelda's artistic ambitions. A few weeks ago, when Squires wrote and told him that Zelda was making speedy progress with her novel, Scott didn't take it entirely seriously. He felt Zelda lacked the aptitude for the longer form and wasn't 'a "natural storyteller" in the sense that I am'. Then, so very quickly, the book is finished! Zelda sends a copy to him and a copy to Max, his editor at Scribner's. By the time Scott has finished reading, he is furious.

This is Zelda's sin, as far as Scott is concerned: she is poaching from him. Parts of her novel overlap and blur with his. He read her extracts from *Tender Is the Night* when they were on holiday in Florida. And when he was away in Hollywood, she wrote him letters confiding how she was studying his work, that she wished she could write like him. She has dabbled in writing in recent years, though the stories she has penned have been published under their joint names. One of her best is *A Millionaire's Girl*, which his agent lavished praise on, not realising initially that Zelda had written it. The *Saturday Evening Post* agreed to pay the handsome $4,000 fee if they published it under Scott's name only.

Zelda's book is about a girl called Alabama who marries an aspiring painter called *Amory Blaine*. Amory Blaine! – she has stolen the name of his protagonist from *This Side of Paradise*. Alabama and Amory live in Connecticut and then France where, dissatisfied by her marriage, she has an affair; determined to rise above being a 'back seat driver' in life, she takes up ballet.

Writing to Dr Squires, Scott complains that 'this mixture of fact and fiction is simply calculated to ruin us both, or what is left of us … My God, my books made her a legend and her single intention in this somewhat thin portrait is to make me a non-entity'.

Zelda writes Scott an apology. She explains her fears for her novel: 'feeling it to be a dubious production due to my own instability I did not want a scathing criticism such as you have mercilessly … given my last stories'. His red pen is savage on the page: *'This is an evasion. All this reasoning is specious.'*

In the end, he makes three demands before publication is allowed to go ahead.

Firstly, parts of the novel will have to be cut – cuts that he will dictate. Secondly, Scribner's are not to give Zelda any praise, as it might result in her suffering 'incipient egomania'. Thirdly, half of any royalties Zelda receives must be used to pay off the debts he owes Scribner's, who have already advanced him money for his unfinished novel; this will continue until $5,000 has been paid off.

Eventually, after Zelda has amended the book according to Scott's demands, the novel is published as *Save Me the Waltz*. Even then, Scott muscles in on the pre-publication hype. After he gives an interview to the Baltimore *Sun*, the result is the headline: 'He Tells of Her Novel', and the subheading 'Work Sent to Publisher is Autobiographical at Suggestion of Her Husband'.

1933: Zelda and Scott are living in Baltimore in a fifteen-bedroom house called 'La Paix'. Scott works on *Tender Is the Night*, and Zelda practises her painting, ballet and writing. Zelda is still receiving some treatment at Phipps. Scott writes to Dr Rennie to complain that Zelda has broken their agreement and is working on a new novel. Her subject matter is madness. This Scott regards as *his* territory.

Zelda has to put a double lock on the room she writes in, for Scott threatens to tear up her work-in-progress.

On 28 May 1933, Scott and Zelda sit down for a three-way discussion with Dr Rennie, who will act as moderator. Scott is determined to assert his authority. One of the doctors at the Phipps clinic, Dr Meyer, previously suggested that the Fitzgeralds should be treated as a *folie à deux*, fearing that

SAM MILLS

Scott's drinking was undermining Zelda's progress. Scott wrote back in protest, asserting that he needed the power to tell Zelda to pack her bags and go back to the clinic whenever necessary. Meyer merely replied: 'The question of authority is simple. We have decided to relieve you of having to be the boss.'

A stenographer announces the time: 2.30 p.m. This fight is being recorded.

'The whole equipment of my life is to be a novelist,' Scott says. 'And that is attained with ... tremendous struggle; that is attained with tremendous sacrifice.' Having asserted that he was a professional, in contrast to Zelda the amateur, he continues: 'Her theory is that anything is possible, and that a girl has just got to get along, and so she has the right, therefore, to destroy me completely in order to satisfy herself.'

Zelda interrupts. She says he is being unfair and argues back: 'I have considered you first in everything I have tried to do in my life.'

Scott carries on putting his wife down: 'Did she have anything to say? She has several experiences to report, but she has nothing essentially to say.' He is gaining momentum now, explaining that his eight-year delay in finishing *Tender* has been caused by dealing with *her* problems, and how he backed her ballet ambitions—

'You mean you were drinking constantly ... It is just one of the reasons why I wanted to be a ballet dancer, because I had nothing else.'

Scott argues against her, and concludes: 'I never drank 'til

I was sixteen years old. The first time I met her I saw she was a drunkard.'

They move onto the subject of mothering, and Zelda accuses him of alienating her from their daughter. Soon they circle back to the issue of their writing and Scott goes for the kill: Zelda's new novel must be stopped. It is plagiaristic. She is sneaking behind his back, stealing his themes: 'You are a third-rate writer and a third-rate ballet dancer.' He goes on to claim that there is no comparison between them, for 'I am a professional writer, with a huge following. I am the highest paid short story writer in the world.'

Zelda retorts: 'It seems to me you are making rather a violent attack on a third-rate talent then.'

Scott declares that she could never earn from her writing, for she is just 'a useless society woman', and concludes: 'You pick up the crumbs I drop at the dinner table and stick them in books.'

'You have picked up crumbs I have dropped for ten years, too.'

(Scott here forgets that he has often incorporated Zelda's ideas and witticisms into his books; years ago, an editor made an offer for Zelda's diaries which Scott rejected, arguing that he wanted to use parts of them in his own novels and stories …)

Zelda replies that she would like to live by her writing herself, but Scott, incensed, cries: 'So you are taking my material, is that right?'

'Is that your material?'

'Everything we have done is mine … I am the professional novelist, and I am supporting you. That is all my material. None of it is your material.'

Zelda is advised by Dr Rennie that Scott is in the right, that in the future, if she wants to bring out a novel, 'it ought to go through his [i.e. Scott's] hands'.

The fight goes on, with Zelda miserably asserting that she is 'so God damned sick of your abuse' until she says something tragic, something that must have whiplashed Scott: she would rather stay in an asylum than go back to him.

'I was told by the doctors they did not want you to go into an asylum because you were not insane,' Scott replies. 'Sometimes I am inclined to think you do these things because you are psychotic, and at other times because … you are just wicked.'

She fights back, and they circle and bicker and bicker and circle and Scott keeps on trying to crush her: 'Don't you think that a woman's place is with the man who supports her, that her duty is to the man who supports her? … I would like you to think of my interests. That is your primary concern, because I am the one to steer the course and the pilot … I am just the captain of this ship, and as long as you watch with the captain the ship goes, and as soon as you stab the captain in the back the ship goes down, and you go down with it.'

Zelda is deflated but she keeps going. She wants to keep writing. She wants to earn. She wants her own independence. Outside, the sky is changing; they have been fighting for hours. 'I am just fighting for my life,' Scott bursts out, 'I have to sacrifice myself for you and you have got to sacrifice yourself for me, and no more writing of fiction!'

Leonard and Virginia Woolf both explored their relationship within their novels; Virginia's debut, *A Voyage Out*, and Leonard's *The Wise Virgins* depicted fears, hopes and insecurities about their own courtship and marriage. But they respected each other as artists and allowed their work to stand side by side, without fighting possessively over ownership of the material. Scott's trouble was that he could only write about himself and, in the words of Zelda's mother, was 'a selfish man'. Zelda, beaten down by Scott's protests, did abandon her second novel and turned instead to painting and writing a play.

Scott drew heavily on Zelda's illness for his novel, *Tender Is the Night*. In the months before publication, the serialisation of *Tender* in *Scribner's Magazine* shocked Zelda, who hadn't realised quite how much Scott had drawn on her life, letters and experiences as a source for his labour of love. Dick Diver, the protagonist of *Tender*, is Nicole's psychiatrist before they marry; in his notes for the book, Scott wrote: 'Only her transference to him saves her – when it is not working she reverts to homicidal mania and tries to kill men ...' adding that this is a 'Portrait of Zelda – that is, a part of Zelda'. He conflated her illness to an extreme. He even included in the novel parts of her doctor's reports from Malmaison, Prangins and Phipps.

All this, together with personal tragedies, such as her brother's suicide, led Zelda to fall into a severe depression. In

February 1934 she suffered her third breakdown. After re-entering Phipps, Zelda wept over Scott's portrayal of her: 'What made me mad was that he made the girl so awful and kept on reiterating how she had ruined his life and I couldn't help identifying myself with her because she had so many of my experiences.'

The ending of *Tender* gave me an insight into Scott's fears. Just as Scott told Zelda and Dr Rennie, 'I am fighting for my life', Dick tells his sick wife: 'I can't do anything for you any more. I'm trying to save myself.' As Dick weakens, Nicole grows stronger. At the end of the book, he 'sacrifices' himself and ends up a small-town doctor, whilst she grows sane and leaves him for Tommy Barban, a French-American soldier who bore similarities to Zelda's ex-lover, Jozan. Barban has a whiff of Ernest Hemingway about him. Once a dear friend to Fitzgerald, Hemingway gradually became a rival whom he envied deeply.

This belied Scott's fear not only of one day losing Zelda, but of her getting better. Scott had a tendency to infantilise her; one of their close friends claimed he treated Zelda like 'a wayward child'. He was perpetually nostalgic for the early days of their marriage. But Zelda was very young then, barely out of adolescence, accepting of her supporting role in his career; as she grew up, as she became a woman, she wanted to express her own talents. Despite his constant demands that Zelda ought to take responsibility, Scott did not appear to want her to become independent, merely to do what he told her. He seemed eager to freeze her natural passage of maturity, to force her into stasis. For Zelda to get better would involve her becoming strong. Perhaps he was happier for her to remain a patient and him the carer. Leonard Woolf was Scott's opposite, so wary of turning Virginia into a patient in her last weeks that he lost her to suicide.

No sooner had my dad been released from Summerfields than he had to go back into hospital for the delayed operation on his aneurism. He would require a general anaesthetic and that was potentially dangerous for him.

I'd witnessed this in June 2015, when he'd had an operation for bowel cancer. The day after his op, I entered the hospital room to find Dad sitting up in bed. Having spent far too much time fretting and googling stats about the odds of elderly patients who die on the operating table, I wanted to cheer at the sight of him. But before I could say hi, a nurse on the ward drew me to one side.

'I'm having trouble getting your Dad to take his medication,' she confided. She shot him a glance as though he was a naughty boy, then passed me a paper cup, asking if I would have a try. I stared down at the two pills, which rattled their colours around the cup. Her request surprised me: it was rare for my father to reject his anti-psychotics. They'd had to stop them for his operation and now they were building them back up again.

Sitting down on a plastic chair by his bed, I asked Dad how he was. He replied that he was fine, but he seemed agitated. There were various plastic tubes coming out of his body and he tugged at them. 'I need to get up.'

'You've just had an operation,' I said, gently pushing him back down.

'If you get the paperwork, I'll be able to leave,' he said, his voice unusually assertive. 'And I can get rid of this.' He tugged at the tubing again.

I tried to give him his pills, but he batted my hand away.

'Look, you need to go down to the living room,' he insisted urgently. 'You'll find the paperwork there, it's in my briefcase, you need to bring it up here. Be quick, it's important, then I can get out of here.'

It was then I realised: my dad thought that he was in his own bed back home. It was one of those symptoms I'd read about in countless textbooks – *paranoid hallucinations* – but not one I had ever witnessed before.

'We're in hospital,' I told him. 'You've had an operation, remember?'

'We're not in hospital,' he argued, 'we're at home and I need you to get the paperwork. I don't know why you're being so difficult.'

'Dad, you had an operation and you're still in hospital. You need to take your medicines and they'll let you out at the end of the week, like the leaflet said.'

'You're lying to me. I don't understand why you'd lie – *get the paperwork*.'

'Dad, look,' I said, pointing to the window and its rather uninspiring view. 'There's a car park there. A hospital car park. See?'

He jumped, startled, his eyes following the line of my

pointed finger to the line of cars parked below. A brief recognition flickered in his eyes; I saw him connect with reality; but then a mistiness fogged his gaze and the moment was lost. He kept telling me to get the paperwork, he refused his medicines, I could not reason with him. After an exhausting thirty minutes that felt like three hours, I passed the paper cup back to the nurse, the pills still intact, and left the ward.

I called my older brother. He heard the panic in my voice. He reminded me that anaesthetic is tough on the body, quoting an expert who compared the impact to a car crash. Then I rang a friend of mine. He was also reassuring. He said that when his dad had gone under anaesthetic for an operation, he'd acted as though he was stoned and had done all kinds of crazy things. And his dad was deemed sane.

The next day, I went in to see Dad again. He was lying down, looking sleepy. The nurse told me he'd tried to get up and leave the ward, but the security guards had put him back in bed; and he'd been sedated.

'Are you better now?' I asked him. He gave me a sheepish grin and nodded. I could see in his eyes that he understood what I was asking. He was aware of what happened. This surprised me and I mulled it over for a while afterwards. I recalled the time I had once suffered a fever with an astronomical temperature, descending into a delirium where I'd laughed so hard I was crying; a part of me had been detached from the illness, watching with quiet sanity, knowing it would pass. My dad's madness had not fully absorbed him; a part of him, underneath it, had been aware what was going on.

This time, thank God, the operation went smoothly. There were no paranoid fits. Within a week he came home to be with us.

In early September we celebrated Dad's birthday with a drive to Littlehampton. Normally I loved our yearly excursions to the beach. This year was different. I sat in the back of the car in a feverish heat, which seemed to have been brought on by a cocktail of travel sickness and general exhaustion. My brother had to stop the car several times whilst I lingered on a grassy verge, cars swishing by, holding a plastic bag and craving the relief of vomiting. On the beach, I stood on the edge of the shore, breathing in the fresh sting of sea air, the tide foaming its frilly edges about my feet, and felt a little better. But a walk over the rocks left me feeling like I'd run several miles, my legs shaky and weak.

I had assumed that I would bounce back quickly now that my dad was home; I felt confused by my body. Why did I seem to be getting weaker? What was the matter with me?

32

What has happened to her? What has she become? Is it his fault?

Scott has run out of funds. *Tender Is the Night* has not sold as he had hoped; it is an even greater failure than *Gatsby*. His earnings are only $5,000, not enough to even cover his debts to his publisher and his agent. He can no longer afford to pay for Zelda to be treated in her current clinic, Craig House, where she has enjoyed a private nurse and grounds sporting a golf course and swimming pools. He has had to move her to the cheaper Sheppard and Enoch Pratt hospital, near Baltimore. There, the windows are barred, the doors locked; it is grim and basic; and when Zelda first enters she endures a rough body search followed by a disinfectant bath.

Zelda begins hallucinating and hearing voices. She hears Scott calling her name, hears him say, 'I have lost the woman I put in my book'. She tries to strangle herself. Throughout 1935, she is categorised as suicidal. The doctors give her Metrazol convulsive treatments, which evoke a state akin to epilepsy. As a side effect, she suffers memory loss and apathy; Scott feels that it has 'washed' her mind 'clean'.

One day, he goes to visit her and they take a walk by the

railway track. The noise of the train grows, a thunderous rattling beast exhaling smoke across the sky. And then he realises: *she is heading for the tracks.*

The train driver can't see what she means to do—

She trips, hurls herself forward—

The train is pounding towards her—

He runs, grabs her with a fierceness that makes her cry out—

Pulls her back.

I imagine Scott holding Zelda tightly, so tightly, her hair billowing against his cheek as the train speeds past. His heart must have hammered with the what-might-have-been, visions of her blood and body parts splayed across the tracks, in his hair, smeared across his face: how has it come to this?

'With each collapse she moves perceptibly backwards,' Scott writes in despair. He now has to face the growing realisation that Zelda's illness is not a temporary problem, but a long-term, perhaps even a lifelong, battle, and her periods of stability do not signal recovery but oases of relief.

Affairs and alcohol are his solace. Affairs are safety valves; like my mother, they allow him to be one who is cared for. One of these affairs is with a married woman, Nora Flynn: 'During the mood of depression that I seem to have fallen into about a year ago she was a saint to me, took care of Scottie for a month one time … and is altogether, in my opinion, one of the world's most delightful women.' But another of his affairs, that with the wealthy Beatrice Stribling Dance, ends in tragedy.

When Scott tells her that he can never leave Zelda, she has a nervous breakdown and is hospitalised. Scott writes to her expressing his grief: 'With all my heart I am sorry to have brought so much sorrow into your life.' But in his *Notebooks*, he muses that he is relatively balanced compared to the 'recklessness' of Nora, Beatrice and Zelda; his wife is 'the most reckless [and the most unbalanced] of all'.

Tony Buttitta, a man Scott befriends at this time, recalls that that summer, 'everything had crashed around him. He was a physical, emotional and financial bankrupt. He smoked and drank steadily, but ate very little … Often when I saw him he cried, suddenly, as if he were an overwrought, indulged child.'

In November 1935, Scott suffers his own mini nervous breakdown. In a state of despair, close to destitution, he flees to a dismal hotel called Skylands in Hendersonville (near Asheville, North Carolina) where he pays just a dollar a day, living off oranges and boxes of biscuits, drinking himself into a stupor. Now both husband and wife are utterly broken.

In *Madness and Civilisation*, Michel Foucault argued that society's great confinement led to the polarisation of sanity and insanity, the drawing of a strong demarcation between the two. This could be applied in microcosm to Scott and Zelda's relationship. Scott once drafted an incredibly harsh (unsent) letter to her where he wrote: 'My talent and decline is the norm. Your degeneracy is the deviation.' By othering her, by playing the quasi-psychiatrist – he was determined to be doctor rather than carer – he remained in the position of power and avoided dealing with his own drink problem. But I am sympathetic to the fact that this avoidance was symptomatic of his era. There was far less support available; Alcoholics Anonymous, for instance, was not founded until 1935. Alcoholism was regarded as a weakness of character, a moral failing, and deemed incurable by many doctors.

In that three-way discussion with Dr Rennie in 1933, it reached such a low point that Zelda concluded several times that she could not carry on living with Scott whilst he was drinking and did not care for her – she would rather be in an asylum. Is this why Zelda carried on being sick? Perhaps Scott did not entirely want her to become well and strong, but perhaps she was also co-dependent in this. Her doctors felt that she began to use the label of her illness as a shield, a way of evading a discussion about the real issues. Equally, her doctors did as much to harm Zelda as they did to help her, with the insulin coma treatments she suffered having some permanent side effects. But perhaps she also grew attached to her diagnosis as a way of resolving a problem that could not be solved between her and Scott – she yearned to be free of him yet found herself trapped in their marriage. 'I can't get on with my husband and I can't live away from him,' she told nurses at Phipps. Being in an asylum became a way of avoiding divorce but evading Scott; of finding an environment which, despite restrictions placed on by her psychiatrists, allowed her creativity to flourish; it is telling that *Save Me the Waltz* was dedicated not to Scott but to Dr Mildred Squires.

Unable to resolve their marital problems themselves, both

drawn to the tragic and the theatrical, Scott and Zelda echo the couple in Edward Albee's play *Who's Afraid of Virginia Woolf*, who need an audience to hear their side of the he said/she said story. Zelda's doctors often ended up in the role of marriage guidance counsellors, which the couple used to manipulate one another. Scott kept on curtailing Zelda's creative activities by getting the doctors to impose time limits on the hours she could spend on them; even in 1934, he was still hoping she might be 'reeducated' out of her creative endeavours.

'Life ended for me when Zelda and I crashed,' Scott once wrote. 'If she would get well, I would be happy again and my soul be released. Otherwise, never.' That image sums up how caring imprisoned him, psychologically, yet the way he treated her only lengthened his own sentence. The relentlessness of her illness exhausted him, made him despair as he realised that Zelda had become 'a case – not a person', but it is tragic that he also perpetuated it by failing to treat her as a person with her own hopes, desires and creative ambitions. In working to destroy her, he destroyed himself in the process.

For me, unexpectedly, the exhaustion hit hardest after my heavy caring duties came to an end. It was as though I had survived on adrenaline and caffeine and my body accepted punishment for as long as it could but at a certain point, it ran out of reserves. My dad's operation had been a success; he seemed relatively stable on his medicines. I just had to do his housework, cook for him and keep an eye on him; I was able to feel more like a daughter than a carer again. But physically and mentally I was burnt out, bent out of shape. I needed time to heal and recover; I needed to do as Leonard Woolf did in 1914 when he got too worn out caring for Virginia and went to stay with Lytton Strachey in Wiltshire.

Instead, I was under pressure to work harder, to make up the time I'd lost to caring, to finish off my crime novel, to keep pushing forward with new publications at Dodo Ink. My insomnia had not settled; it was getting worse. I was recording my bad nights and good nights, and their weekly ratio was normally six bad to one good. I had pains in my eyes like knives stabbing, woke every morning around three, worked through the days in a fug, found my memory was a sieve and lists were essential.

When I found out the Society of Authors had awarded me a grant, I cried with relief. They sent me a generous cheque for £2,000. Now I could remain solvent, have breathing space, maybe earn more money and repair my tatty finances. But work was no longer a joy. I had reached a point where my body felt so worn out and fragile that every activity felt like a blow that weakened it further. The week that our third Dodo title was launched, I could barely get out of bed. Exhaustion was mummifying me. So I forced myself to do what I had been putting off for so long: I dragged myself to see the GP.

The doctor who saw me listened carefully to everything I told him and replied that I'd been doing far too much. He said I needed time to recover from my caring duties. Sleeping pills were not the answer, he warned, as I would not be tackling the root problem of overwork at a time when my body craved recovery. We compromised: I would take a month or so off, and he gave me a short supply of melatonin tablets.

His advice came as a great relief. I felt bad at having to let go of some of my authors and pass them over to Thom and Alex. But for the first time in a long, long time, I had three nights of good sleep in a row, aided by melatonin and my own supply of Sominex.

Even with the contingency grant, I could not afford to stop work entirely – or perhaps, as a workaholic, I didn't want to. Each morning I would scribble about 1,000 words. Writing was not therapy but it was therapeutic; usually it gave me energy, but now it wiped me out for hours. I kept thinking that it would surely only take a few weeks to feel better. I was puzzled by how slowly my body, which had always been so robust and flexible, was recovering.

Just before Christmas, I made the mistake of travelling up north. The journey was long and tiring, the cold seared into me and over the next few days the insomnia kicked off again. My old body had never minded travel; I had zigzagged all over the place without a care. This new body disorientated me in its inability to adapt, its shock at the slightest change; I felt as though I'd aged ten years in the space of one. I took a cocktail of pills, herbal and conventional, in an attempt to hammer my body back into a sleep routine.

Since my mother's death, Christmas had become a day our family wanted to speed through. All of us acted strangely.

Diversion – films, alcohol, books, sleep – was crucial. My older brother favoured DIY. In one particularly fraught year, he decided to replace Dad's kitchen across the three days of holiday. John is extremely dynamic and he crammed about three weeks' of work into seventy-two hours. I remember that at one point, I had to wash up our plates, greasy with Christmas dinner, in the bath, because there was no kitchen sink; a half-cooked Christmas pudding somehow ended up stored on a shelf in the toilet, and as rows raged, I felt guilty – my brother meant well, was doing a helpful task, giving Dad an amazing present. It was just his way of both grieving and avoiding grief.

Christmas 2016 marked the passing of five years since my Mum's death. We were a little more relaxed than previous years, watching TV and playing board games together. Yet I found myself muddling up which piece was mine and getting confused about simple rules. *I'm going senile*, I thought. The one advantage of my new memory problems was being able to rewatch movies I'd seen before without remembering any details of their plots; I guess it saved on buying new DVDs.

A few months later, when the pain in my eyes became so severe that to read or watch a film was agony, I went to the optician. My left eye had a temporal haemorrhage at the back, she said in alarm, waving an X-ray at me. For a fortnight, I rested my eyes, avoided screens and paper, lay down and substituted reading with listening to Radio 4, until my eyes healed. On one of these days, I happened to be looking at the patient leaflet that came with my sleeping pills, which I'd not bothered to read before. Serious side effects, it warned, might include: 'Blurred or reduced vision or pain in the eye.' It advised to stop taking them and seek immediate medical guidance.

I had originally been told by the chemist to only take the pills for a fortnight, but I'd been taking them for six months. But – how to give them up? According to the patient leaflet, they weren't addictive, but without them, sleep fled and my eyes burned with the fire of tiredness. Every night, I tried to shave a little off my pills with a knife, so that a slightly bigger slice of white powder went tumbling into the bin. My sight was deteriorating, for little black floaters pierced my vision and when I read the left-hand side of a book, a blurry smudge obscured the type.

The sort of problems I was suffering from are not uncommon among carers. Seventy-two per cent suffer poor mental health as a result of caring and sixty-one per cent report that their physical health has worsened. You can feel very alone when you fall sick, especially if there is no one to step in and cover for you, and you will always suffer people who try to diminish your illness. One relative – who had little involvement in my father's care during this period except from visiting him once a week – looked mystified when I explained to him I was ill. Another friend kept telling me: 'But you look fine, I can't believe there's anything really wrong with you.' Sometimes I wished I had suffered a broken leg rather than insomnia, exhaustion, despair: it would be there on the outside, a visible sign, clear and easy for everyone to understand.

I was advised that I could put my dad into respite care if I was desperate for a break. But this was the snag: there was an emotional element to my dad's catatonia, and he was a man obsessed with routine. If he got disorientated and unhappy, it might cause another catatonic collapse, which would only increase the demands on me as a carer in the long run.

An example of how exhaustion can blur things: about a year after my dad was home, I came across some carers leaflets that I'd set to one side during the depth of his illness, far too fraught to focus on them. Perhaps I'd been worried that they might include guidelines in the guise of help, pointers that I wasn't living up to. But the leaflets really were written to offer assistance. Thanks to a local charity, I could have had help with my fares when visiting my father at Summerfields. Another advised that I could have had free counselling (though I doubt I'd have had time to go). I also remember a careworker advising me that I could have something called a carer's assessment, where someone from the local council assesses your needs and whether you qualify for support. But, again, it washed over me, forgotten by the next day in my single-minded focus on my father.

That is the trouble with being a carer: you can end up rather like the players in *Rosencrantz and Guildenstern are Dead*, the sidekicks, the support act, and the focus of all discussions and attention is on the one who needs you rather than on yourself.

Over Christmas and New Year 2016 it seemed as though Dad had stabilised. I was hopeful that the narrative of his illness had come to its conclusion, that I could put a full stop on it and a new phase of life would begin in which I had no caring responsibilities. But, of course, that didn't happen: there were more complications to come.

33

It is a summer's evening in 2017, and nearly time for bed. I watch my dad pop medicines out from their pill sheets whilst I stand by the stove, feeling delightfully witchy. I am boiling up a potion.

To the milk in the pan, I add poppy seeds, cardamom and coconut sugar. It bubbles up into a sweet, rich, calming concoction. It is one of the remedies I've been given by a Danish doctor, who specialised in Ayur Veda medicine. After a year of trying to get off the sleeping pills, I've found her sleeping remedy the only thing that matches their power. It is as potent as a pill, but without the damage. My dreams are unusually euphoric, imbued with a kind of childhood magic, as though my body is celebrating being free of the pills. I've also attended a meditation retreat and the bliss I enjoyed there has dissolved the months of stress. When I came back, several people told me I looked years younger.

Finally, I was healing. I hadn't collapsed in 2016 as I'd feared, I hadn't broken: years of practising meditation had given me a foundation of strength. My luck was back. I'd got a deal for my crime novel; it seemed a miracle that I'd written anything even publishable in 2016, given the state I had got into. Dodo

Ink was good too: the three of us, Alex and Thom and I, had meshed into a close-knit team, and we were working hard to bring out three more novels.

My dad had been stable for over twelve months now. I still looked after him, taking care of his house, giving him emotional support, cooking him at least one meal a day. I remained alert to the danger signs of catatonia. The words of his doctor rang in my ears, spoken just before his discharge: 'We must make sure this never ever happens again.'

But then came a new set of signs, ones I failed to recognise. When my father called the GP, he listed them: stomach pains, nausea, vomiting. They told him not to worry. It was just his gastritis bothering him. He asked for an emergency appointment. They gave him an appointment that was fourteen days away. He tried phoning again a few days on, but they wouldn't give him anything earlier; a doctor came on the line and simply advised that he eat soft food.

Ten days later, Stefan came over. He saw the state of my father and insisted that we take him to A&E.

Dad was kept in hospital whilst they debated whether or not to operate. He had a bowel obstruction, a potentially life-threatening condition. I still felt hot with shame that I had believed the rationale of our GP. I knew that with austerity cuts, they were struggling, underfunded, too many patients and not enough slots. And someone like my father, elderly and mentally ill, was easily fobbed off. It was a medical survival of the fittest. By listening to them, believing in their white-coated authority, I had neglected to see the truth of the situation. I was his translator for the world he lived in; I was his protector. And I had failed to fight for him, just when he needed me to be at the vanguard. My assumption had been that I'd got the hang of this caring thing, that I knew the ins and outs of his condition, but in fact caring is rarely simple because its nature is not static. It creates routines, crafts the days into set shapes, lulls you into states of false security, and then mutates, slaps you with fresh challenges, leaves you lost just when you feel you have gained wisdom.

A week went by and we were relieved that no operation was necessary, though Dad had suffered four days of no food and no water, everything delivered to his body via tubes. The block was clearing.

Unable to take his anti-psychotic medication, he was a different man. Once again, he surprised me and my brother with flashes of wicked wit, cynicism, insight. It highlighted just how blurred his personality was by the drugs he took, like a man perpetually underwater.

Clozapine is a drug that can't be stopped or started suddenly. Over the next month, twice a day, a careworker from the home recovery team visited Dad at home and gave him a titrated dose, slowly building him up to full dose and zombie consciousness.

I took a short trip to Appley Bridge and went into Manchester for a day of writing. As always, it was raining. Sitting in Waterstones Deansgate, I tried to pinpoint the emotion in

the backdrop of my heart. An anticipation for something …
someone … Then I clicked. I'd sat in this very seat for many
years, waiting for Thom to finish work, to catch sight of him
coming up the escalators, greeting me with a kiss hello before
we went for a meal or a movie. Recently I'd gone for pizza
with a friend and gently tossed my olives onto their plate on
autopilot, until their look of surprise had led me to collapse
into embarrassed laughter. *It's what I used to do with Thom*,
I'd explained: *I hated olives; he loved them.*

I'd had no time to grieve back in 2016. Now I felt a bitter-
sweet sadness, finding memories of him woven into the streets,
into the rain we used to shelter from, in cafes we'd lounged
in, in cinemas where we'd watched movies.

Recently, I had seen Z. It had not felt like a rebound fling
or a consolation. There was always a connection between us
and our rare meetings brought it alive. It had been a night of
happy laughter and electric passion. But in the morning, as
we parted, there was a sadness for my future, traced in the
skyline: being with Z always left me feeling both sated and
frustrated. It was that most satisfying and unsatisfying of all
relationships.

But any hope of a proper relationship seemed impossible.
Romance and caring would always end up in the boxing ring;
I could probably never have anything more.

My dad's hospital stint brought new changes. One Saturday,
when he needed to go back for a check-up, my brothers and
I began to bicker about who ought to take him. The match

struck, the flame began to dance and spread and soon we were rowing furiously about who was doing the most caring for Dad, which was an awful subject, as though we were competing over who loved him the most.

Once things had settled, however, life did improve. I noticed the burden of caring became more evenly distributed. My younger brother took him to hospital and psychiatric appointments. My older brother drove him to the supermarket twice a month, took care of the garden and DIY in the house. I was in charge of his day-to-day emotional care and played doctor. His medical team had decided to take him off his long-term drug, for fear of more bowel disasters, and try him on a new drug, Olanzapine. Within weeks, our worst fears materialised: he had a catatonic collapse. But it was only a brief one. We discovered a secret weapon in the form of Valium. It seemed the best way to prevent a collapse; a doctor explained that when catatonia descends, the muscles in the body lock up and seize, whilst Valium is the antidote that softens the body into relaxation.

It was a big responsibility. But, just as Leonard Woolf gained confidence in detecting when Virginia might be on the verge of collapse, I felt that I had developed sensitive antennae towards my father. I had to watch him carefully each day for the subtle signs: slowing down when he was doing the washing up or climbing the stairs; or becoming just a shade more inward. I developed a Pavlovian response to the sound of drumming fingers.

My older brother organised a power of attorney for Dad,

for both health and welfare, and property and financial affairs. They can only be set up when the loved one is in sound mind, in preparation for an emergency; once the emergency happens, it's too late. A friend of mine was in power of attorney hell because her parent had Alzheimer's and she had to apply to the Court of Protection to become a deputy: a long-winded, expensive and stressful process.

Still, I felt a little uneasy: I didn't want to take any more control over Dad's finances than was necessary. I was grateful for the clause in the guidelines that laid out principles for taking care of the finances, such as: 'A person should not be treated as lacking capacity just because they make an unwise decision, and, actions carried out should limit their rights and freedom of action as little as possible.'

One day my older brother called me to say he was concerned about Dad's spending. I digested his concerns and said I would bring up the matter with Dad when we went for a walk around the garden.

These walks had become our post-lunch ritual. I thought back to how the garden had looked just after Mum died: more stark than flower, more fence than green leaf. Now it was lush, crawling, flowering, a battleground of ripeness. John and I had worked on it together; I had designed the new raised bed and trellis at the far end and he had constructed it. As I took my father around, I supplied a commentary, as if I were a presenter on a nature programme. New pink roses; a yellow waterfall of rock rose; the flowers on the ceanothus like fat blue bees; the rich-leafed branch-muddle of the crab apple.

My dad loved being guided through it, loved having seasonal patterns explained and confirmed. When we stopped by two tall pines – ones he had planted decades back – he suddenly sparked up and reeled off their names: *Pinus strobus* and *Pinus cembroides*. His memory was normally such a blur that these moments of lucidity surprised me.

'Dad,' I began, then paused, pondering how to broach the issue.

Sometimes my father made bad spending decisions, such as mistakenly thinking his clock was broken when it just needed new batteries, then splashing out on a ridiculously expensive new item. Whilst Dad was in receipt of some generous pensions, they were not quite covering his living costs, which meant he was dipping into the money Mum had left him. John felt it would be wise to save this money for the future vicissitudes of old age: a stairlift, a walk-in shower, nurses. I had always admired my older brother's skill with money. He was sharp and money-smart. It was a good idea to stop Dad overspending; but I didn't want him to be like Mum, saving his money only to pass it all to us when he died. I wanted him to enjoy it. The trouble was keeping a balance, and of course not knowing how long he was going to live.

'Don't worry, Dad, it's nothing,' I said, wondering if I was being kind or just irresponsible.

Later that afternoon, Dad came back from Sainsbury's with a bottle of elderflower and rose pressé.

'Dad, that's too expensive,' I berated him gently, but he beamed, telling me it was his gift because he knew it was my favourite. Whenever I went away – I risked no more than a week at a time, once a month – I would call him every day and he'd tell me he'd bought me some apples, or some nice cheese, as though he wanted not just to spoil me, but to lure me back home with treats.

There had been just one occasion when I hadn't managed to call him every day. In the summer of 2018, I took my first holiday abroad in years. In Oslo, I fretted over roaming charges (in theory they shouldn't have been applied yet my balance seemed to be rocketing). I attempted to call him via Skype, only to get a message from the very phone blocker we'd installed on the phone saying: 'This number has chosen not to accept this type of call.' When I got back, ten days later, my dad was in a terrible way – swaying, drumming, barely speaking. It was the only time that year that he came close to a descent back into catatonia and I realised then that I couldn't ever miss a day's call. I was his rock. His stability wasn't just dependent on that rainbow array of pills he took day and night; it was about feeling safe, feeling loved, about knowing I was there.

34

I stood outside Covent Garden tube station, scrutinising every dark-haired man who swiped and exited through the gates, wondering if reality would match the promises of technology.

A tall Italian man wearing glasses approached me.

'Hey.' He had a lopsided smile. 'Are you Sam?'

In the local pub, we sat together to eat and drink and chat and size each other up.

Around this time, people often asked me if I wanted to join a carers' support group. I always said no. Instead, I joined a dating site. I made sure that I didn't tick the 'long term' relationship box. I was still romantically hungover from my breakup with Thom. Moreover, I knew that a relationship was incompatible with caring; I still felt a bit grumpy about that. But flings would be better than nothing. No, I didn't want to join a carers' group even though I knew they brought a lot of people solace and help and assuaged their loneliness. I felt that I needed *escape* in my spare time. I needed activities that were the complete opposite of caring. I liked disappearing into the dark hush of a cinema and entering someone's story; I swam in the beauty of art galleries. I needed fun, adventure, freedom, anything to help to eradicate the restlessness that prickled me from time to time as I struggled with my responsibilities

And, for a brief time, it worked. I half-feared my flings would be soulless and empty; instead, they were fun and uplifting and sweet. They infused into the lightness of summer, the romance of kissing as the twilight set in, ventures to a strange flat, repressing giggles so as not to wake up flatmates.

I had anticipated that the man I was sitting next to in the pub would follow the pattern. But it was becoming clear that he hadn't read my profile properly. He seemed to have assumed that, being female, I must be looking for a long-term relationship. I felt too awkward to correct him. He looked at my lips, my throat. He listened carefully to all I said, making judgements, weighing pros and cons, assessing whether I was Girlfriend Material.

He was a handsome man and I felt a flicker of interest stirring. What if I could have a relationship again; what if I just gave it a try?

A new question: he wanted to know why I was still living with my dad.

'Well, he's got schizophrenia,' I said. 'I'm his carer.'

His beer froze mid-air. 'That's hereditary, isn't it?'

Shaken by his response, I replied in a stiff, scientific voice that genes could play a part, but there was also the issue of epigenetics: genes that could be switched on or off depending upon environmental factors. Lifestyle, upbringing, treatment plan, all contributed too.

Silence. He downed his beer. 'I think I should head off.'

I was stung. I walked out into the streets of London feeling tainted.

The next day I was scribbling a shopping list and at the word *ginger* my pen froze. I recognised the distinctive loop of the g. I thought back to the week after my mother's death, when a relative had phoned me and gasped at the sound of my voice. 'You sound *exactly* like her,' they'd said, making me feel like a medium carrying her ghost. I had her voice, I mimicked her handwriting flourishes, I cooked recipes that she had left behind, cared for my dad in the same way she had. I had her father's blue eyes. She'd repeatedly asserted that I took after *her* side of the family, as though I was exclusively her daughter, as though she had generated both sperm and egg.

Perhaps she'd been afraid I would inherit my father's illness. When I had visited him in Summerfields, I had been able to empathise deeply in part because I knew that I could have ended up in that ward myself, had life and luck gone differently. I also sensed that my creative energies might have been inherited from him, though this was intuitive and I had no evidence that this was true.

I was in Waterloo with a little time to spare, browsing in a station bookshop. I looked for titles on schizophrenia and found none, but I did find a self-help book that gave advice on how to make use of your inner psycho to achieve corporate success: *The Good Psychopath's Guide to Success.* I considered that my father, whilst not contributing economically to society, was one of the kindest, most sensitive men I had ever known. Yet the chances of a self-help book about developing one's inner schizophrenic appearing on a bookshelf any time soon seemed slim.

In a capitalist regime, being a useful member of society is defined as being productive. 'To be mad is to be idle,' Andrew Scull observes. Capitalism has taken this to such an extreme that psychopathy is re-labelled sanity if it is seen as something that can make money. Meanwhile, a lack of productivity might be pinned on the vulnerable – in 2017 the Chancellor Philip Hammond linked low levels of productivity in the UK with a higher percentage of disabled people in employment. The idea is a regression to the Victorian era. In 1872, *Good Words* ran an article by a reporter who had paid a visit to Caterham Asylum, who observed that many of the patients 'are evidently drafted from the poorest portion of the population'. He celebrated that they had been set to work, for many of them, 'prior to their entrance into the Asylum, had never done a day's useful labour in their lives'. Meanwhile, he observed the condition of the children there was to be 'deplored ... because no healthy occupation could be found for them'.

In Germany, the eradication of schizophrenics and bipolar patients by the Nazis remains a lesser-known feature of the Holocaust. It is estimated that around a quarter of a million people with schizophrenia were killed or sterilised between 1939–45. The Nazi regime thought that people with mental illnesses were 'life unworthy of life'. The Nazis argued that poverty and disease arose from hereditary conditions, and ran a propaganda campaign highlighting the cost to the state. In the 1930s, Hitler declared: 'It is right that the worthless lives of such creatures should be ended, and that this would result in certain savings in terms of hospitals, doctors and nursing staff.' The only exceptions were those patients who were doing economically important work in the institutions; in 1939 the directors of German hospitals were asked to fill in forms for their patients detailing their diagnosis and capacity for work. But no exception was made for those with schizophrenia. The Nazis were determined to wipe out every last one of them. Schizophrenics were disproportionately targeted because – according to the historian Henry Friedlander – 'the overriding criterion' for selection for death in the T-4 mass murder programme was 'the ability to do productive work'.

Had I been alive at that time, I would have been sterilised. In 1935, Franz Kallman, a Berlin psychiatrist and geneticist, made a speech calling for the examination of all relatives of schizophrenics in order to identify the non-affected carriers. This they did by noticing minor anomalies. But all of these theories were based on wrongful scientific ideas. The Nazis mistakenly thought that schizophrenia was caused by a single gene. In reality it is caused by hundreds of genes; such variants may be carried by a large number of people, most of whom will never develop schizophrenia. The Nazis did not succeed in wiping out schizophrenia, despite their mass exterminations; it still remains in 1 per cent of the population in Germany, a standard percentage worldwide.

And if schizophrenia is such a terrible genetic cocktail to inherit (and I am not convinced it is), then why has it remained in the gene pool at all? Why hasn't Nature bred it out entirely?

At a recent social gathering, I met a psychiatrist who said to me: 'If you have a little of the schizophrenic gene, it's useful for becoming a writer – but if you have a lot, then it's terrible.' He was speaking metaphorically, but I understood what he meant. I was reminded of a paper which argued that people with mild features of schizophrenia who do not experience breakdown often enjoy high levels of creativity.

Being the healthy relative of a family member with psychosis has its advantages. Jon Löve Karlsson, based at the Institute of Genetics in Reykjavik, conducted a study in Iceland which examined the first-degree relatives of people with a history of psychosis. They were 30 per cent more likely to be in the Icelandic *Who's Who*, with many of them excelling in academia, politics and the arts; they were 50 per cent more likely to have published a book. Think of numerous famous creatives who were on the knife edge between genius and madness: Virginia Woolf, Sylvia Plath, Richard Dadd, William Blake, Robert Schumann, Vincent van Gogh, Herman Melville, to name but a few.

The academic David Horrobin also cites studies showing that 'families with schizophrenic members seem to have a greater variety of skills and abilities, and a greater likelihood of producing high-achievers'. Einstein's son suffered from schizophrenia, as did Carl Jung's mother. When James Joyce's daughter Lucia developed schizophrenia, Joyce took her to see

Jung, who said that they were like two people going to the bottom of a river, 'one falling and the other diving'. It sounded like an apt description of me and my father. My meditation and my writing felt so similar: dives into deep waters, a place of both silence and infinite possibility.

I had inherited my father's extreme sensitivity, which meant that I was easily hurt; but I knew that the flipside of this was a kind of hyper-empathy; I identified with Virginia Woolf's 'Cut me anywhere, & I bleed too profusely. Life has bred too much "feeling" of a kind in me.' I found it easy to slip into the mindset of someone of another gender, another job, another age; I had turned up at numerous literary events to find people amazed to find that I was female, fooled by my first-person novels written from the viewpoints of young men. The experience of the poet Theodore Roethke, a manic depressive, was one I recognised: 'Suddenly I knew how to enter into the life of everything around me. I knew how it felt to be a tree, a blade of grass, even a rabbit ...' When I was a teenager, on the verge of collapse, this had nearly been fatal, but now that I was a writer, stabilised by meditation, it was a creative asset I treasured.

There are biological similarities between the brain chemistry of schizophrenics and creatives. Researchers at the Karolinska Institutet in Sweden cite that both healthy, highly creative people and schizophrenics have a lower density of dopamine D2 receptors in the thalamus. The thalamus is a relay centre. It filters information before it reaches the cortex, which is responsible for decision making; if less is filtered, more creative ideas can spark. As Professor Ullén, one of the researchers concluded: 'Thinking outside the box might be facilitated by having a somewhat less intact box.'

Creativity is about making connections. Dr Johnson defined metaphysical poetry as 'heterogeneous ideas … yoked by violence together'. When Zelda Fitzgerald was recovering in Prangins, the doctors noted that in her speech she tended to make sudden, jerky jumps from one subject to another. Again, this was one of Zelda's characteristics that was seen as a quirk before she was incarcerated, then labelled a symptom once she was sick. In her debut novel *Save Me the Waltz,* there are similarly surreal imaginative jumps, such as the moment her heroine Alabama details her amorous feelings for her lover, David Knight – and then, in the next sentence, imagines herself crawling inside his ear: 'Like a mystic maze the folds and ridges rose in desolation; there was nothing to indicate one way from another. She stumbled on and finally reached the medulla oblongata'.

And this is why the gene perpetuates, it has been argued: in order for society to move forward, we need innovation, and with innovators there comes a little madness.

Of course, there is a danger of romanticising mental illness, as the Romantic poets once did, equating madness with genius. It feels more than a little arrogant, if not cruel, for me to suggest that my father's great suffering has been worthwhile because I am able to wake up every morning brimming with creative ideas and to make a living from them. For those with severe psychosis, there is no romance to their tragedy. But learning more about these genetic advantages did save me from an uneasy, lingering feeling that I had bad genes, that I was tainted in some way, that having children at some point in the future might not be a good idea. And, I hope, they might help us, as a society, to treasure the benefits of schizophrenia and psychosis, rather than seeing those who suffer from them as the Other.

There was no need for my dad to come with me to the vet. He was too old to help carry Leo; if anything, it made the walk there more painful because I had to go slowly to match his pace whilst lugging the carrier. But I said I needed his 'moral support'. My dad did so few things in the outside world and this was a way of making him feel more integrated.

A year ago, my vet had said my cat had only six months to live. But here she was, still thriving and purring and playful. The vet looked amazed and said she'd made a miraculous recovery.

'Fantastic news!' I cried, kissing Leo's furry head. Dad smiled, looking quietly pleased.

Out in the foyer, we went up to pay the bill. The receptionist, I suddenly noticed, was giving my dad a weird look. Why? There was nothing wrong with him, no symptoms of catatonia. Then my perspective shifted and I saw him as she did, as a stranger viewing a man who looked a bit odd, who was trembling slightly, twitching. I had stopped noticing this, because these things had normalised for me. I gave the receptionist a cross look. It didn't make any difference. She was still judging him, and I resolved not to go back to that particular vet.

On the way home, it struck me that things had changed since the days when I'd been embarrassed to travel into London with my dad on the tube. Caring had collapsed the distance between us. He had stopped being a ghost in the house and had become my father again. I was no longer ashamed of him; I had become his protector. I felt proud to be his daughter; proud to be his carer. Because I knew that underneath his twitches, the side effects of his medicine, was a wonderful man who had once been a boy who walked in the streets loving the dawn's magic.

35

And what of F. Scott Fitzgerald: did he ever rise to the challenge of caring for Zelda?

It is 1938 and Zelda has been in Highland Hospital, Asheville for two years. She has been in and out of clinics for nearly a decade. Scott has not failed her financially: the colossal fees have always been paid. But over the course of the year, Scott and the Sayre family get into a fiery dispute over Zelda. She has improved; on holiday with her mother, Minnie, Zelda seems radiant, blooming and back to her old self. Now they want her released. Minnie writes to him: 'I feel that contact with those she loves is good for her and gives her a sense of protection … if Zelda can live here with me I am not afraid to try it.' Her sister Rosalind also petitions him: 'continued hospitalisation, against her will, will be detrimental'.

Scott regards their optimism as naivety. In the early days of their courtship his letters fondly depicted Zelda as his princess in a tower. Now he feels the tower *is* the right place for her, the safe place, where she can be looked after, perhaps for the rest of her life. 'Cure her I cannot and simply saying she's cured must make the Gods laugh,' he declares. He drafts a sarcastic, angry letter to Marjorie, Zelda's other sibling: '[it is a] preposterous idea that Zelda's sanity can be bought with a one way ticket to Montgomery ... You have nothing to offer.' He holds back from sending it, but composes another rude missive to Rosalind. He still hasn't forgotten the letter Rosalind sent him when Zelda was first put away. She wrote to him saying she ought to adopt Scottie, as though Scott wasn't even capable of parenting his own daughter. On the top of the letter he adds: 'When you people stink you certainly stink.'

Scott contacts Zelda's current doctor, Dr Carroll, and advises him that Zelda should not be released. That is the position they must maintain whilst her family froth and make a fuss. Then, as though he is a helpless observer with his hands tied, he writes to her family again, advising that Dr Carroll has said no, and if Zelda is released, she will not be able to return if the experiment goes wrong.

Why has Scott given up on hope of Zelda's recovery? He seems tired, worn out, jaded by alcohol and personal failures. He writes to Zelda and tells her to stop harassing him for her freedom – he has to look after their daughter, pay her school fees and work on his new novel. No doubt Scott's decision is influenced by the disasters of the past. His most recent novel, *Tender Is the Night*, was completed in La Paix, the house they stayed in after she was released from Phipps, in a smoggy, half-burnt study with watermarks staining the walls – the result of Zelda setting alight to the house after burning some old clothes in the fireplace upstairs. Living with her is like residing next to a volcano, a place of lush beauty, where lava can flow at a minute's notice. They gave an interview with the papers after the fire, claiming it was due to faulty electrics. They are keeping up a good act. But Scott must feel he can not keep up the show for both of them in squeaky-clean Hollywood. It is already tiring enough for him to keep it up for himself.

Hollywood: it is the third time Scott has tried to make it here. MGM gave him a contract and now he is freelancing. He lives in the San Fernando Valley and he is paying off his debts and living a quiet life. Having dried out in a clinic, his drinking is under control. Most of the time. He feels on probation. When he first arrived here, he could detect the pity in people's gazes, as though he was some kind of has-been. One guy even looked at him in surprise; he thought Scott had died long ago. Scott is conscious that he looks a little rough around the edges; the drink has softened his face and greyed his skin and his hair is receding. He is doing his best to be polite, to be professional, to make his living, to clean up his reputation. He has a new girlfriend, Sheilah, and her good influence helps. But the years have worn him down. It is all he can do to survive, to pay off his debts, to make the most of his final years; to produce a few more first-rate novels and leave behind some mark on the world.

And then comes the surprise.

A letter from Dr Carroll. Zelda is ready for release. Scott is surprised – and positive – but then doubt comes. Zelda and Hollywood would be a dangerous combination. He writes to Zelda and shares the good news with her. But in a subsequent letter, he warns her: 'I wish you were going to brighter surroundings but this is certainly not the time to come to me.'

Scott has resigned from caring. He cannot play the role anymore; he has given up in defeat.

F. Scott Fitzgerald was a man who tried to make the best of a difficult situation, but in the end, he was a terrible carer. But then I wonder what it would have been like if my father's catatonic attacks had gone on and on. Just one year was enough to run me into the ground; after a decade, it would have finished me off. I fear that after eight years of being ground down, I might have abandoned Dad to a home and given up like Scott. That said, I can't imagine ever forcing my father to stay locked up if, say, my brothers had said they wanted to take care of him. Scott allowed his family feud, the ongoing blame game as to who was responsible for her illness, to colour his decision on what was best for Zelda.

As Scott's alcoholism worsened, there were direct echoes between his illness and Zelda's schizophrenia. His liver eventually became so poisoned that he suffered delirium tremens and could not eat solid food. Once, in 1935, he saw beetles and pink mice scurrying all over him; unlike Zelda, however, his hallucinations were not deemed madness or grounds for incarceration. When he finally, finally decided to get clean, it was his choice. He did it the way he wanted. He hired nurses and a doctor who looked after him, feeding him intravenously whilst he went cold turkey and suffered severe spells of vomiting. Writing to Harold Ober afterwards, he reported that he could finally sleep 'and tho my hair's grey I feel younger than for four years'.

In the end, the only reason Zelda did manage to escape from Highland Hospital was because Dr Carroll had been implicated in a rape case involving one of his patients. Writer Sally Cline has unearthed evidence that Carroll was also abusing several other female patients; Zelda was possibly one of them. This became Zelda's ammunition; she used it to fight her way to freedom. On 15 April 1940, she climbed onto a bus leaving for Montgomery and headed home to live with her mother.

At first, Zelda found it hard to adapt. She couldn't write; she couldn't paint. As she explained to Scott, 'it requires most of my resources to keep out of hospital'. But as the months went by, she began her artwork again, exhibiting locally and working on a new novel entitled *Caesar's Things*. This is what I love about Zelda: despite all the doctors telling her to swallow her ambition and be a good wife, and Scott trying to beat down her creativity, she refused to surrender.

Like my mother, Scott found himself fragmented in his relationships. He did not divorce Zelda. He did not want her to ever feel deserted. Sheilah was unaware of how frequently he was in contact with his wife, via letters to her. His love for Zelda always lingered with a nostalgia that was part of the romantic, destructive impulse in his personality; in his (unfinished) final novel, *The Last Tycoon*, he immortalised Zelda as Minna, the beautiful dead wife of the protagonist, a woman he mourns.

When you read about what happened to Zelda and the

way she was punished, controlled, labelled 'mad' for not fitting into society's ideal of a good wife, then you can understand why the closing down of asylums had such traction in the 1960s. The transition to care in the community that followed seemed a positive step forward – a way of freeing the vulnerable and allowing them to lead more independent lives. But it is important to remember that this process was underpinned by the expansion of the welfare state. In the States, President Lyndon Johnson introduced a Great Society programme in the sixties, which meant that discharged mental health patients would have a guaranteed income; in Britain, Edward Heath's government brought in a raft of social security payments, such as Invalidity Benefit, in 1971.

It seems to be a tragic pattern in society that during times of austerity, it is the vulnerable in society who suffer the most. One of the worst examples of this occurred during the First World War. A loss of staff, budget cuts and harsh rationing meant that patients in asylums in Britain and France starved to death; in 1918 a third of patients died in one hospital in Buckinghamshire as a result.

With the savage cutting of benefits after 2010, and the snags and snares of Universal Credit, many people who are mentally ill are falling through the safety net. When the welfare state was reformed, all of those on sickness benefit were reassessed. Private companies ran the assessments, with a fit-for-work test that has been deemed far too crude by various charities. Over £100 million has been wasted on the appeals process for disability benefits; over 60 per cent of appeals have been upheld.

During the appeals process, during the long waits without benefits, the stress is catastrophic for carers – not just the financial strain, but the isolating stress of effectively being told that their lives are a fantasy. The carer's daily reality might be the grind of washing and feeding and dispensing medicines and love, yet all the time, haunting them, is a dry, short letter telling them that their 'patient' is fit for work, that they ought to be in a nine-to-five job, a mismatch between real life and state indifference that provokes a sense of deep dislocation. A recent ITV news report said that many carers are simply too 'exhausted' to go through the appeals process.

In June 2018, I noticed *#CarersActionDay* trending on Twitter. The government had brought in a series of new measures to help carers. They were a positive step forward. Carers would have dedicated employment rights: workers would be offered flexible working hours, including extended lunch breaks, ten extra days off a year, and the freedom to start work earlier and finish later. They could also enjoy paid carer's leave so that they could attend hospital appointments. Carers, I read, save the UK economy £132 billion a year, and since 6,000 people become a carer every day in this country, they deserved greater support.

I was pleased that new measures had been introduced but since I was self-employed, none would make the slightest impact on me. When I did a google search, I noticed that many people had had the same reaction as me: what carers need most is more money. The Carer's Allowance was inadequate, was the general consensus. A full-time carer earns less than the minimum wage; most carers combine their caring with full-time work, choosing exhaustion over poverty.

I read another piece, in the *Guardian*, that discussed the impending care crisis. Struggling to break even, care homes were going bankrupt at a record rate. An elderly 'self-funder' in a home will usually pay around £845 per week; the council will only pay £621 on average. Once again, the government were suggesting that we take care back into the community, into our homes, with families acting as carers. But in the comments section of the article I saw worries and objections: 'How can we provide for our children if we give up work to look after our parents?' Another: 'How will we have the energy to do this if many of us will be in our sixties ourselves when we start needing to look after our parents?'

There are currently over a million elderly people who are not getting the help that they need, who require assistance with going to the toilet, dressing, washing, and who have been left to flounder. With an ageing population, this is a group which is rapidly increasing. The more the state recedes, the less we are free to make a choice as to whether or not we want to be a carer. And even with the thousands of us who become carers on a daily basis, stepping in as the state steps back, there will not be enough of us. The numbers don't add up. Three in five informal carers are over the age of fifty, which means that soon they will be the ones needing care, and with so many of us living longer, there will be too many old and too few young, a chasm between supply and demand.

* * *

I felt shocked when I recently revisited Manchester and Liverpool after a long time away; every few feet I found myself passing someone on the pavement with a cup in hand, desperate for money. I'd never seen so many homeless people on the streets.

My dad, who doesn't get out much into the city, kept reading reports about this in the newspapers. One stated that 80 per cent of rough sleepers in London who died in 2017 had mental health care needs. Then I received a call from my older brother, who said Dad had been writing too many cheques for charities: £20 here, £20 there. Too much for a man on a pension, my brother said – he'd have to cut back. Though I agreed, I was touched by my father's compassion, his social conscience: most of the cheques were for homeless charities.

As Patrick Cockburn, a journalist whose son suffers from schizophrenia, notes; we are in an era where those who are vulnerable have never had so many rights, but at the same time, so little care. Thankfully, it is much harder for someone to do what Scott Fitzgerald did to Zelda and keep them locked up month after month because they cannot face caring for them. The Mental Health Act (1983) means that even if you are sectioned for twenty-eight days, you have a right to appeal against the decision. However, reductions in the numbers of NHS beds for those who are mentally ill has been the biggest of any sector: a 72 per cent fall from 67,112 to just 18,730 beds between 1987 and 2016/17.

Back at Dad's, whilst doing the washing up, I listened to

a Radio 4 discussion about care homes. Many of the residents hadn't expected to live as long as they had. They'd had to sell their houses to be there, and some were terrified of running out of funds. For those without money, the council was sending a meagre payment to the care home – but not enough to cover costs. Care home managers were therefore faced with a terrible dilemma: should they lower their fees, which might risk closure some way down the line, or force some residents to leave? I heard the fear in those quavering, elderly voices, a genuine terror of being thrown out on the streets and abandoned.

What was the solution to the problem, the presenter asked? One elderly woman declared fiercely that we should all look after each other; we should act as one big family.

I've noticed that being a carer has increased my empathy towards vulnerable people. When I see people living on the streets, when I hear radio discussions, I feel a great sadness; I want to do something to help. I read about a scheme where you can take in a homeless person for the night, but I knew I wouldn't be taking in anyone extra in our spare room; my dad would find it an invasion and wouldn't be able to cope. There is only so much caring we can do as individuals, and when the state steps back too much, we're left feeling overwhelmed by the number of people who need help. The right balance needs to be struck between charity and state intervention: if we need to care more as individuals, we also need collectively to care more as a nation.

36

'Look,' my dad said. We were sitting at the dining-room table; I was doing my emails and he was gesturing at a page in the fat white album that contained his wedding photos.

I wasn't sure why he'd suddenly picked up the album. He hadn't looked at it for years.

It was a photo of him and my mother. They both looked radiant and young and full of promise. Mum's hair flowed like dark wine over her white gown; Dad's grin was boyish, and his chest was puffed up, as though he was proud to have got her. Then he added in a vexed tone: 'My brothers and sister didn't come to the wedding …'

'Oh,' I said, feeling disturbed. I thought again of my father as a boy, creeping out at dawn, taking his sister by the hand, and walking through the morning twilight magic. I'd seen another childhood photo of him recently. He looked like a mischievous cherub.

My dad was still stable. But it was haunting me again, the urge to know a cause. Yes, I understood why he'd had catatonia, but not why he'd developed schizophrenia in the first place. On Radio 4, I heard an expert, Sir Robin Murray, discussing a paper he'd written outlining that schizophrenics were more likely to have suffered a childhood 'hazard', such as meningitis or not doing as well as their siblings. It left me wondering if my father had been the outsider in his family, growing up, and this was why they'd all missed his wedding. My imagination started to conjure up all sorts of plots: sibling rivalry, a tragic mistake, parental hierarchies of favourite children.

I was back to reading about schizophrenia again: I'd discovered a book by Eleanor Longden. It was 'a story about finding meaning in madness'. She had been studying at university when she'd woken up one day and found she was hearing a voice. It was narrating her life in the third person, observing and recording her actions. The voice felt natural; she didn't feel afraid of it; not until she told a friend, who insisted she seek medical help. For Eleanor: 'It was as if my friend had picked up a baton, which was handed to a doctor, then ultimately to a psychiatrist.' Hospital admissions followed, the voices she heard were labelled scary, and the more she fought them, the more they multiplied and became aggressive. She ended up on what she calls 'the Schizophrenia Scrapheap' – 'diagnosed, drugged, discarded'.

But Eleanor felt that the voices were messengers. They were carrying important messages about the child abuse she had suffered growing up: deep traumas that lay buried inside her.

The story of Eleanor's recovery was one of the most inspiring things I'd ever read. With the help of a supportive doctor who told her that she could recover, she bound her shattered self back together. She dealt with her voices by setting aside a slot each day when she would listen to them, accepting them rather than resisting them, and recognising that 'the most menacing, aggressive voices actually represented the parts of me that had been hurt the most – and as such, it was these voices that needed to be shown the greatest compassion and care'. She continued her studies and achieved the highest first ever awarded on her degree course, followed by an MA course which landed her the highest mark in her year. She has argued that psychiatry should not ask the question 'What's wrong with you?' but 'What happened to you?' She champions the Hearing Voices Movement, which believes that voice hearing is a survival strategy, 'a sane response to insane circumstances', and that voice-hearers can live rich, fulfilling lives and contribute to society.

Severe abuse in childhood trebles the risk of schizophrenia (and other related psychoses) descending later in life. Dissociation – the splitting away of yourself from experience – is a powerful form of defence. I discussed it with Tomazi, a friend of mine and a psychotherapist on Harley Street, over coffee in St Pancras. He pointed out that a fractured self, though weakened, is harder to attack. He waved his hands here and there and here and said: 'If you're in pieces, then where can you be attacked? It's harder to pinpoint a place *to* attack.' For a schizophrenic, that shattered self might manifest in the form of voices, which seem external. But tests show that they are really internal voices masquerading as separate identities, for they are accompanied by heightened activity in

Broca's area, the brain's speech centre – just as we do when we hear external voices.

We all experience a Heraclitan flow of inner monologue all day, and sometimes the voice in our mind splits into parent/child as we debate a key decision or a moral issue, for example. Yet we like to maintain the illusion of one I, a Self that is a sole Me. As Christopher Bollas notes, for the schizophrenic: 'In their plurality, the voices that now contain the function of the I are existentially closer to the truth than our "normal" illusion of unitary mental status. The fact is that the I has never been a unified perspective but has always represented many differing views. We are heterogeneous, full of contradictions …' To preserve a sense of sanity, the illusion of 'I' prevails.

In *The Crack-Up*, Scott Fitzgerald writes about his breakdown – 'there was not an "I" any more' – and describes various friends who represent aspects of his conscience: Edmund Wilson is his intellectual conscience, Hemingway his artistic conscience. Once he snapped at Zelda: 'Can't you stop your "I"s? Who are you? You are a person of six or seven different parts. Now, why don't you integrate yourself?', projecting onto his wife a neurosis of his own. This sense of a loss of self, a fragmentation of his psyche, was also echoed in his demand that Zelda rewrite an essay from her first person to the perspective of 'we', and so 'Show Mr and Mrs F–' became an essay narrated by them as a couple. Later in life, Scott reflected with nostalgia: 'Once we were one person and always it will be a little that way.' With his flagging sense of 'I', Zelda's strong, independent 'I' was a threat; he needed to collapse them both into one.

Eleanor Longden's story lingered. It uplifted me and yet it troubled me.

A week later, I suffered a bout of flu. Several days were spent in bed, drifting in and out of sleep. I felt as though I was somehow sweating out a repressed grief for my father, in the heat of fever and the pounding in my temples. It seemed such a waste, his life. If only he had been born in a different era, when his voice might have been accepted rather than labelled a sickness he had to fight. The medications he'd taken were not cures, just compromises, putting him in purgatory, half-awake, half-alive. One drug he'd been given, years back, had been dispensed in too high a dose and left chunks of his memory missing, like bridges with bombed-out parts, roads that couldn't be crossed. My dad wasn't the only victim; the drug had been rebranded and sold under a different name after the controversy. If only in his early life he'd learnt to meditate like I had. Why had I enjoyed such good luck and redemption – why not him? My mother had been convinced that his schizophrenia had begun *within* the psychiatric ward he entered after his breakdown, as if the place tore at his spiderweb-fine cracks and made the shattering permanent.

I fell into sleep, into the pit of nightmare. My dream self was standing in the hallway. My father was climbing the stairs. I put my arms around him with an intimacy I would never do in waking life. He was crying. I asked him: *Why did you get ill?* He said: *I can't ever tell you.* He went into his bedroom and shut the door.

I woke up.

The wedding album! Downstairs I sat before the dining-room table in my pyjamas and opened it up again. I recalled my dad saying: 'My brothers and sister didn't come to the wedding …' I wondered if I dare call them and ask why they hadn't gone.

Then I came across a photo: Mum and Dad, just married, standing right next to his brothers, and his sister with her husband and baby.

They *had* all been there.

'Dad!' I called out.

'They came!' he beamed, looking astonished. Sitting down, he flicked through all the photos again, rewriting his memory.

'I can't seem to find out *why*,' I concluded, after relaying the whole story to Tomazi. My father would probably always remain an enigma, suggested Tomazi. When I spoke to him about Eleanor Longden, he also reassured me. The fact that being off medication had worked for her did not mean it was the right solution for everyone, he said. Everyone had to find their own way. Some might need medication, some counselling. There was no definitive cure. Longden herself had argued that each person's journey was unique.

I felt at peace after our talk. Of course my father needed his medication: he would be catatonic without it. For him, it was the scaffolding around his life that allowed him to sleep and eat and talk and be.

But I still believed that Longden's experience was the way forward. I kept coming across case studies where clinicians had successfully treated schizophrenia solely through therapy. And then I discovered why schizophrenics in developing countries are shown to have better rates of long-term recovery than those in developed: at first it was thought to be the result of cultural differences, attitudes, family ties, but in the end they realised that it was medical. Those in developing countries took less anti-psychotic medicine and in the long term they did better without it. A 2015 study demonstrated that anti-psychotics cause brain damage/atrophy and the shrinking of brain tissue.

Perhaps we place too much emphasis on pills in our current society; I suppose it is simpler, cheaper and less time-consuming to medicate a patient and sedate them rather than offer them weeks of therapy. An over-reliance on pills reinforces the idea that mental illness is purely biological. I looked into environmental factors, desperately searching for reasons that might chime with my dad's history. I found out that even the time of year that you are born can influence the onset of schizophrenia: those born in winter or early spring in the northern hemisphere are more likely to develop it later in life than those born any other time of year. Maternal stress or sickness can play a part; ironically, given the Nazi determination to wipe out those with the illness, the children of mothers born during the German invasion of the Netherlands in the 1940s, where the mothers suffered food deprivation due to the Nazi blockade, had higher rates of schizophrenia. Cannabis can trigger the illness in those predisposed to the disorder. Living in the city rather than the countryside apparently increases risks; and being in a minority group is also a factor, with some ethnic minorities showing higher rates of the illness, just as people who are single are more likely to develop psychosis if they live in areas with fewer single people compared to those living in places where being single is more common.

However, my father was born in August and claimed he had never smoked cannabis. I don't know if rationing might have affected his gestation. I don't know if something hidden in his childhood, something he could never face or admit, might have caused it.

When Scott explored Zelda's madness in *Tender Is the Night*, he gave Nicole (Zelda) a defining reason: that her father had abused her as a child. As far as we know, this wasn't the case in real life. It reflects his desire to control the narrative of her illness, to have the last word in the blame game and assert that her family was responsible rather than his drinking. It can also be a solace to create an alternative reality where illness has one clear reason. As a novelist, I craved that neatness too. But I never found that puzzle piece that made everything fall into place. I had to accept that my father's illness was a riddle; all I had were fragments that I could not put together. I would never know its roots, but I could still be a good carer to him. He didn't need me to know or understand one key cause: he just needed me to be there for him.

37

'FOR SALE' said the sign that poked out of our neighbours' front garden. We felt sad that they were going. They were the loveliest people – warm, generous, friendly without being nosy, and if I was ever away and they thought something was wrong with my dad, they'd give me a call. But they were an elderly couple and both were becoming frail now; the husband had fallen over and had had a hip operation, and his wife had such a bad knee that she could only walk slowly.

Their daughter had stepped in as carer. She had persuaded them to sell the house so they could move over to Norfolk to be with her. Fleetingly, I wondered if this might be my answer – getting Dad to move somewhere else with me if and when the time came. But then I remembered how anxious he got just taking a train to a new place. He was anchored to our family home.

At least I could get away now and again. I escaped for a one-week trip to Romania, making sure I called my dad every day. I was now able to detect possible catatonia just from the tone of his voice, at which point I'd tell him to take a Valium.

Whilst I was away, I received a text from a friend, Dylan, asking if he could stay at ours for the night. I knew Dylan had been going through a tough time recently. He was down on his luck and lacked a permanent home. I texted back: **'I'm on holiday, but I've called Dad and he says it's fine for you to stay!'**

I was a little nervous. Whenever Dylan had come to stay with me in the past, he'd got on well with my dad. But it would be different with just the two of them. Recently one of Dad's careworkers had persuaded him to attend a social group, but it hadn't worked out. All Dad did was go there for twenty awkward minutes, have a cup of tea, and flee home. Making conversation was not his forte. I feared a house guest might all be too intrusive for him to handle.

On my return home, I found that Dad had been the perfect host. I hadn't realised at the time, but Dylan had been in a deep state of depression when he'd asked for somewhere to stay. Dad had recited a menu of what they were going to have for lunch, proudly served up the meal, and engaged with him at the table (I think it had been a typical conversation, whereby my dad had to be asked questions and gave cautious answers, but Dylan had still enjoyed it). He had shown such hospitality, warmth and kindness that Dylan had felt lifted up out of the fug of his misery and poverty, applied for an emergency grant and got one. It had been a turning point for him, after weeks of trouble: and all because my dad had been so lovely.

I felt so touched by the story: I saw in my dad's ability to care for someone else not just a sign of compassion, but also good health. For a fleeting moment, I even wondered if my dad might be becoming more self-sufficient. Then I opened the cupboard and saw it was stuffed full of Belgian buns after his recent trip to the supermarket. Whilst I'd been away, he'd fallen into bad habits.

'*Dad!*' I admonished him gently, pointing. 'You know you're not allowed sugar.' It was another one of the hellish side effects of his medicines: his new anti-psychotic had made him border-line diabetic.

'But there's not much sugar in them,' he protested, and looked pleased when I said I'd make him some sugar-free cakes with xylitol. The thought came to me: *I'm going to be looking after him till the day I die,* and then the troubling caveat: *actually, I may not be able to; finances might not allow it.* If Dad became immobile, if he needed constant support and I stopped work, my Carer's Allowance would not be enough for me to live on and pay off my debts; thus, being a full-time carer could potentially bankrupt me. I had to hope that, in the future, there might be better financial support so that I had a choice to care for him to the very end.

'Thanks, I love you. This is a picture of the beautiful Wilson's Bird-of-Paradise of Papua New Guinea. I bequeath this bird to you.'

I had to read over Z's email twice to be sure I hadn't imagined the first sentence. I love you! What was this? I rewound time back thirteen years to 2005, the first night we'd spent together, roaming around London, dancing together at a club, sharing our first kiss as music hammered into our heartbeats. Z had asserted that our liaison should just be a casual thing. There's so much fire between us, he said, that it can't be sustained, it will just burn out and we'll have a beautiful friendship. I had been disappointed. For all my smiles and shrugs and 'oh yes, casual sounds a good idea', I had hoped for more. But he was so charismatic, and I was so enamoured by him, that I had been ready to accept our affair on his terms. And later, when I was more self-aware and a little more cynical, I became happy with it this way, both committed and casual, everything and nothing all at once.

I love you. Maybe he was just drunk, I told myself, feeling anxious. How should I reply?

'Your dad's doing really well,' Tony, his careworker, remarked to me, looking pleased.

We were attending one last follow-up meeting. My dad had made such good progress that he was going to be discharged by the mental health crisis team. On the bus home, I sat next to him; I could not stop smiling.

I realised then that I wasn't caring for him out of guilt anymore, or because I had made a promise to my mum: I was doing it because I felt a responsibility to do so, because I loved him and wanted to look after him.

A few weeks earlier I had started working on this memoir. I remember telling a friend of mine that I was worried being a carer might be seen as a boring topic to explore. Unglamorous. I said that perhaps I ought to choose a sexier subject. He replied that this was exactly why I ought to write it, because there are numerous books out there about doctors and high-flying surgeons and so few about those for whom caring is an unpaid, everyday duty. There are currently 6.5 million carers in the UK, which means that 1 in 8 of us are carers; the number is set to rise quickly, increasing by 60 per cent by 2030. In spring 2019, the government announced that their green paper on social care would be delayed – the fifth delay in two years. And so the crisis keeps deepening, without a resolution in sight.

We live in a society where being a carer is undervalued, not just financially, but in terms of status. Inequality is growing in our country – at a faster pace than the rest of Europe – and its documented effect on our national psyche is to make us all suffer more status anxiety, more fear, more suspicion and feel less compassionate to those in need. Being a carer might be a strain, it might make you feel trapped, anxious, tired, but it does also have its positives: the development of love, kindness, compassion. But I'm not sure these qualities are valued that much, in part because they were once associated with women, and with women being forced to play the role of angel in the house. As a feminist, I celebrate women being strong, assertive, forging their own path in life. But I can't help thinking: why do we have to label love, compassion, kindness as sickly 'feminine' qualities – why can't we overturn that? Why can't they be qualities that we just value in both women *and* men? Why can't men be encouraged to have those more? This is why it is crucial that the government gives carers both practical and financial support. The lack of the latter renders caring unattractive, maintaining its status as lowly, unpaid 'woman's work'.

I love you, I wrote to Z, and left it hanging on the screen.

Sometimes I worried about Z dying. How awful it would have been if he did pass away and I had never said I loved him. Ever since my mum's death, I had a sharper awareness of mortality, and sometimes suffered paranoid phases where I was convinced I was going to lose a loved one. But if I did reply in the positive to Z, our relationship might shift to a different realm and come into conflict with caring, and then it might shatter. I would rather keep it as it was, compart-mentalised, than lose it at all.

So I deleted the words and just sent him a warm, friendly reply as though he'd never said it. His reply was equally breezy, and we carried on as before.

I am in the gift shop of the Tate Modern. I'm picking out a postcard for my dad. I've just seen the Picasso exhibition and I feel drunk on its colours. It's a shame that my father is too scared of travelling into the capital to ever venture out to exhibitions. Every time I visit one, I bring him back a postcard, as though I've been on a trip abroad.

On the train home, the setting sun spills its gold onto the screen of my mobile. I receive a text from a friend who's adventuring in Berlin. There are still days when I feel restlessness jiggling inside me. Days when I feel envious of friends who are free to travel, wonder if my love life will ever be viable. And then there are days when I treasure the experience of looking after my father, feel a bliss in my heart when I cook him a meal and see the joy in his face when he tucks in, or when I call him and I hear the affection in his voice. These oscillating states are typical of bearing any great responsibility for another person; it has its rewards, it has its restrictions. My father may not have accomplished great things; his life has been more of anti-life, in a way. But I believe that he is a very special man, and it has been a privilege to look after him.

Home. I open the door, find my dad sitting in his armchair. When I pass him the postcard, his face lights up. He gazes at it, drinks it in. For him, this is as meaningful as a trip to the Louvre, the Met, or the Tate. Then, carefully, he adds it to the pile of postcards that I've given him. It has become a record of the years gone by since my mother died, starting with a Da Vinci and ending with a Picasso, and in that moment, I feel how lucky I am to be here with him, and I want to freeze time, stop all change. But I notice the lines that thicken about his eyes as he smiles, his white hair a little thinner than last year, and through the window the sunset is fading into the first dark of night.

Dad and me, August 1984

ACKNOWLEDGEMENTS

A huge thank you to my wonderful editor, Helen Garnons-Williams, for steering me through numerous drafts of this book, and my excellent agent, Will Francis at Janklow & Nesbit.

Thanks to my family for being supportive of the book. And thank you to friends who offered help, support, chat, inspiration: Tom Tomaszewski, Joe Thomas, Harald, Jude Cook, David & Leesha, Venetia Welby, Seraphina Madsen, James Higgerson, Susan Barker, Alexander Spears, Simon Lewis, Thom Cuell, Jenny, Anna Maconochie, Vanaja and Kumar Mahadevan, Dylan Evans, Neil Griffiths, Lola Jaye, Samantha Ellis, Sam Byers, Zakia Uddon, Emily Midorikawa, Jonathan Ruppin and Emma Claire Sweeney.

Thank you to those who helped during my parents' illnesses, from the wonderful Macmillan nurses to the hard-working, dedicated staff at St Helier hospital and the various psychiatric wards that my father stayed in, to our lawyer, David Lunn.

Thanks to the Society of Authors for their assistance,

particularly the contingency grants that they gave me in times of need. I also owe thanks to the Arts Council England for awarding me a grant to develop the final draft of the book.

PERMISSIONS

SELECT BIBLIOGRAPHY

Leonard and Virginia Woolf

Sowing, Growing, Beginning Again, Downhill All the Way, The Journey Not the Arrival Matters, Leonard Woolf (Hogarth Press 1960–1969)

Letters of Leonard Woolf, ed Frederic Spotts (Bloomsbury 1989)

Leonard Woolf: A Biography, Victoria Glendinning (Simon & Schuster 2006)

Mrs Dalloway, Virginia Woolf (Hogarth Press 1925; Penguin Classics 2000)

A Room of One's Own, Virginia Woolf (Hogarth Press 1929)

Moments of Being, Virginia Woolf (Pimlico edition 2002)

Virginia Woolf, A Writer's Diary 1918–1941, ed Leonard Woolf (Hogarth Press 1953; repr Persephone Books 2012)

The Diary of Virginia Woolf, i-v, ed Anne Olivier Bell and Andrew McNeillie (Hogarth Press 1977–1984)

The Letters of Virginia Woolf, vol. i-vi, ed Joanna Trautmann and Nigel Nicholson (Hogarth Press 1975–1980)

Selected Writings, Vita Sackville-West (St Martin's Press 2015)

Virginia Woolf, Hermione Lee (Chatto & Windus 1996)

Virginia Woolf: A Biography, Quentin Bell (Hogarth 1972)

Virginia Woolf, Selected Essays, ed David Bradshaw (OUP 2008)

Virginia Woolf, A Literary Life, John Mepham (Macmillan 1991)

The World Broke in Two: Virginia Woolf, T. S. Eliot, D. H. Lawrence, E. M. Forster and the Year that Changed Literature, Bill Goldstein (Bloomsbury 2018)

All that Summer She Was Mad: Virginia Woolf and Her Doctors, Stephen Trombey (Junction Books 1981)

Vanessa Bell, Selected Letters, ed Regina Marler (Bloomsbury 1993)

Zelda and Scott Fitzgerald

Zelda Fitzgerald: Her Voice In Paradise, Sally Cline (Faber & Faber 2002)

Save Me The Waltz, Zelda Fitzgerald (Charles Scribner's Sons 1932; Vintage edition 2001)

Zelda, Nancy Milford (Harper & Row 1970)

A Constant Circle: H. L. Mencken and his Friends, Sara Mayfield (Delacorte Press, 1968)

F. Scott Fitzgerald: A Life In Letters, ed Matthew J Bruccoli (Charles Scribner's Sons, 1994; Simon and Schuster 1995)

The Letters of F. Scott Fitzgerald, ed Andrew Turnbull (Harpercollins 1994, Charles Scribner's Sons, NY 1963; Bodley Head London 1964)

Dear Scott, Dearest Zelda – The Love Letters of F. Scott

and Zelda Fitzgerald, edited by Jackson R. Bryer and Cathy W. Barks (Bloomsbury 2003)

Scott Fitzgerald, Andrew Turnbull (Charles Scribner's Sons 1962)

Paradise Lost: A Life of F. Scott Fitzgerald, David S. Brown (Harvard University Press 2017)

Scott Fitzgerald, A Biography, Jeffrey Meyer (Harpercollins 1994)

The Crack-Up, F. Scott Fitzgerald, ed Edmund Wilson (New Directions, New York 1945–1956; Alma Classics Edition 2018)

This Side of Paradise, F. Scott Fitzgerald (Charles Scribner's Sons, New York 1920; Penguin, Harmondsworth 1963)

The Beautiful and the Damned, F. Scott Fitzgerald (Charles Scribner's Sons, New York 1922; Grey Walls Press, London 1950, Penguin, Harmondsworth 1966)

Tender Is the Night, F. Scott Fitzgerald (Charles Scribner's Sons, New York 1934, 1962; Penguin, Harmondsworth 1955, 1986)

The Last Tycoon, F. Scott Fitzgerald (Charles Scribner's Sons, New York 1941, 1969; Penguin, Harmondsworth 1960)

Emily Dickinson

Emily Dickinson: The Complete Poems, ed Thomas H. Johnson (Faber & Faber edition 2016)

Letters of Emily Dickinson, ed Mabel Loomis Todd (Franklin Classics edition 2018)

A Loaded Gun: Emily Dickinson for the 21st Century, Jerome Charyn (Bellevue Literary Press 2016)

Emily Dickinson: A Literary Life, Linda Wagner-Martin (Palgrave Macmillan 2013)

Lives Like Loaded Guns: Emily Dickinson and Her Family's Feuds, Lyndall Gordon (Virago 2011)

My Wars Are Laid Away In Books, Alfred Habegger (Modern Library 2001)

Florence Nightingale

Florence Nightingale: The Woman and Her Legend, Mark Bostridge (Penguin 2009)

Cassandra, Florence Nightingale (1859)

A history of mental health / schizophrenia

The Yellow Wallpaper, Charlotte Perkins Gilman (The New England Magazine 1892)

Dementia Praecox and Paraphrenia, Emil Kraepelin, trans R. M. Barclay (Edinburgh: E & S Livingstone 1919)

When the Sun Bursts, Christopher Bollas (Yale University Press 2016)

Living With Schizophrenia, Neel Burton (Acheron Press 2012)

The Voices Within, Charles Fernyhough (Wellcome Collection 2016)

The Myth of Mental Illness, Thomas Szasz (Harpercollins 1961)

Madness and Modernism: Insanity in the Light of modern art, literature and thought, Louis Sass (Oxford University Press; revised edition 2017)

Madness in Civilisation, Andrew Scull (Thames & Hudson 2015)

Madhouses, Doctors and Madmen: The Social History of Psychiatry in the Victorian Era, Andrew Scull (University of Pennsylvania Press 1981)

Psychiatry and Its Discontents, Andrew Scull (University of California Press 2019)

Bedlam: London and Its Mad, Catharine Arnold (Simon & Schuster 2008)

Madness: A Brief History, Roy Porter (OUP 2003)

The Female Malady: Women, Madness, and English Culture, 1830–1980, Elaine Showalter (Virago 1987)

Strong Imagination: Madness, Creativity and Human Nature, Daniel Nettle (OUP 2002)

The Divided Self, R. D. Laing (Penguin Books 1965)

The Gene: An Intimate History, Siddhartha Mukherjee (The Bodley Head 2016)

The Madness of Adam & Eve: How Schizophrenia Shaped Humanity, David Horrobin (Transworld 2001)

The Quantity Theory of Insanity, Will Self (Bloomsbury 1991)

Learning From The Voices Inside my Head, Eleanor Longden (TED Books 2013)

NOTES

Authors' original spelling and punctuation marks have been retained in quotation, even when they contained spelling mistakes.

Page 1
'The world of human beings grows too complicated' VW to Emma Vaughan 23 April 1901, *Letters* vol I. p.42

Page 15
'The books transported her into new worlds' *Matilda*, Roald Dahl, p. 21(Puffin Books, 1989)

Page 18
'A stodgy parent is no fun at all!' *Danny The Champion of the World*, Roald Dahl, epilogue (Puffin Books, 1975)

Page 21
'the world seen by the sane and the insane' 14 October 1922, VW, *Diaries* vol. II

Page 22

'had nothing whatever seriously the matter with him' *Mrs Dalloway*, p.23

'To love makes one solitary' *Mrs Dalloway*, p.25

Page 47

'an outsider to this class …' *Beginning Again*, LW, p.74

'the most precious flower and fruit' *International Government*, LW (1916)

'one of the most inveterate and gross vulgar errors' *Beginning Again* p.107

Pages 48–49

'as it does when in a picture gallery you suddenly come face to face with a great Rembrandt or a Velásquez' *Sowing*, LW, p.183

'a look of great intelligence, hypercritical, sarcastic, satirical.' *Sowing* p.184

'innocent imperialist' quoted in *Leonard Woolf*, Victoria Glendinning, p.77, from *Growing* by LW.

'*She's the only woman in the world with sufficient brains*' LS to LW, 21st August 1909, *Letters*, *LW* (ed. Spotts) p.149

Page 50

'Leave the ground …' *Beginning Again* p. 30

'seems to bring things from the centre of rocks, deep streams that have lain long in primordial places within the earth.' *Leonard Woolf*, Victoria Glendinning p.135

'I see the risk of marrying anyone and certainly me' LW to VW, 12 Jan 1912, *Letters*, *LW*, p.169

'fucking' and 'copulation', *LW*, Victoria Glendinning, p. 132

Page 51
'a touch of my usual disease, in the head' VW to Ka Cox, 7 Feb 1912, no 602., *Letters* vol I

'all the horrors of the dark cupboard of illness' 8 August 1921, *Diaries* Vol II. p.125

'I shall tell you wonderful stories of the lunatics. By the bye, they've elected me King' VW to LW, 5 March 1912, *Letters* Vol. I

Pages 52
Quotes from Seneca and Dryden are taken from *Beginning Again* pp.31–32

'most sensitive and sophisticated mind' *Beginning Again* p.77

Page 53
'the greatest disaster that could happen' *Reminiscences, Moments of Being*, VW p.11

Page 54
'to drift through a beautiful, vivid dream' *Beginning Again* p.69

Page 55

'L in his stall, I in mine.' 30 Nov 1937, *Diaries,* vol V p. 120

Page 56

Leonard's fears about whether or not they should have children is detailed in *Beginning Again* p.82 and *LW*, Victoria Glendinning p.161

'one does plunge into a new and unknown state of affairs' Quoted in *LW*, Victoria Glendinning p.160

'I want everything – love, children, adventure, intimacy, work.' VW to LW, 1 May 1912, *Letters* vol. I

Page 57

'A little more self control on my part' 5 Sept 1926, *Diaries* vol III p. 107, and letter from VW to Ethel Smyth, 8 Feb 1927, *Letters* vol. III

'that her mental condition was due to her own fault – laziness, inanition, gluttony' *Beginning Again* p.79

Page 58

Feeling less 'coerced', 15 October 1923, *Diaries* vol. II

Page 62

'the life of a vagrant' *Dementia Praecox and Paraphrenia*, Emil Kraepelin (1919)

Page 63

'a heightened consciousness of memories and experiences' *Living With Schizophrenia*, Neel Burton p.3

Page 64

'he feels both more exposed' *The Divided Self*, R. D. Laing p.37

Page 65

'Most people I know who have talked with schizophrenics' *When the Sun Bursts,* Christopher Bollas p.3

'Those on the verge of schizophrenia' *When the Sun Bursts*, Christopher Bollas p.75

'a new significance to everything …' ZSF to FSF, Summer 1930, Letter no 53, *Dear Scott, Dearest Zelda* pp.81–82

Page 66

'It as if he is gradually leaving our world' *When the Sun Bursts*, Christopher Bollas p.77

'Our type of mourning is unique' *When the Sun Bursts*, Christopher Bollas p.77

Page 69

'maniacs often recover much sooner' *The Practice of Physick: Two Discourses Concerning the Soul of Brutes*, Thomas Willis, 1684

Page 70

'the most blessed manifestation' quoted by Andrew Scull in *Psychiatry and Its Discontents*, p.43

'England, pre-eminent in art' *The Female Malady*, Elaine Showalter, p.24

Page 78

'a peculiar "headache" low down at the back of her head, insomnia, and a tendency for the thoughts to race' *Beginning Again* p.76

'some strange feeling of guilt' *Beginning Again* p.79

'artistic integrity and ruthlessness' *Beginning Again* p.149

'the shock of severing as' *The Journey Not the Arrival Matters* p.79

Page 79

'life was opening out for him' *LW*, Victoria Glendinning p.171

Page 80

'one of those appalling nightmares' *Beginning Again* p.150

'one revisionist biography even suggested that he dictated her suicide note' – see Irene Coates *Who's Afraid of Virginia Woolf: A Case for the Sanity of Virginia Woolf* (Soho Press 1998)

Page 81

'Went Savage w V morn said she ought to go Jean' quoted in *LW*, Victoria Glendinning p.171

'liked her up to a point' *Beginning Again* p.150

'a long serious letter with it, exhorting me to Christianity' VW to Vanessa Bell, Christmas Day 1910, letter 546, *Letters* vol I.

'a multitude of sins, symptoms and miseries' *Beginning Again* p.76

Page 82

'in service' LW to VW, 1 August 1913, *Letters, LW,* p.186

'I believe, Great One, you do want' LW to VW, 1 August 1913, *Letters, LW,* p.186

'Only rest quietly & dont worry' LW to VW, 25 July 1913, *Letters, LW,* p.184

Page 83

'I want to see you, but this is best' VW to LW, Aug 1913, *Letters* Vol II, pp.32–6

'Never talk again, dearest, of causing me anything but the most perfect happiness' LW to VW, 27 July 1913, *Letters, LW,* p.185

'I don't think that Woolf can go on for long alone' quoted in *Letters, LW,* Victoria Glendinning p.173

Page 84

'in a hopeless quandary' *Beginning Again* p.151

'full of delusions' *Beginning Again* p.151

Page 85

'I had to be on the alert continually' *Beginning Again* p.154

Page 86

'her condition was due to her own faults' *Beginning Again* p.155

'she should put her case to him' and 'undergo what treatment he might prescribe' *Beginning Again* p.155

'that terrible quality' *Beginning Again* p.15

Page 88

'For the previous two months I had had' *Beginning again* p.157

'You can't realise how utterly …' LW to VW, 13 March 1914 *Letters of Leonard Woolf* p.205

Page 92

'a role that one in five children now play' https://www.nottingham.ac.uk/education/news/news-items/news1718/child-carers.aspx

Page 96

'to her fate' Lytton Strachey to Lady Ottoline Morrell, 23 April 1916

Page 97

'If a man is mad, he shall not be at large in the city' cited in *Madness: A Brief History*, Roy Porter p.89

Page 100

'Alzheimer's patients, for 50,000 of them end up in the NHS' *The Independent 17 May 2018* https://www.independent.co.uk/news/health/dementia-alzheimers-hospital-emergency-admission-cuts-services-social-care-elderly-a8354946.html

Page 101

'deranged patients can hardly ever be cured in the bosom of their family' quoted in *Madness in Civilisation*, Andrew Scull p.205

— 371 —

Page 104

'innumerable young women in love difficulties...' VW to JT, 28th July 1910, Letter 531, *Letters* vol I.

'a long line of imbeciles' and 'they should certainly be killed' VW, Jan 9th 1915 *Diaries* vol I.

'the feeble-minded' cited in Victoria Brignell *The Eugenics Movement Britain Wants to Forget, The New Statesman* 9th Dec 2010 https://www.newstatesman.com/society/2010/12/british-eugenics-disabled

'Her own half-sister, Laura Stephen, had been incarcerated in institutions since early adulthood' https://www.tandfonline.com/doi/abs/10.1080/0013838X.2017.1423207

Page 105

'Thackeray's grand-daughter' *Old Bloomsbury, Moments of Being,* p.44

Page 111

'appalling nightmare' and 'collapse of one's everyday life' *Beginning Again* p.150

'In the first weeks at Dalingridge' *Beginning Again* pp.162–163

Page 112

'dreadful, large gloomy buildings enclosed by high walls, dismal trees, and despair' *Beginning Again* p.158

'the word 'manic' is a dangerous one' *VW,* Hermione Lee, p.791, note 58; *LW,* Victoria Glendinning, p.177

'in the warm, peaceful, soft and sunny evening' *Beginning Again* p.165

'look towards the long hazy line' *ibid.*, p.165

Page 113

'I've never been alone with anyone else ...' and 'you can day after day & all day give me perfect happiness' LW to VW, 13 March 1914, *Letters of Leonard Woolf* p.205

Pages 113–114

'I believe, however, that the good sense of the proceeding' VW, 13 Jan 1915, *Diaries* vol I.

Page 114

'we could not turn her house into a mental hospital' *Beginning Again* p.172

Page 115

'immense solidity with grace, lightness and beauty' *Downhill All the Way* p.11

Page 116

'I remember how I hoped that he would stop' *Moments of Being*, Virginia Woolf p.82

'to comfort' *ibid.*, p.44

'a violent state of excitement' Gerald Brenan to Rosemary Dinnage, 4 Nov 1967 'dislikes the possessiveness and love' *Vita Sackville-West, Selected Writings* p.144

'Leonard, though I should say a strongly sexed man' Gerald Brenan to Rosemary Dinnage, 4 Nov 1967

Page 117
'labyrinth' and 'private nightmare' *Beginning Again* p.176

Page 118
'years we simply lost out of our lives' *Beginning Again* p.166

'nervous exhaustion' Dr Craig's letter, dated 10 May 1916, is quoted in *LW*, Victoria Glendinning p.201

'shell-shocked already' *LW*, Victoria Glendinning, p.203

Page 122
'were walking around buried up to [his] waist' Will Self, *New Statesman*, *'Will Self on Astral Weeks by Van Morrison'* 18 December 2017

Page 123
'Virginia's imagination, apart from her artistic creativeness' Alix Stratchey, reminiscing on her conversation with Leonard, quoted in *My Madness Saved Me: The Madness and Marriage of Virginia Woolf*, Thomas Szasz

Page 124
'I, Mandril Sarcophagus Felicissima var. Rarissima' LW to VW, June 19th 1914, Monk's House Papers, University of Sussex

Page 125

'what they knew amounted to practically nothing' *Beginning Again* p.160

'be in bed no less than 10 hours out of the 24' quoted in *LW*, Victoria Glendinning p.180

'a quiet, vegetative life, eating well, going to bed early, and not tiring herself mentally or physically' *Beginning Again* p.76

'She is absolutely forbidden by the doctors' LW to Lady Robert Cecil, 8 March 2016, *Letters of Leonard Woolf* p.214

Page 126

'In the legend that has grown up around Virginia Woolf' *The New York Times*, 'This Loose, Drifting Material of Life' by Daphne Merkin 8 June 1997

Page 127

'Virginia Woolf was a sane woman who had an illness' *VW*, Hermione Lee p.175

'As an experience, madness is terrific I can assure you, and not to be sniffed at' VW to Ethel Smyth, 22 June 1930, *Letters* vol. IV p.180

Pages 127–8

'there is no doubt that after her suicide attempt "he made her into an invalid" in order to prevent a recurrence' *VW*, Hermione Lee p.336

Page 128

'Leonard made me into a comatose invalid' VW to Violet
Dickinson, June 1912, no. 625 *Letters* Vol. I p. 502

Page 129

'she found Leonard absolutely dependable' quoted in *VW*,
Hermione Lee p.337

'one's personality seems to echo out across space, when he's
not there to enclose all one's vibrations' 2 Nov 1917, *Diaries*
vol. I p.70

Page 134

'The Gods … were taking us seriously', *Sketch of the Past,
Moments of Being*, p.141

Page 140

'Because I could not stop for Death' *Emily Dickinson – The
Complete Poems* p.350

Page 161

'the menace … under which she always lived' *Beginning Again*
p.75

'nerve-wracking' *Beginning Again* p.166

Page 162

'Dearest, I feel certain that I am going mad again.' VW to
LW, 18? March 1941, as quoted in *The Journey Not The Arrival
Matters* pp.93–4

Page 163

'red from weeping, his face haggard beyond description', quoted in *LW*, Victoria Glendinning p. 368

Page 164

'If one is in the exact centre of a cyclone or tornado' *The Journey Not the Arrival Matters* p.69

'the depression struck her like a sudden blow.' *The Journey Not the Arrival Matters* p.79

'in the desolate ruins of my old squares: gashed; dismantled; the old red bricks all white powder, something like a builder's yard', VW, Jan 15th 1941, *Diaries* vol. V

Page 165

'Rodmell life is very small beer' VW, 26 Jan 1941, *Selected Diaries* p.502

'It was essential for her to resign herself to illness' *The Journey Not the Arrival Matters* p.91

Page 166

'I know that V. will not come across the garden from the Lodge' quoted in *LW* Victoria Glendinning p.373

'I suppose I ought to say I was wrong' LW to Margaret Llewelyn Davies, 1st April 1941, *Letters* p.254

Page 171

'literature does its best to maintain that its concern is with the mind' *On Being Ill, Selected Essays* p.101

Page 174

'...we often found ourselves helpless' *When the Sun Bursts*, Christopher Bollas p.35

'but because of how they deconstruct' *When the Sun Bursts*, Christopher Bollas p.36

Pages 188–189

'If Leonard were to seek sexual solace with anyone' *LW*, Victoria Glendinning p.193

Page 189

'psychologically fascinating...she found it almost impossible to refuse anyone anything' *Beginning Again* pp.173–174

Page 193

'It was a well-known joke among their friends' *VW*, Hermione Lee p.366

Page 194

'Studies show that women frequently become snared in the role because caring is often a gradual responsibility' Emer Begley and Suzanne Cahill, *Studies: An Irish Quarterly Review*, Vol. 92, No. 366 (Summer, 2003), pp.162–171

'Yet when men care for children, their testosterone levels fall by around a third' https://www.sciencemag.org/news/2011/09/fatherhood-decreases-testosterone

'It is more likely that women end up caring because girls are brought up to be more compliant' based on quotes by clinical

psychologist Linda Blair, interview in https://www.telegraph.
co.uk/women/womens-life/11043452/Caregivers-are-more-likely-
to-be-women-says-American-study-as-daughters-take-respon
sibility-over-sons.html

'in the UK, women have a 50:50 chance of becoming a carer
by the time they are 59; men have the same odds by the time
they are 75 years old' https://www.carersuk.org/images/Facts_
about_Carers_2015.pdf

'In the US, women are twice as likely to end up in the role'
https://www.telegraph.co.uk/women/womens-life/11043452/
Caregivers-are-more-likely-to-be-women-says-American-study-
as-daughters-take-responsibility-over-sons.html

'Women are four times more likely to reduce their working
hours than men due to multiple caring responsibilities' https://
www.carersuk.org/news-and-campaigns/features/10-facts-about-
women-and-caring-in-the-uk-on-international-women-s-day

'That said, for elderly carers, the figures shift – carers over the
age of 85 are more likely to be men' https://www.carersuk.org/
images/Facts_about_Carers_2015.pdf

'Men do make their contribution and they make it well: 42%
of informal carers are male' https://carers.org/key-facts-about-
carers-and-people-they-care

Page 195
'decrease of labour market participation levels, especially
among women' *The Guardian* 6 August 2018 https://www.

theguardian.com/society/2018/aug/06/carer-shortage-after-brexit-will-force-women-to-quit-jobs

'under house arrest' https://web.archive.org/web/2010012712 1657/
http://www.carersuk.org/Aboutus/MoreaboutCarersUK/OurHistory

Pages 195–196
'the accumulation of nervous energy ... makes them feel ... when they go to bed, as if they were going mad' *Cassandra*, Florence Nightingale, 1852

Page 196
'all that ministering angel nonsense' *Florence Nightingale: The Woman and Her Legend*, Mark Bostridge p.502

Page 197
'how wearing...the incessant cares and the anxious necessities of your situation are' Judge Lord's 1877 letter is to Vinnie Dickinson, Emily's sister, but relates to the heavy duty of care the two sisters shared. Quoted in *The Life of Emily Dickinson*, Richard B. Sewall, p.657

'I don't doubt if they live they will be ornaments to society. I think they are both to be considered as embryos of future usefulness' Letter to Mrs A. P. Strong, 1845, postmarked 4 August, Amherst, *Letters of Emily Dickinson* p.11

Page 198
'Literature cannot be the business of a woman's life' Robert Southey to Charlotte Brontë, 12 March 1837

'In the evenings, I confess, I do think, but I never trouble anyone else with my thoughts' Charlotte Brontë to Robert Southey, 16 March 1937

'we feel that our presence is negated' *When the Sun Bursts*, Christoper Bollas, p.77

Page 218
'But the effect of her being on those around her was incalculably diffusive' *Middlemarch*, George Eliot p.896 (1871-2; Penguin paperback edition 1965)

Pages 219–220
'Each life is a game of chess that went to hell on the seventh move' *Money*, Martin Amis p.119 (1984, Jonathan Cape, Vintage paperback edition 2005)

Page 222
'I never did enough for him' quoted in *Virginia Woolf*, Hermione Lee p.172

Page 225
'tore through her body as if it were late for an important meeting with a lot of other successful diseases' *The Quantity Theory of Insanity*, Will Self, p.1 (1991 Penguin, paperback edition)

Page 236
'lack-of-care-home' https://www.theguardian.com/uk-news/2017/mar/06/mossley-manor-liverpool-care-home-latif-brothers-fined

Page 237

'there are currently 100,000 unfilled jobs in social care' https://www.independent.co.uk/news/health/social-care-uk-tory-women-children-elderly-a8812991.html

'Retaining staff is also …' https://www.caretalk.co.uk/how-to-solve-the-care-sectors-staff-retention-problem/

'Whilst only 3% of care homes are rated outstanding, 17% have been given a rating that they could do better' https://www.theguardian.com/society/2018/nov/25/care-home-patients- england-wales-malnutrition-dehydration-bedsores

Page 243

'The brain imaging of a schizophrenic' *A Trip Inside the Schizophrenic Mind, Scientific American*, Taylor Beck, 1 March 2017

Page 246

'In China, they'd brought in a law in 2013 called the Elderly Rights Law' https://www.bbc.co.uk/news/world-asia-china-23124345

Page 247

'schizophrenics had a much better chance of recovery in developing countries' *A Schizophrenia Mystery Solved?* Robert Whitaker, *Psychology Today,* 18 May 2010 https://www.psychologytoday.com/gb/blog/mad-in-america/201005/schizophrenia- mystery-solved

Page 249

'with the inexorable, monotonous motion of a machine' article by John Galt in *The American Journal of Insanity* (1855), quoted in Chapter 1, *Madhouses, Doctors and Madmen: The Social History of Psychiatry in the Victorian Era*, Andrew Scull

'In the mid-fifties, there were over 150,000 patients' http:// news.bbc.co.uk/1/hi/health/229517.stm

Page 250

'sluggish schizophrenia' *Psychiatry and the Dark Side: Eugenics, Nazi and Soviet philosophy*, Jason Luty, *Advances in Psychiatric Treatment vol 20, Issue 1,* pp.52–60, January 2014

'the elimination of by far the greater part of this country's mental hospitals' Enoch Powell, Address to the National Association of Mental Health Annual Conference, 9 March 1961

Pages 250–251

'In the animal kingdom, the rule is, eat or be eaten' *The Myth of Mental Illness*, Thomas Szasz (Secker & Warburg 1962)

Page 251

'If you talk to God, you are praying; if God talks to you, you have schizophrenia.' *The Second Sin,* 'Schizophrenia', Thomas Szasz, p.113 (Doubleday 1973)

For Szasz, mental illness was not disease but a reflection of 'problems in living' *The Myth of Mental Illness*, Thomas Szasz

But he was not entirely against psychiatry – he simply felt that it was too coercive and should be replaced with trust and consent, adhering to the Hippocratic injunction to 'do no harm'. *Coercion As Cure: A Critical history of Psychiatry*, Thomas Szasz (Transaction Publishers 2009)

'People go into hospital with mental disorders and they are cured' Department of Health and Social Security 1971, quoted in *Madness in Civilisation*, Andrew Scull p.367

'no-man's land' of community care, described it as 'everybody's distant cousin but nobody's baby', Sir Roy Griffiths, 1988

Page 252
'in a splendidly original variation on the ancient practice of treating the mad like cattle' *Madness in Civilisation*, Andrew Scull p.377

'In US jails, a 2006 report showed that 24% of patients met the criteria for a psychiatric disorder' *Madness in Civilisation*, Andrew Scull p.378

'There is the CareRooms scheme, for example, which has been dubbed the 'air bnb for social care' scheme' https://www.thetimes.co.uk/article/carerooms-carebnb-to-offer-home-for-patients-62crxqdob

Page 253
'The Homeshare network, for example, was set up in 2015' https://www.theguardian.com/society/2015/mar/03/young-person-live-older-person-cheap-rent-live-in-care

Page 256

'Sometimes I don't know whether Zelda and I are real or whether we are characters in one of my novels' FSF said this to a visitor at La Paix in 1933; quoted in *F Scott Fitzgerald*, ed. Harold Bloom p.85

'I would almost rather she die now' Rosalind Sayre Smith, 8 June 1930, Box 53, Folder 14A, Princeton University Library.

'the best in Europe' FSF to Judge Sayre and Mrs Sayre, 1st December 1930, *Life In Letters* p.202

Pages 256–257

'Yet, when Zelda's doctors write and ask the Sayres about this genetic aberration' *Zelda*, Nancy Milford, p.162

Page 257

'the necessity of an arbitrary and unmotivated, often *an even undesired self-assertion'* quoted in *Scott Fitzgerald*, Andrew Turnbull p.195

'the schizophrenogenic mother' https://www.thelancet.com/journals/lancet/article/PIIS0140-6736(12)60546-7/fulltext

Page 259

'My latest tendency is to collapse about 11.00' FSF to Hemingway, 9 Sept 1929, *A Life in Letters* p.169

Page 260

"Are you under the illusion that you'll ever be any good at this stuff?" *Scott Fitzgerald*, Andrew Turnbull p.191

'replace Isadora Duncan now that she was dead and outshine me at the same time' quoted in *Zelda*, Sally Cline, p.213

'he needed to drink in order to write' *Zelda*, Sally Cline p.216

'I think I'll turn off here', quoted in *Married to Genius*, Jeffrey Meyers p.234

Page 261
'During my young manhood for seven years I worked extremely hard' FSF to Dr Oscar Forel, circa summer 1930, *A Life in Letters* pp. 196–7

Page 262
'In 1928, after messing up a speech he was supposed to make at the Princeton Cottage Club dinner' *Zelda*, Sally Cline, p. 217

'the face I knew and loved' FSZ to ZSF c. July 1930, *Dear Scott, Dearest Zelda*, p.88

'She was sedated recently' this is detailed in *Zelda*, Sally Cline, p.272

Page 263
'The mortality rate is 1% and side effects are serious' https://journals.sagepub.com/doi/pdf/10.1177/014107680009300313

'*Please* help me. Every day more of me dies with this bitter and incessant beating I'm taking' ZSF to FSF August/Sept 1930 *Dear Scott, Dearest Zelda*, p.90

Pages 263–264
'You can choose the conditions of our life.' ibid

Page 266

'Now the standard cure for one who is sunk is to consider those in actual destitution or physical suffering' March 1936, *Pasting it Together, The Crack Up* p.64

Page 270

'a call upon physical resources that I did not command, like a man overdrawing at his bank' March 1936, *Pasting it Together, The Crack Up* p.67

Page 272

'the first time in two years + 1/2', FSF to Maxwell Perkins c. 15 January 1932 *Life In Letters* p.208

'is for Americans, a place of dissipation' *Paradise Lost*, David S. Brown, Chapter 13, p.186

Page 273

'do not worry about us' ZSF to FSF, 18 Nov 1931, *Dear Scott, Dearest Zelda*, p.124

"I think you'll always pay your bills, Scott" quoted in *Zelda*, Sally Cline, p.296

'my whole fortune depends' FSF to Dr Oscar Forel, 1st February 1932

'she has come to regard me as the work horse and herself as the artist.' FSF to Dr Thomas Rennie, October 1932, *Letters, FSF* p.220

Pages 273–274

'Almost one in three providing substantial care have seen a drop of £20,000 or more a year' https://www.carersuk.org/images/Facts_about_Carers_2019.pdf

Page 274

'almost half end up cutting back on essentials such as food and heating' http://www.carersuk.org/images/News_and_campaigns/Carers_Rights_Day/CUK-Carers-Rights-Day-Research -Report-2018-WEB.PDF p.8

Page 288

'PLEASE DO NOT JUDGE OR IF ALREADY DONE' FSF to Maxwell Perkins, March 16, 1932 *Dear Scott, Dearest Zelda* p.165

'a 'natural storyteller' in the sense that I am' 8 March 1932, FSF to Dr Mildred Squires

Page 289

'this mixture of fact and fiction is simply calculated to ruin us both' FSF to ZF, March 14 1932, *Dear Scott, Dearest Zelda*, p.165

'feeling it to be a dubious production due to my own insta-bility' ZSF to FSF late March 1932, *Dear Scott, Dearest Zelda*, p.163

'This is an evasion. All this reasoning is specious' quoted in *Zelda*, Nancy Milford p.220

Page 290

'incipient egomania' quoted in *Zelda*, Sally Cline p.309

'After he gives an interview to The Baltimore *Sun,* the result is the headline: 'He Tells of Her Novel' and a subtitle 'Work Sent to Publisher Is Autobiographical at Suggestion of Her Husband' *Zelda*, Nancy Milford, p.256

Page 291

'The question of authority is simple. We have decided to relieve you of having to be the boss' Dr Adolf Meyer to FSF, 18th April 1933, quoted in *Zelda*, Sally Cline p.324

Transcript between F Scott Fitzgerald and Zelda, quoted in *Zelda*, Sally Cline p.324-333 and *Zelda*, Nancy Milford pp.272–276

Page 292

'years ago, an editor made an offer for Zelda's diaries which Scott rejected, arguing that he wanted to use parts of them in his own novels and stories' *Zelda*, Nancy Milford p.71 and p.80

Page 294

'a selfish man' Helen Blackshear, *Mama Sayre, Scott Fitzgerald's mother-in-law, Georgia Review*, winter 1965 p.467

'Only her transference to him saves her' quoted in *Zelda*, Nancy Milford p.218-9, from the Fitzgerald Collection at Princeton University Library

'Portrait of Zelda, that is, a part of Zelda' *ibid*

Page 295

'What made me mad was that he made the girl so awful' ZSF Feb-Mar 1934, quoted in *Zelda*, Nancy Milford p.286

'I am fighting for my life,', Dick tells his sick wife, 'I can't do anything for you any more. I'm trying to save myself.' *Tender Is the Night* p.301

'a wayward child', Sara Mayfield, *Exiles* (Dell Publishing Co. 1974) pp.151-2; see also *A Life in Letters* p.299, where FSF writes to Sara Murphy and says of Zelda, 'she was always my child.'

Page 300

Scott feels that it has 'washed' her mind 'clean' FSF to Gerald and Sara Murphy, quoted in *Paradise Lost*, David S.Brown, Chapter 19, p.265

Page 301

'With each collapse she moves perceptibly backwards' quoted in *Scott Fitzgerald: A Biography*, Jeffrey Meyers p.268

'During the mood of depression that I seem to have fallen into about a year ago, she was a saint to me, took care of Scottie for a month one time... and is altogether, one of the world's most delightful women' FSF to Mrs William Hamm October 28 1936

Page 302

'With all my heart I am sorry to have brought so much sorrow into your life' FSF to Beatrice Dance, 6 March 1936 'recklessness' of Nora, Scott and Zelda; his wife is 'the most unbalanced of all' *The Notebooks of F. Scott Fitzgerald*, ed. Matthew J. Bruccoli (New York: Harcourt Brace Jovanovich/ Bruccoli Clark, 1978)

'That summer in Asheville everything had crashed around him.' *The Lost Summer: A Personal Memoir of F. Scott Fitzgerald*, Tony Buttitta (Viking, NY, 1974)

'My talent and decline is the norm. Your degeneracy is the deviation.' FSF to ZSF, unsent letter, c.late 1939, Princeton University Library, quoted in *Zelda*, Sally Cline p.373

Page 303

"I can't get on with my husband and I can't live away from him," ZSF Feb-Mar 1934, quoted in *Zelda*, Nancy Milford p.286

'Her doctors felt that she began to use the label of her illness as a shield' – see *Zelda*, Nancy Milford p.256 – 'Dr Meyer wanted Zelda to face her sickness squarely, not passively in the fixed terms of dementia praecox and schizophrenia that she would prattle about as an evasive tactic.'

Page 304

'even in 1934, he was still hoping she might be 'reeducated' out of her creative endeavours' *Zelda*, Sally Cline p.346

'Life ended for me when Zelda and I crashed.' Quoted in *Married to Genius*, Jeffrey Meyers (Southbank Publishing 2005; Trafalgar Square Publishing US) p.242

'a case – not a person' *Scott Fitzgerald: A Biography*, Jeffrey Meyers p.232

Page 308

'72% of carers suffer poor mental health as a resulting of caring and 61% report that their physical health has got worse' 2018 research report https://www.carersweek.org/images/Resources/CW18_Research_Report.pdf

Page 322

'To be mad is to be idle', *Madness in Civilisation*, Andrew Scull p.122

'Philip Hammond linked low levels of productivity in the UK with a higher percentage of disabled people in employment' https://www.theguardian.com/politics/2017/dec/07/philip-hammond-causes-storm-with-remarks-about-disabled-workers

'are evidently drafted from the poorest portion of the population' – *Good Words* article by William Gilbert can be found in full here http://www.workhouses.org.uk/MAB-Caterham/

'It is estimated that around a quarter of a million people with schizophrenia were killed or sterilised' https://www.ncbi.nlm.nih.gov/pmc/articles/PMC2800142/

Page 323

'It is right that the worthless lives of such creatures should be ended' *Psychiatric Genocide: Nazi Attempts to Eradicate Schizophrenia*, by E. Fuller Torrey and Robert H. Yolken, *Schizophrenia Bulletin*, Volume 36, Issue 1, January 2010, pp.26–32 'the overriding criterion' for selection for death in the T-4 programme was *'the ability to do productive work.'* Henry Friedlander, *The Origins of Nazi Genocide* (The University of North Carolina Press, 2000), quoted in *Psychiatric Genocide: Nazi Attempts to Eradicate Schizophrenia,* by E. Fuller Torrey and Robert H. Yolken, *Schizophrenia Bulletin*, Volume 36, Issue 1, January 2010, pp.26–32

'In 1935, a Berlin psychiatrist called Kallman made a speech' – *Psychiatric Genocide: Nazi Attempts to Eradicate Schizophrenia,* by E. Fuller Torrey and Robert H. Yolken, *Schizophrenia Bulletin*, Volume 36, Issue 1, January 2010, pp.26–32

'but in reality it is caused by hundreds of genes' such variants may be carried by a large number of people, most of whom will never develop schizophrenia. David Horrobin, *The Madness of Adam and Eve* p.181

Page 324
'Jon Löve Karlsson, based at the Institute of Genetics in Reykjavik' source: Daniel Nettle, *Strong Imagination: Madness, Creativity and Human Nature* p.150

'families with schizophrenic members seemed to have a greater variety of skills and abilities, and a greater likelihood of producing high achievers' David Horrobin, *The Madness of Adam and Eve* p.181

Page 325
'one falling and the other diving' Richard Ellman interview with Carl Jung, 1953

'Cut me anywhere, & I bleed too profusely. Life has bred too much 'feeling' of a kind in me' Virginia Woolf, 9 February 1924, *Diaries* vol II

'Suddenly I knew how to enter into the life of everything around me. I knew how it felt to be a tree, a blade of grass, even a rabbit ...' Theodore Roethke

'Researchers at the Karolinska Institutet in Sweden' https://www.bbc.co.uk/news/10154775

Page 326

"Thinking outside the box might be facilitated by having a somewhat less intact box." https://news.ki.se/creativity-linked-to-mental-health

'heterogeneous ideas ... yoked by violence together.' Dr Samuel Johnson, *Lives of the Most Eminent English Poets vol I* (1779)

'Like a mystic maze the folds and ridges rose in desolation...' *Save Me The Waltz*, Zelda Fitzgerald p.38

Page 329

'I feel that contact with those she loves is good for her and gives her a sense of protection' Minnie Sayre to FSF, 26 April 1938, quoted in *Zelda*, Sally Cline p.369

'continued hospitalisation, against her will, will be detrimental' Rosalind Sayre, quoted in *Zelda*, Sally Cline p.370

'Cure her I cannot and simply saying she's cured must make the Gods laugh' FSF to Rosalind Sayre, 21 December 1938

Page 330
'[it is a] preposterous idea that Zelda's sanity can be bought with a one way ticket to Montgomery...You have nothing to offer.' FSF to Marjorie Brinson *c.* end Dec 1938, co187, Box 53, Folder Marjorie Brinson (Sayre) PUL, quoted in *Zelda*, Sally Cline p.371

'When you people stink you certainly stink'. FSF to Rosalind Sayre Smith, *c.* end of Dec 1938 co187, Box 53, Folder 14, Princeton University Library

'He writes to Zelda and tells her to stop harassing him for her freedom' FSF to ZSF, 6 Oct 1939, *Life In Letters*, pp.412–3

Page 331
'One guy even looked at him in surprise; he thought Scott had died long ago' – based on Arnold Gingrich, editor of *Esquire,* saying that 'sixteen years after his fame, a lot of people thought he was dead', quoted in *SF,* Jeffrey Meyers p.264

'A letter from Dr Carroll. Zelda is ready for release' FSF received the letter from Dr Carroll dated 4 March 1940, *Zelda,* Sally Cline p.375

Page 332
'I wish you were going to brighter surroundings' 11 April 1940, *Dear Scott, Dearest Zelda* p.334

Page 333

'and tho my hair's grey I feel younger than for four years' FSF to Harold Ober, May 1937, *Life in Letters* p.323

'Sally Cline has unearthed evidence that he was also abusing several other female patients' *Zelda*, Sally Cline p.375

'it requires most of my resources to keep out of hospital' ZF to FSF, September 1940, *Dear Scott, Dearest Zelda* p.365

Page 334

'in 1918 a third of patients died in one hospital in Buckinghamshire as a result' *Madness in Civilisation*, Andrew Scull p.364

Pages 334–335

'£100 million has been wasted on the appeals process; over 60% of appeals are upheld' https://www.theguardian.com/politics/2018/feb/12/disability-benefit-appeals-department-for-work-and-pensions-figures

Page 336

'Three in five informal carers are over the age of fifty' https://www.ons.gov.uk/peoplepopulationandcommunity/birthsdeathsandmarriages/ageing/articles/livinglongerhowourpopulationis changingandwhyitmatters/2019-03-15

Page 337

'One stated that 80% of rough sleepers in London who died in 2017 had mental health care needs' https://www.theguardian.com/society/2018/jun/19/deaths-of-mentally-ill-rough-sleepers-in-london-rise-sharply 'we're in an era where those who are vulnerable have never had so many rights, but at the same time, so little care' https://www.independent.co.uk/life-style/health-and-families/health-news/the-demise-of-the-asylum-and-the-rise-of-care-in-the-community-8352927.html

'the biggest of any sector: a 72% fall from 1987 to 2016/7, from 67,112 to just 18,730' https://www.theguardian.com/society/2018/jul/21/mental-heath-crisis-beds-shortage-detentions-soar

Page 338
'There is evidence that antipsychotics' https://www.sciencedirect.com/science/article/abs/pii/S0924933815300559

Page 339
'On Radio 4, I'd heard an expert, Sir Robin Murray' BBC Radio 3, *The Life Scientific*, 7 February 2012

Page 340
'a story about finding meaning in madness.' *Learning From the Voices Inside My Head*, Eleanor Longden

'It was as if my friend had picked up a baton, which was handed to a doctor, then ultimately to a psychiatrist.' Eleanor Longden, interviewed by Jon Ronson, *Guardian* 8 August 2013 https://www.theguardian.com/technology/2013/aug/08/ted-talk-eleanor-longden-schizophrenia

'diagnosed, drugged, discarded' ibid

Page 341

'the most menacing, aggressive voices actually represented the parts of me that had been hurt the most – and as such, it was these voices that needed to be shown the greatest compassion and care' *ibid*

She has argued that psychiatry should not ask the question 'what's wrong with you?' but 'what happened to you?' *Learning From the Voices Inside My Head,* Eleanor Longden

Page 341

'a sane response to insane circumstances' Eleanor Longden, interviewed by Jon Ronson, *Guardian* 8 August 2013 https://www.theguardian.com/technology/2013/aug/08/ted-talk-eleanor-longden-schizophrenia

Pages 341–342

'for they experience heightened activity in Broca's area, the brain's speech centre – just as we do when we hear external voices' https://www.nytimes.com/2003/05/06/science/experts-see-mind-s-voices-in-new-light.html

Page 342

'In their plurality, the voices that now contain the function of the I' *When the Sun Bursts,* Christopher Bollas p.106

'there was not an "I" any more' *The Crack Up*, FSF p.68

'Can't you stop your 'I's? Who are you? You are a person of six or seven different parts. Now, why don't you integrate yourself?' from the threeway discussion between Scott, Zelda and Dr Rennie on 28th May 1933 at La Paix, quoted in *Zelda*, Sally Cline p.328

Pages 342–343
'Once we were one person' FSF to Zelda, April 1938, *A Life In Letters* p.355

Page 345
'Those in developing countries took less anti-psychotic medicine' https://www.theguardian.com/commentisfree/2008/mar/02/mythoftheantipsychotic

'I found out that even the time of year that you are born can influence the onset of schizophrenia' Orfhlaith McTigue and Eadbhard O'Callaghan, *International Journal of Mental Health*, Vol. 29, No. 3, Risk Factors for Schizophrenia and Implications for Prevention—1 (Fall 2000), pp.66–78

Pages 345–346
'the children of mothers born during the German invasion of the Netherlands' *Environmental Risk Factors for Psychosis,* Kimberlie Dean and Robin M. Murray, Dialogues Clin Neurosci. 2005 Mar; 7(1): 69–80 https://www.ncbi.nlm.nih.gov/pmc/articles/PMC3181718/

Page 346
'Cannabis can trigger the illness, in those predisposed to the disorder' https://www.psychologytoday.com/gb/blog/not-the-whole-person/201801/can-marijuana-trigger-schizophrenia

'Living in the city rather than the countryside increases risks' *Schizophrenia and Urbanicity: A Major Environmental Influence—Conditional on Genetic Risk,* Lydia Krabbendam, Jim van Os, *Schizophrenia Bulletin,* Volume 31, Issue 4, October 2005, pp.795–799

'being in a minority group is also a factor, with some immigrants/ethnic minorities showing higher rates of the illness' *Ethnic Identity and the Risk of Schizophrenia in Ethnic Minorities: A Case-Control Study,* Wim Veling, Hans W. Hoek, Durk Wiersma, Johan P. Mackenbach, *Schizophrenia Bulletin,* Volume 36, Issue 6, November 2010, pp.1149–1156

'people who are single are more likely to develop psychosis' *Environmental Risk Factors for Psychosis,* Kimberlie Dean and Robin M. Murray, Dialogues Clin Neurosci. 2005 Mar; 7(1): 69–80 https://www.ncbi.nlm.nih.gov/pmc/articles/PMC3181718/

Page 351
'There are currently 6.5 million carers in the UK…' https://www.carersuk.org/news-and-campaigns/press-releases/facts-and-figures